# Jammu & Kashmir

# Jammu & Kashmir

*Levels, Issues, and Prospects
of Employment Generation*

DR. BILAL AHMAD KHAN
*Ph.D. & PDF*
*Special Centre for the Study of North East India*
*School of Social Sciences*
*Jawaharlal Nehru University, New Delhi*

OXFORD
UNIVERSITY PRESS

# OXFORD
## UNIVERSITY PRESS

Great Clarendon Street, Oxford, OX2 6DP,
United Kingdom

Oxford University Press is a department of the University of Oxford.
It furthers the University's objective of excellence in research, scholarship,
and education by publishing worldwide. Oxford is a registered trade mark of
Oxford University Press in the UK and in certain other countries

© Oxford University Press 2022

The moral rights of the author have been asserted

First Edition published in 2022

Impression: 1

Published in the United States of America by Oxford University Press
198 Madison Avenue, New York, NY 10016, United States of America

British Library Cataloguing in Publication Data

Data available

Library of Congress Control Number: 2022931623

ISBN 978-0-19-284965-6

DOI: 10.1093/oso/9780192849656.001.0001

Printed in India by Rakmo Press Pvt. Ltd.

# Foreword

I would very strongly recommend this book to anyone interested in gaining an insight into the issues pertaining to the prospect for employment generation in Jammu and Kashmir in present times. The book is original in content. The author is one of India's best-known scholars on Jammu and Kashmir. We get here a fresh perspective that boldly shifts the focus from the past demographic and developmental dimensions to the present dynamics of the state, or, rather, the Union Territories. In spelling this out the author, Dr. Bilal Khan, explains in great detail the varied and diversified geographic, agro-climatic, and topographic features of the region that pose peculiar and unique problems of development. The author dwells on how the state has been subverted from time to time. The work draws attention to the trends and issues concerning the work force. The policy implications of this work are immense. The book is focused on finding innovative methods to enable the young youth to exercise as well as realize their full potential.

The author shows with corroborating evidence that the Central Government not only deployed security forces in large numbers but also spent huge sums of money on building infrastructure and providing economic assistance to Jammu and Kashmir. Instead of addressing the problems of the peasantry and the common people and expanding the employment of the restive youth, this led to the creation of neo-rich strata within the state. Dr. Bilal presents the much neglected dimensions of the economy of Kashmir by showing how the widening gulf over decades has generated mass discontent against the Indian government and created the social basis of separatism and militancy in the 1990s. He points out with much evidence that a radical shift in its policies, especially in the education sector, is an absolute prerequisite for the birth of a capable workforce. The remedy lies in revamping the education sector by crafting appropriate policies for suitable skills in line with the socio-economic requirements of the society. Underdevelopment and unemployment in Jammu and Kashmir is the manifestation of a mismatch between physical and human resources, technically known as structural unemployment. This exists when a large segment of the working age population does not possess the appropriate skills and knowledge to be gainfully employed.

The author has shown how a window of opportunity would open up when the atmosphere for peace is restored. Dr. Bilal does well in reminding us that former Prime Minister Vajpayee's peace process proposal and the composite dialogue framework had genuinely turned the tables and facilitated the growth and development of the state. This goes to show that given the right combination of well thought out policy and effective implementation, one may still expect positive results at the ground level.

Professor Pulin Nayak
Formerly Director/Chairperson, Delhi School of Economics
University of Delhi

# Preface

I felt my serious inclination towards writing this book when my first article 'Unemployment: An Ample and Serious Problem' was published in the local newspaper Greater Kashmir way back in 2014 while pursing Doctor of Philosophy. My interaction with students inside and outside the state in 2015–2016, when the state of Jammu and Kashmir faced a serious unemployment problem, made me realize that there was an immediate need of a book on Jammu & Kashmir: Levels, Issues, & Prospects of Employment Generation which could educate the young youth about the various aspects and challenges in a simple and lucid manner. It took nearly 5 years to fulfil this dream of mine. The book has been designed to cater to the requirement of General Studies for civil services. It would also be useful for graduate and post-graduate courses in Economics of various universities. The book on Levels, Issues, & Prospects of Employment Generation also takes cognizance of latest developments that take place in the state economy from time to time. Adequate and required notes and references have been given after consulting and referring to an array of sources. I have taken care of both the objectives as well as the subjective aspects based on the current issues. The book also presents a comprehensive treatment of economic problems. It takes care of recent data of workforce wherever it is required. For convenience, the book is furnishing in seven chapters.

I am grateful to Professor Nisar Ali for the inspiration and motivation I got from him to complete this work. I have especially learnt the art and importance of work, punctuality, and honesty in a very practical way from him. I am grateful to my colleagues who have helped in this endeavour with valuable suggestions.

I must also put on record my gratitude to my institution, that is, Jawaharlal Nehru University, for all that I learnt as a student and as a teacher of this Premier University. It is hoped that this book will prove handy and useful to students and teachers of State Economy. Moreover,

I am sanguine that work will prove useful to researchers. Suggestions for further improvement of the book are solicited.

Seamlessly blending facts and incisive analysis, this book raises and conceives about the nature of employment and unemployment in the region. It will be of great interest of researchers and scholars of Indian economy, especially on Jammu and Kashmir as well as government bodies, think tanks, and the interested general reader.

Dr. Bilal Ahmad Khan
Ph.D. & PDF
School of Social Sciences
Jawaharlal Nehru University, New Delhi

# Contents

# Abbreviations

| | |
|---|---|
| ADS | Agriculture Department of State |
| AHD | Animal Husbandry Department |
| CAG | Comptroller and Auditor General |
| CSO | Central Statistical Organization |
| CV | Coefficient of Variation |
| DAC | Department of Agriculture and Cooperation |
| DECC | District Employment and Counseling Center |
| DES | Directorate of Economics and Statistics |
| DI | Disparity Index (David Sopher's Disparity Index) |
| DLHS | District Level House Hold Survey |
| EUS | Employment and Unemployment Survey |
| FYP | Five Year Plan |
| GK | Greater Kashmir (Newspaper) |
| GSL | Gereral Studies Manual |
| KSG | Kashmir Study Group |
| LFPR | Labour Force Participation Rate |
| MCWS | Modified Current Weekly Status |
| MHFW | Ministry of Health and Family Welfare |
| NFHS | National Family Health Survey |
| NSS | National Sample Survey |
| NSDP | National State Domestic Product |
| ORF | Observer Research Foundation |
| RTFD | Report of Task Force on Development |
| SFC | State Finance Commission |
| UPS | Usual Principal Status |
| UPSS | Usual Principal Subsidiary Status Approach |
| WTO | World Trade Organisation |

# 1

# Historical Perspective of Jammu & Kashmir Economy

The history of Kashmir is intertwined with the history of the broader Indian subcontinent and the surrounding regions, comprising the areas of Central Asia, South Asia, and East Asia. Historically, Kashmir referred to the Kashmir Valley. Today, it denotes a larger area that includes the Indian-administered state of Jammu & Kashmir (which consists of Jammu, the Kashmir Valley, and Ladakh), the Pakistan-administered territories of Azad Kashmir and Gilgit–Baltistan, and the Chinese-administered regions of Aksai Chin and the Trans-Karakoram Tract.

The mythological traditions supported fully by the research of geologists confirm that the valley originally was a huge lake called 'Satisar' (the land of goddess Sati) and its waters were blocked near Baramulla (ancient Varahmulla) hundred million years ago *(Kalhan 1148 AD)*. There are various historical legends for the State of Jammu & Kashmir in general and for Kashmir Valley in particular. According to the oldest extant book on Kashmir, *Nilmat Puran*, in the Satisar lived a demon called Jalod Bowa, who tortured and devoured the people, who lived near mountain slopes. Hearing the suffering of the people, a great saint Kashyap by name, came to the rescue of the people here. He was able to cut the mountain near Varahmulla, which had blocked the water of the lake from flowing into the plains below. The lake was drained, the land appeared, and the demon was killed. The saint encouraged people from India to settle in the valley. The people named the valley as *Kashyap-Mar.* The name Kashmir also implies land desiccated from water (ka-water and shimeera-desicate). The Chinese pilgrim Hien-Tsang who visited the valley around 631 AD called it Kashi-Mi-Lo. In modern times, the people of Kashmir have shortened it into 'Kasheer' in their tongue. In Persian terminology Kashmir is combination of two words 'kash' and 'mir', kash means to attract and mir means the rich, there by Kashmir means attracting the rich.

*Jammu & Kashmir.* Bilal Ahmad Khan, Oxford University Press. © Oxford University Press 2022.
DOI: 10.1093/oso/9780192849656.003.0001

The abundant resources, beauty, and the salubrious climate of the Kashmir valley were known even from the ancient times. This northern most state of India is bounded in the north-east by China, in the north-west by Afghanistan, and in the west by Pakistan. The southern boundary is contiguous with the states of Punjab and Himachal Pradesh. The State is broadly grouped into three main regions, namely Jammu, Kashmir, and Ladakh. Geographically, the Pir Panchal range separates Jammu from Kashmir Valley, the Zojila intervenes between the latter and Ladakh. The State has a geographical area of 222,236 sq. km comprising 6.93 per cent at national level 2011–12).

## Nature of Population Growth in J&K State

The size of population and its growth have a direct bearing on the economic development, social wellbeing, and political stability of a region. Population growth is, thus, pivotal in the region's demographic dynamism.

At the time of the partition of British India, the state had a population of slightly more than *four million, one million* of whom were in the areas that were occupied by *Pakistan* during the first Kashmir war of 1948–1949. The remaining *three million* lived in the part of the state that was to be controlled by *India*. The population in the Indian part of Kashmir increased at a rate of less than 1 per cent annually till 1971. After that, the growth rate increased threefold to 2.6 per cent a year. It stayed at that level for three decades. The sudden jumps in some periods reflect some migration into the area from other parts of India (Burki, 2007).

Although, growth rate of population of J&K State has a record of constant impulses of immigration from the north-west, west-south, and east directions. The alien races, ethnic groups, and various religions have influenced the cultural ethos and mode of life of this region. State has great diversity in its terrain, climatic conditions, and resource base which resulted uneven distribution of population. The heavy increase of population from past seven decades is reflected in Table 1.1.

Prior to 1921, the population of the State grew at a slow rate because the State experienced number of famines and epidemics (Census of India, 1921). After 1921, however, the population increased steadily.

**Table 1.1** Population Trend for J&K State, 1941–2011, (Lakhs)

| Year | T. Pop | Male | % | Fem | % | Rural | % | Urban | % |
|---|---|---|---|---|---|---|---|---|---|
| 1941 | 29.46 | 15.77 | 53.51 | 13.69 | 46.49 | 25.60 | 86.88 | 3.86 | 13.12 |
| 1951 | 32.53 | 17.16 | 53.36 | 15.17 | 46.64 | 27.96 | 85.95 | 4.57 | 14.05 |
| 1961 | 35.60 | 18.96 | 53.25 | 16.64 | 46.75 | 29.67 | 83.34 | 5.93 | 16.66 |
| 1971 | 46.16 | 24.58 | 53.25 | 21.58 | 46.76 | 37.58 | 81.41 | 8.58 | 18.59 |
| 1981 | 59.87 | 31.64 | 52.84 | 28.22 | 47.16 | 47.26 | 78.95 | 12.60 | 21.05 |
| 1991* | 77.18 | 40.14 | 52.00 | 37.04 | 48.00 | 58.79 | 76.17 | 18.39 | 23.83 |
| 2001 | 100.69 | 53.00 | 52.63 | 47.36 | 47.36 | 75.64 | 75.12 | 25.05 | 24.88 |
| 2011 | 125.48 | 66.65 | 53.11 | 58.83 | 46.88 | 91.34 | 72.79 | 34.14 | 27.20 |

*Source:* (1) Census of India 1981, 2011; (2) Digest of Statistics 20000/201112.

*Notes:* (i) 1951 figures of population are the arithmetical mean of 1941 & 1961 populations, as in 1951, Census was not held in J&K State; (ii) The 1991 Census was not held in J&K. The population figures are as projected by the Standing Committee of Experts on Population Projections (October 1989).

In 1941, the population of the State was 29.46 lakhs, out of which 15.77 lakhs (53.51 per cent) were males and 13.69 (46.49 per cent) females. In 1951, soon after the partition, the population of the State reached to 32.53 lakhs. During 1961–71, the population of the State proliferated from 35.60 lakhs to 46.16 lakhs, thus showing an increase of 10.56 lakhs. As per 1981 Census, the total population of the State was 59.87 lakhs with 52.84 per cent males and 47.16 per cent females (Census of India, 1941).

The figures of *2001 Census* showed that the population of the State crossed one crore mark showing a total population of 100.69 lakhs with 53.00 lakhs males (52.63 per cent) and 47.36 lakhs females (47.36 per cent). Again, census 2011 showed that the population of the State increased 125.48 lakhs with 66.65 lakhs males (53.11 per cent) and 58.83 lakhs females (46.88 per cent). Thus, it becomes articulate fixing the data that population in the State has increased by 96.02 lakhs from 1941 to 2011.

Agriculture is investigated the main stay of state economy as more than 75 per cent of the population derives their income directly or indirectly from the agriculture sector. The J&K State is basically agrarian and rural in nature. The rural population in the State is three times more than the urban population shown in the Table 1.1. According to the Census report of 1941, 86.88 per cent of the total population of the State was residing in the villages and the remaining 13.12 per cent in urban areas. During 1961–71, the percentage of urban population increased from 16.66 per cent to 18.59 per cent and the trend continued increased as shown in the Table 1.1. According to 1991 estimates, the rural population was 76.17 per cent while as that of urban population was investigated 23.83 per cent The *Census 2011* showed 72.79 per cent of rural population while as 27.20 per cent urban population.

The provincial level analyses revealed that Kashmir province accounts higher proportion of rural population than in Jammu province. However, population living in villages has declined decade after decade. In fact, people from rural areas have migrated to urban areas (*more in Jammu province as people from Kashmir province tried to settle in Jammu (city) due to lack of security and confidence*) because of security reasons, education, medical facilities, and employment opportunities.

## Population Growth in J&K State, 1901–2011

Yet, an analysis of the development process over the past decades shows that one of the major causes for slow economic and social development has been unplanned population growth. Its optimum size, growth, composition, and quality of population play an important role in the development process. A large population undergoing hyper growth in a poor economy with limited resources and rudimentary technology can be a liability. Contrary to the population productively employed, it can be an asset. Thus, stabilization of population is the most important factor (Annual Report, MHFW, 1997–1998).

The state has witnessed a fluctuating population growth rate since 1901. The population trend is examined since the beginning of this century using the census data. The beginning of the century witnessed breakouts of cholera, pneumonia followed by floods and earthquakes which took a heavy toll of life in Kashmir Division. In Jammu division also, plague, enteric fever, and famine remained active throughout this period. In the first two decades of the 20th century, the population growth was below 10 per cent. After 1931, it raised at a constant rate of 10 per cent per decade up to 1961, thereafter, an unprecedented rise of 29 per cent per decade was highest growth rates among the all states in the country.

During the decade 1921–31, there was a severe famine in the Jammu division followed by cholera, small pox, and plague in the state. The census year 1931 marks a watershed in the demographic history of the state with a discernible change between the decades since 1931 (Census, 1941). This can be attributed to the fact that the general population itself has grown rapidly through natural increase; this growth has occurred in all regions and affected almost all population groups in the towns and villages. The accentuated growth rate is recorded only after 1960s. Data shows sudden spurt in population from 9.44 per cent in 1961 to 29.65 per cent in 1971, then 29.69 per cent in 1981, 28.92, 30.46, and 23.71 per cent in 1991, 2001, and 2011. The population growth of J&K State during the reference periods of 1901 to 2011 is reflected in Table 1.2.

However, since 1971, there was great change in absolute terms. In 1971 census, J&K stands 46.16 lakhs, and then proliferated to 59.87, 77.18, 100.69, and 125.48 lakhs in 1981, 1991, and 2001 and in 2011, reflects more than 25 per cent decadal variation since 1971 against nation

**Table 1.2** Population Growth of Jammu and Kashmir,

| Year | Population (in Lakhs) | Absolute Change (Lakhs) | Decadal Variation | | Average Annual Growth Rate |
|------|------|------|------|------|------|
| | | | J &K | India | |
| 1901 | 21.39 | – | – | – | – |
| 1911 | 22.92 | 1.53 | 7.16 | 5.75 | 0.69 |
| 1921 | 24.24 | 1.31 | 5.75 | –0.31 | 0.56 |
| 1931 | 26.70 | 2.45 | 10.14 | 11.0 | 0.97 |
| 1941 | 29.46 | 2.76 | 10.36 | 14.22 | 0.99 |
| 1951 | 32.53 | 3.07 | 10.42 | 13.31 | 1.00 |
| 1961 | 35.60 | 3.07 | 9.44 | 21.64 | 0.91 |
| 1971 | 46.16 | 10.55 | 29.65 | 24.80 | 2.63 |
| 1981 | 59.87 | 13.70 | 29.69 | 24.66 | 2.63 |
| 1991* | 77.18 | 17.31 | 28.92 | 23.86 | 2.57 |
| 2001 | 100.69 | 23.51 | 30.46 | 21.34 | 2.69 |
| 2011 | 125.48 | 26.51 | 23.71 | 17.70 | 2.63 |

*Source*: Census of India, J&K.

*Note*: *The 1991 census was not held in J&K. The population of India includes projected population of J&K (excludes area under occupation of Pakistan and China) as on 1 March 1991 made by the Standing Committee of Experts.

experienced below than 25 per cent in the same periods. The annual growth rate is more than 2 per cent since 1971. The annual growth rate of 2.63, 2.63, 2.57, 2.69, and 2.63 per cent is reflected during the same period of 1971, 1981, 1991, 2001, and 2011 respectively. According to the *2001 census*, the size of J&K's population is 100.69 lakhs, that is, 0.98 per cent at all India level and 1.01 per cent (125.48 lakhs), according to the 2011 census.

## District-Wise Growth Rate of Population, (1951–2001)

The distribution of population since 1951 shows almost the same trend. In 1951, seven districts had 5–10 per cent of the state population. Due to the decline in the share of population in Rajauri district, in 1961 and 1971, six districts remained in the category of having 5–10 per cent of the growth rate of state's population. In Leh and Kargil district, a little more than 1 per cent of the population is found. This is because of undulating topography and harsh climate has restrained people from settling there.

There is also a great deal of variation in the rate of growth of population in terms of spatial dimension. Major districts experienced an average annual growth rate ranging around 1 per cent and some around 14 per cent during the reference periods from 1951 to 2001. Most of these districts form a pocket surrounding Srinagar district. It is very important to note that the districts having influence of the urban agglomerations have a better average annual growth compared to other districts. Four districts Srinagar, Anantnag, Baramulla, and Jammu experienced average annual growth rate ranging 10 to 15 per cent from 1951 to 2001. The Jammu district ranks the top among all the districts in the average growth rate of population. From 1971 to 2001, Jammu district accounts more than 15 per cent of average growth rate of population. During the period between 1951 and 2001, Leh and Kargil district found only 1–2 per cent of the average growth rate of population due to harsh climate that has restrained people from settling there. In other districts, it can be assumed that male members have migrated to cities where employment opportunities are better compared to the villages. The district-wise growth rate of population since 1951 (up to 2001) in the J&K State is depicted in Table 1.3.

Table 1.3  District-wise Growth Rate of Population, 1951–2001, Percent

| District | 1951 | 1961 | 1971 | 1981 | 2001 |
|---|---|---|---|---|---|
| Kupwara | 5.75 | 5.73 | 5.58 | 5.49 | 6.36 |
| Baramulla | 11.05 | 11.01 | 11.10 | 11.19 | 11.59 |
| Srinagar | 12.01 | 12.36 | 12.22 | 11.83 | 12.30 |
| Badgam | 5.84 | 6.01 | 5.83 | 6.13 | 5.90 |
| Pulwama | 6.87 | 6.95 | 6.80 | 6.75 | 6.28 |
| Anantnag | 11.13 | 11.27 | 11.22 | 10.96 | 11.62 |
| Leh | 1.24 | 1.22 | 1.12 | 1.14 | 1.17 |
| Kargil | 1.29 | 1.27 | 1.16 | 1.10 | 1.14 |
| Doda | 7.06 | 7.37 | 7.41 | 7.10 | 6.86 |
| Udhampur | 7.32 | 7.31 | 7.42 | 7.58 | 7.34 |
| Punch | 4.53 | 4.34 | 3.70 | 3.74 | 3.69 |
| Rajauri | 5.46 | 4.82 | 4.71 | 5.05 | 4.75 |
| Jammu | 14.43 | 14.41 | 15.70 | 15.76 | 15.61 |
| Kathua | 6.01 | 5.92 | 6.02 | 6.17 | 5.40 |
| J&K | 100.0 | 100.0 | 100.0 | 100.0 | 100.0 |

*Source*: Calculated from the census data (Various Issues).

## District-Wise Size and Growth of Population, 2011

According to census 2011, total population of state stands 125.48 lakhs. District Jammu accounts highest proportion (15.26 lakhs) followed by Srinagar (12.69 lakhs) due to rapid migration from rural areas. According to *census 2011*, sex ratio stands at 883 per thousand. The population density of state varies highly among the districts. District Ganderbal (1151 per sq. km) accounts highest proportion followed by and Bandipora (1117) whereas district Leh and Kargil accounts only 3 and 10. The district-wise population of J&K State, as per Census 2011 is depicted in Table 1.4.

## Demographic Features of J&K State

Demographic transition is the important indicator for conceiving State's development, that is, studying various aspects of development.

**Table 1.4** District-wise population of J & K State, census 2011

| District | Total Pop (Lakhs) | | | Decadal Growth Rate (2001–11) | Sex ratio | Pop Density Per Sq. Km | Proportion of District Pop to State Total Pop | |
|---|---|---|---|---|---|---|---|---|
| | M | F | T | | | | M | F |
| Kupwara | 4.75 | 40.04 | 8.75 | 34.62 | 843 | 368 | 3.79 | 3.19 |
| Baramula | 5.42 | 4.73 | 10.15 | 20.34 | 873 | 305 | 4.32 | 3.77 |
| Srinagar | 6.75 | 5.94 | 12.69 | 23.56 | 879 | 703 | 5.38 | 4.73 |
| Badgam | 3.90 | 3.55 | 7.35 | 21.18 | 883 | 537 | 3.11 | 2.75 |
| Pulwama | 2.97 | 2.72 | 5.70 | 29.18 | 913 | 598 | 2.37 | 2.17 |
| Anantnag | 5.52 | 5.17 | 10.70 | 37.48 | 937 | 375 | 4.40 | 4.13 |
| Leh | 0.92 | 0.54 | 1.47 | 25.48 | 583 | 3 | 0.74 | 0.43 |
| Kargil | 0.80 | 0.62 | 1.43 | 20.18 | 775 | 10 | 0.64 | 0.50 |
| Doda | 2.13 | 1.96 | 0.40 | 27.89 | 922 | 79 | 1.70 | 1.57 |
| Udampur | 2.98 | 2.57 | 5.55 | 20.86 | 863 | 211 | 2.38 | 2.05 |
| Punch | 2.52 | 2.24 | 4.76 | 27.97 | 890 | 285 | 2.01 | 1.79 |
| Rajauri | 3.32 | 2.86 | 6.19 | 28.14 | 863 | 235 | 2.65 | 2.29 |
| Jammu | 8.15 | 7.10 | 15.26 | 12.48 | 871 | 596 | 6.50 | 5.66 |
| Kathua | 3.27 | 2.87 | 6.15 | 20.38 | 877 | 232 | 2.61 | 2.29 |
| Samba | 1.68 | 1.49 | 3.18 | 16.90 | 886 | 318 | 1.35 | 1.19 |
| Reasi | 1.66 | 1.48 | 3.14 | 27.06 | 891 | 184 | 1.33 | 1.18 |
| Kishtwar | 1.20 | 1.10 | 2.31 | 21.06 | 917 | 125 | 0.96 | 0.88 |
| Ganderbal | 1.58 | 1.38 | 2.97 | 36.30 | 869 | 1151 | 1.27 | 1.10 |
| Kulgam | 2.16 | 2.06 | 4.22 | 7.30 | 951 | 925 | 1.73 | 1.64 |
| Ramban | 1.49 | 1.34 | 2.83 | 31.81 | 901 | 213 | 1.19 | 1.07 |
| Shopian | 1.36 | 1.29 | 2.65 | 25.85 | 951 | 852 | 1.09 | 1.03 |
| Bandipore | 2.01 | 1.83 | 3.85 | 26.31 | 911 | 1117 | 1.61 | 1.46 |
| J&K | 66.65 | 58.83 | 125.48 | 23.71 | 883 | 124 | 2.47 | 1.98 |

*Source*: Census of India (2011); Directorate of Statistics and Economics, Govt. (2011–12).

Note: In 2006 new eight (8) districts were created in the Azad-led government, Kishtwar, Samba, Reasi, and Ramban new districts in the Jammu division and Bandipore, Kulgam, Ganderbal, and Shopian in the Kashmir valley.

It represents past achievements and makes some firm statements about the future where the state is going. Furthermore, attempts to explain why the economies have more or less passed through the same three stages of population growth (Theory of Demographic Transition). Prior to the economic modernization, national economies had stable or very slow growing population combination of high birth rate and high death rate. With economic development resulting in higher incomes, improving health facilities, there was marked decline in mortality that gradually raised life expectancy. With declining death rate but birth rate not falling correspondingly, these economies passed through stage two, marking slow growing population to rapidly increasing number. Finally, stage third is reached when the influences of modernization and economic development cause fertility to decline so that eventually falling of birth rate converge with lower death rate leaving little or no population growth (Dyson, 1988).

The workforce of a state is closely controlled by a large number of demographic factors. The size of population, the birth rate, the death rate, the longevity, migration, literacy, education, general health of people, the occupation of the people, per capita income attitude towards life, and standard of living influence the availability of workforce in a society (Roy, 2008).

In this context, we propose to discuss the following demographic trends in view of historical perspectives of J&K State like sex composition of population, population density, literacy rate, etc. The salient demographic characteristics of the J&K State have been elaborated in the following paragraphs:

## Sex Composition, 1981–2011

The sex composition of a population helps in understanding the demographic processes of fertility, mortality, and migration. The spatial pattern of sex ratio reveals a high degree of variation at district level. Samba followed by Udhampur recorded highest sex ratio in 1981 census and replaced by Kulgam and Shupian in 2011 census. Kargil registered least sex ratio of 775 per thousand.

### District-Wise Sex Ratio 1981–2011
An important concern in the present status of Jammu & Kashmir's demographic transition relates to adverse sex ratio. Since 1981 nothing has happened to change the attitude of the people in respect

of their preference for sons. The low sex ratio in the state may be attributed to the high mortality rate among the females on account of negligence of female children. Girls receive less medical attention than boys. Study further argues that there is mounting evidence of sex-selective abortion in some districts of the state (Annual Report: MHFW, 2013–2014). The district-wise sex ratio since 1981 is shown in Table 1.5.

**Table 1.5** District Wise Sex-Ratio of J & K State, 1981–2011, *Per 1000*

| District | 1981 | 1991 | 2001 | 2011 |
|----------|------|------|------|------|
| Kupwara | 858 | 882 | 906 | 843 |
| Badgam | 880 | 906 | 931 | 88 |
| Leh | 886 | 854 | 823 | 583 |
| Kargil | 853 | 845 | 837 | 775 |
| Punch | 889 | 904 | 919 | 890 |
| Rajouri | 906 | 892 | 878 | 863 |
| Kathua | 917 | 908 | 898 | 877 |
| Baramulla | 876 | 891 | 905 | 873 |
| Bandipora | 858 | 876 | 894 | 911 |
| Srinagar | 873 | 857 | 841 | 879 |
| Ganderbal | 871 | 894 | 917 | 869 |
| Pulwama | 906 | **919** | 942 | 913 |
| Shupiyan | 876 | 913 | **950** | **951** |
| Anantnag | 888 | 900 | 911 | 937 |
| Kulgam | 887 | **916** | **945** | **951** |
| Doda | 904 | 909 | 913 | 922 |
| Ramban | 867 | 878 | 889 | 901 |
| Kishtwar | 896 | 900 | 904 | 917 |
| Udhampur | **934** | 876 | 846 | 863 |
| Reasi | 864 | 872 | 880 | 891 |
| Jammu | 912 | 889 | 865 | 871 |
| Samba | **945** | 896 | 897 | 886 |
| J & K | **892** | **892** | **892** | **883** |
| India | **934** | **927** | **933** | **943** |

*Source*: Compiled from Census of India.
*Note*: Data of newly Created districts in 2006 stands at Tehsil level in 1981 & 2001.

Based on the census 1981, sex ratio in the State is adverse in the sense that in 1981 there were 892 females per 1000 males against 934 at national level. The sex ratio as per census 2001 is 892 against 933 at national level. The sex ratio as per *census 2011* was 883 against 940 at national level which is a matter of great concern and needs to be addressed on priority. It also depicts higher mortality rates for females in the state due to low level of social development.

Furthermore, the Division of Kashmir has only 878 females per 1000 of males, while in Jammu and Ladakh Divisions, the sex ratio stands at 925 and 879 respectively. The Division of Kashmir having over 95 per cent of Muslim population has a low sex ratio. In fact, many of the Muslim boys are not getting married and in many cases the bridegrooms have to pay a substantial amount to the parents of brides (Annual Report: MHFW, 2008–9).

## Age Structure or Age Composition, 1981–2011

Age structure is an important characteristic of population which determines the workforce and dependency ratio. Now considering J&K State, the dependency ratio is significantly high which reflects feature of developing societies. The age groups of State Population at national level since 1981 have been given in Table 1.6.

According to *census 1981*, age group 0–14 possess somewhat large proportion (13.34 per cent) then declined 9.49 per cent (2001) and 7.7 per cent (2011). Fortunately age group of 15–59 continuously maintains the

**Table 1.6** Age Structure of Population, 1981–2011, (Per cent)

| Jammu and Kashmir State | | | | All India | | |
|---|---|---|---|---|---|---|
| Age Group | 1981 | 2001 | 2011 | 1981 | 2001 | 2011 |
| 0-4 | 13.34 | 9.49 | 7.3 | 14.3 | 12.8 | 9.7 |
| 5-14 | 25.95 | 26.15 | 17.6 | 26.4 | 22.6 | 19.7 |
| 15-59 | 54.97 | 57.23 | 65.9 | 54.1 | 57.1 | 62.5 |
| 60 & Above | 5.67 | 7.13 | 8.4 | 6.2 | 7.5 | 8.0 |

*Source*: Compiled from Census of India (Various Issues).

dominance since 1981. According to census 2011, large proportion of population are trapped in the age group of 15–59 (65.9per cent) followed by group 5–14 (26.15 per cent). Thus, the state's potential for creating job opportunities can meet the increasing demand for employment as a consequence of increasing proportion of adult population.

## Birth Rate and Death Rate of J&K, 1971–2011

J&K state has performed well in providing health and medical facilities to the people. The number of health institutions has increased substantially in the recent past. The health indicators have improved and indicate the following position over the last five decades as shown in table. The birth rate and death rate for the state from 1971 to 2011 is shown in Table 1.7.

From the above estimates, it can be inferred that vital indicators BR, DR, & IMR have come down, reflect a satisfactory picture of health status of J&K State. However, death rate is lower in urban areas which can be attributed to better health care and health standards in urban areas. Similarly, table shows the high birth rate in rural areas which can be attributed to illiteracy and less acceptance to family planning measures.

**Table 1.7** Birth Rate, Death Rate and IMR for J&K State, (Per 1000)

| Years | Birth Rate | | Death Rate | | Infant Motility Rate | |
|-------|------------|-------|------------|------|----------------------|----|
| 1971 | Combined | 21.44 | Combined | 7.19 | Combined | 71 |
|       | Rural    | 22.19 | Rural    | 11.7 | Rural    | 84 |
|       | Urban    | 20.89 | Urban    | 6.02 | Urban    | 57 |
| 1981 | Combined | 31.6  | Combined | 9.0  | Combined | 72 |
|       | Rural    | 33.9  | Rural    | 9.7  | Rural    | 81 |
|       | Urban    | 21.4  | Urban    | 6.0  | Urban    | 63 |
| 2001 | Combined | 20.2  | Combined | 6.1  | Combined | 50 |
|       | Rural    | 21.1  | Rural    | 6.1  | Rural    | 51 |
|       | Urban    | 16.4  | Urban    | 6.1  | Urban    | 45 |
| 2011 | Combined | 18.6  | Combined | 5.7  | Combined | 45 |
|       | Rural    | 19.9  | Rural    | 6.0  | Rural    | 48 |
|       | Urban    | 13.7  | Urban    | 4.7  | Urban    | 34 |

*Source*: Indicators of Economic Development, 2015–16 (DES).

Table 1.8  Birth Rate and Death Rate of J & K State, 1981 & 2011.

| Year | Birth rate/1000 Population | | Death rate/1000 Population | |
|------|------|-------|------|-------|
| | J & K | India | J & K | India |
| 1981 | 20.2 | 28.4 | 6.1 | 9.3 |
| 2001 | 19.9 | 25.8 | 5.4 | 8.4 |
| 2011 | 19.9 | 21.8 | 5.5 | 7.2 |

*Source*: Compiled Census of India.

Birth Rate (BR) and Death Rate (DR) at National Level

The difference between birth rate (BR) and death rate (DR) gives the estimate of growth rate of population. The most encouraging and important fact is that both the birth and death rates in the state remained quite below than national average. The birth and death rate at both levels dwindled during 1981–2011; however, nation experienced faster speed than state.

## Density of Population

The density of population in the state has shown tremendous increase after independence. It has increased from 32 to 124 persons per km² in 1951–2011 generally by the rapid rate of population. The density of population has increased more than two-fold in the last 50 years only. Srinagar and Jammu districts recorded high density of population of 703 and 596 persons per km² respectively, mainly on account of being the state's administrative capitals which have made them the hub of socio-economic activities. The lowest population density is found in the Leh district with only 3 persons per km².

The population density of J&K State since 1981 shown in Table 1.9.

In the Kashmir division, highest density of population is recorded in Srinagar district followed by Badgam. In Jammu division, high concentration and high density of population is found in Jammu plains consisting of Jammu and Kathua districts. On the other hand, Leh, Kargil, and Doda districts recorded least density of population due to harsh environment control and the absence of social and economic development activities. Since 1981, Srinagar is the most thickly populated district followed by Jammu district.

**Table 1.9** Population Density of J & K State, 1981–2011

| State/Districts | Area sq. kms | Density (Persons per sq. km of area) | | | |
|---|---|---|---|---|---|
| | | 1981 | 1991 | 2001 | 2011 |
| Anantnag | 3984 | 165 | 207 | 294 | 375 |
| Pulwama | 1398 | 289 | 369 | 464 | 594 |
| Srinagar | 2228 | 318 | 401 | 531 | 703 |
| Badgam | 1371 | 268 | 263 | 461 | 537 |
| Baramulla | 4588 | 146 | 188 | 252 | 305 |
| Kupwara | 2379 | 138 | 175 | 269 | 368 |
| Leh | 82665* | 2 (a) | 2 (a) | 3 (a) | 3 |
| Kargil | 14036 | 5 | 6 | 8 | 10 |
| Jammu | 3097 | 305 | 390 | 508 | 596 |
| Udampur | 4550 | 100 | 132 | 162 | 211 |
| Doda | 11691 | 36 | 45 | 59 | 79 |
| Kathua | 2651 | 139 | 186 | 205 | 232 |
| Rajouri | 2630 | 115 | 159 | 182 | 235 |
| Poonch | 1674 | 134 | 175 | 222 | 285 |
| J & K | 222236 Sq Kms | 59 (a) | 76 (a) | 99 (a) | 124 |
| All India | 3287263 Sq Kms | 240 | 298 | 324 | 382 |

*Source*: Census of India, J&K.

*Note*: *Including 78114 sq. kms under Pakistan, 5180 sq. kms handed over by Pakistan to China.

As per *2001 Census*, Srinagar district has 531 souls per sq. km, while as Jammu has 508 souls per sq. km. Leh has the lowest density of 3 souls per sq. km. Srinagar, Jammu, Pulwam, and Badgam districts constitute the zone of highest density in the State. This is due to variety of factors such as level of land, fertile character of the soil, moderate climate, and availability of adequate irrigational facilities besides higher level of economic development. The J&K State stands at 124 souls per sq. km in 2011 against 382 at national level.

## Literacy Rate of J&K, 1981–2011

Literacy rate is a vital parameter to gauge the socio-economic transformation of the population. The process of education in terms of improved qualification and skills would help in the formation of human capital stock which has an overwhelming influence on the socio-economic development of a region as it determines the rate and pattern of resource utilization.

District wise literacy rate of State is examined since 1981. During 1981 only four districts, namely Jammu (42.86 per cent), Srinagar (33.90 per cent), Kathua (31.90 per cent), and Leh (25.17 per cent), the literacy rate was over 25 per cent, while in other three districts, namely Badgam (17.86 per cent), Kargil (18.86) and Doda (18.50) possess less than 20 per cent of literacy rate (J&K in Indian Economy, 2017, DES). The literacy rate in the remaining districts varied between 20 and 25 per cent. However, with the passage of time, the literacy rate increases steadily due to several schemes and backward and economically deprived areas were given special attention. It increased almost two-fold. According to *census 2011*, literacy rate of J&K stands 68.74 per cent. The district wise literacy rate, 1981–2011 is reflected in Table 1.10.

Literacy Rate at National Level
According to the *census of 1981*, literacy rate stood only 26.67 per cent against national average of 41.43 per cent. During 1981–2011, the literacy rate increased by 42.07 against 31.57 per cent at national level shown in Table 1.11.

As per *census 2011*, the literacy rate of the state is 68.74 per cent against 74.04 per cent at national level. Male and female literacy rate accounts 78.26 per cent and 58.01 per cent against the national average of 82.14 per cent and 65.46 per cent. The district-wise pattern of literacy rate indicates high rate for Jammu, Samba, and Leh district, while low literacy rates for Ramban, Bandipora, and Badgam districts in the State. Female literacy rate is low in all districts. This reflects a poor social awareness for female education due to existing socio-cultural beliefs.

## Religious Composition

The basic needs like food, clothing, shelter, and occupations of the people are closely influenced by the religious values. Religion has been divisive as well as unifying force. The religious composition has great social and

**Table 1.10**  District wise Literacy Rate of J & K State, 1981

| Districts | 1981 | 2001 | 2011 |
|---|---|---|---|
| Anantnag | 22.93 | 51.27 | 64.32 |
| Pulwama | 20.47 | 54.62 | 65.00 |
| Srinagar | 33.90 | 50.57 | 71.21 |
| Budgam | 17.86 | 47.60 | 57.98 |
| Baramulla | 20.62 | 51.12 | 66.93 |
| Kupwara | 16.82 | 51.36 | 66.92 |
| Leh | 25.17 | 68.84 | 80.48 |
| Kargil | 18.86 | 68.35 | 74.49 |
| Jammu | **42.86** | 77.87 | 83.98 |
| Udhampur | 23.50 | 66.97 | 69.90 |
| Doda | 18.50 | 63.74 | 65.97 |
| Kathua | 31.90 | 71.68 | 73.50 |
| Rajouri | 24.73 | 71.02 | 68.54 |
| Poonch | 23.39 | 68.62 | 68.69 |
| Jammu & Kashmir State | 26.67 | 54.46 | 68.74 |

*Source*: Census of India. J&K in Indian Economy—Various Issues (DES).

*Notes*: In 2006 new eight (8) districts were created in the Azad-led government, Kishtwar (58.54), Samba (82.48), Reasi (59.42), and Ramban (56.90) new districts in the Jammu division and Bandipore (57.82), Kulgam (60.35), Ganderbal (59.99), and Shopian (62.49) in the Kashmir valley according to census 2011.

**Table 1.11**  Literacy Rate of Jammu and Kashmir at All India Level

| | Jammu and Kashmir State | | | All India | | |
|---|---|---|---|---|---|---|
| Year | Literacy Rate | Male | Female | Literacy Rate | Male | Female |
| 1981 | 26.67 | 36.29 | 15.88 | 41.43 | 53.46 | 28.47 |
| 2001 | 54.46 | 65.75 | 41.82 | 65.38 | 75.85 | 54.16 |
| 2011 | 68.74 | 78.26 | 58.01 | 73.0 | 80.9 | 64.6 |

*Source*: Census of India, Socio-Economic Profile of J&K, 2008, DES.

economic relevance. The religious composition for state of 1981 has been given in Table 1.12.

It is examined nearly 66 per cent of the total population of the J&K state consists of Muslims and 30.41 per cent of Hindus. Buddhists with 1.26 per cent constitute the third largest religious group followed by Sikhs

Table 1.12 Religious Composition of Jammu and Kashmir State, 1981

| Division | Muslims | Hindus | Sikhs | Buddhists | Others |
|----------|---------|--------|-------|-----------|--------|
| Kashmir | 94.00 | 4.42 | 1.20 | 0.05 | 0.33 |
| Jammu | 33.81 | 62.06 | 3.67 | 0.11 | 0.35 |
| Ladakh | 44.66 | 0.01 | — | 51.82 | 3.51 |
| Total | 65.84 | 30.41 | 1.06 | 1.26 | 0.19 |

Source: Victoria Schofield (2001). *Kashmir in Crossfire*. London: B Taurus Publishers.

Table 1.13 Religious Composition of J&K State, 1981–2011

|  | 1981 | 2001 | 2011 |
|--|------|------|------|
| Muslim | 64.19 | 66.97 | 68.31 |
| Hinduism | 32.24 | 29.63 | 28.44 |
| Sikhism | 2.23 | 2.04 | 1.9 |
| Buddhism | 1.16 | 1.12 | 0.9 |
| Christianity | 0.19 | 0.20 | 0.30 |
| Jainism | 0.03 | 0.02 | 0.01 |
| Others | 0.02 | 0.01 | 0.01 |

Source: The First Report on Religion Data, New Delhi, 2004; Victoria Schofield (2001). *Kashmir in Crossfire*. London: B Taurus Publishers; and Census of India (2011).

(1.06 per cent) in the state. There are however, significant spatial variations in the concentrating of different religious groups. In the Kashmir Division, Muslims have an overwhelming majority constituting 94 per cent of population and in Jammu Division about 62 per cent are Hindus, while in Ladakh Division 51.82 per cent are Buddhists (Victoria, 2001). Thus, spatial variation in the population of different regions is quite significant. The Religious composition of State since 1981 is depicted in Table 1.13.

Expectedly, very large variations are found in the percentage of different religious communities since 1981. The State possesses large proportion of Muslims and India followed by Hindu proportion (Religion Data, 2004). As per the last *2011 census*, J&K is Muslim majority state in

India with approximately 68.31 per cent of population following Islam. Hinduism is the second popular religion in the State with approximately 28.44 per cent following it. While 1.9 per cent followed Sikhism and small proportion follow Buddhism (0.9 per cent), Christianity (0.3 per cent), Jainism (0.01), and other (0.01).

## Life Expectancy of J&K

J&K has surpassed Kerala as the state with the highest life expectancy in India, according to the latest data released (on 19 October 2016) by Registrar General of India custodian of census data. The report from *Sample Registration Survey* provides life expectancy at birth for year 2002–06 and 2010–14 for J&K 72.6 and 74.6 against All India figure of 67.9 and 63.5. This hasn't happened overnight as it took more than three decades to reach to this level along with constant efforts from the state. While going to the retrospection, in 1970–75, J&K had a total life expectancy of 56.1 years with 56.9 for men and 55.2 for women whereas Kerala in the same period of 1970–75 had a total life expectancy of 62.0 with 60.8 for men and 63.3 for women. J&K State was behind Kerala, Punjab (57.9), and Haryana (57.5).

According to *National Family Health Survey, 2016–17*, J&K stands at the rank two with 2,812 hospitals after Rajasthan. The J&K has higher number of health institutions than neighbouring Himachal Pradesh (160), Punjab (240), and Haryana (159). J&K has a total of 637 Primary Health Centres, 84 Community Health Centres, and 23 district hospitals.

## Occupational Structure

Estimates with regard to sectoral structure reveal that in consistent with the declining contribution of primary sector towards GSDP, the labour absorption of this sector shows a dwindling trend. And, the tertiary sector occupied this place as the employment generation and secondary sector has remained more or less constant over the period except for the decade 1971–81.

Table 1.14  Sectoral Structure of Work force, 1961–2011

| Occupation | 1961 | 1971 | 1981 | 2001 | 2011 |
|---|---|---|---|---|---|
| Primary Sector | 78.62 | 71.05 | 64.28 | 50.1 | 43.10 |
| Secondary Sector | 9.03 | 8.94 | 14.27 | 6.2 | 8.4 |
| Tertiary Sector | 12.35 | 20.01 | 21.45 | 43.7 | 48.5 |

*Source*: Compiled from Census of India (Various Issues).

Table 1.15  Occupational pattern of workforce, (1961–2011) Percent

| Occupation | 1961 | 1971 | 1981 | 2001 | 2011 |
|---|---|---|---|---|---|
| Cultivators | 75.81 | 64.27 | 56.85 | 43.40 | 36.12 |
| Agricultural Labours | 2.81 | 6.78 | 7.23 | 6.70 | 6.12 |
| Household Industry | 9.03 | 10.94 | 14.47 | 6.20 | 6.52 |
| Other | 12.35 | 18.01 | 21.45 | 43.70 | 51.24 |
| Total | 100 | 100 | 100 | 100 | 100 |

*Source*: Compiled from Census of India (Various Issues) J&K in Indian Economy (Various Issues), DES.

It is an interesting to note that during 1961 and 2011, the sharp fall of workforce took place by 35.52 per cent in primary sector which has been compensated by a sharp and unprecedented increase in the tertiary sector by 36.15 per cent.

The number of cultivators shows the consistent decline from 1961 to2011 and the direct labour absorption capacity of agriculture during the five decades of planning is reduced by one half. The agriculture can be attributed to sharp decline in the size of holdings during 60s as compared to 50s and absence of industrialization during the said decade (J&K in Indian Economy, 2017). It has been confined to small scale household industry whose progress over the period has seen many ups and downs revealed by the cyclical nature of the figures.

The occupational pattern is also reflected into various categories since 1961 below in Table 1.15.

## Urbanization and the Development Process

Urbanization is a part of development process. Its process is fast in rapidly growing economies where newly established industries and ancillary activities continuously provide jobs to people who migrate to cities (Dyson, 1988).

The development experience of various economies reveals that the growth process and structural transformations move concurrently. The decline in the contribution of agriculture and growth in the contribution of manufacturing and tertiary sector give fillip to process of urbanization. While analysing urban population since 1961 in terms of percentage, it has steadily increased from 16.66 per cent to 27.21 per cent up to 2011 (Indicators of Regional Development, 2011–12, DES). The J&K economy too has experienced similar structural changes and this is evident from the analysis of Table 1.16.

At the provincial level similar pattern is examined yet some interesting aspects call for special attention. In Kashmir division, the process of urbanization has increased by 11.49 per cent during 1961 and 2011 respectively. While as in the Jammu division correspondingly is 18.84 per cent. Interestingly Jammu division experiences the highest increase in urban population particularly after 1981 as the violence result migration from Kashmir to Jammu division.

The district-wise proportion of urban population indicates huge disparity. District Srinagar with 98.60 per cent urban population on the top

Table 1.16  Urban population and density of population for J&K State, (1961–2011), Percent

| Year | Urban Population (J&K) | Kashmir Division | Jammu Division | Density Population |
|------|------------------------|------------------|----------------|--------------------|
| 1961 | 16.66 | 20.21 | 12.18 | NA |
| 1971 | 18.59 | 23.14 | 13.81 | 45 |
| 1981 | 21.05 | 25.20 | 14.61 | 59 |
| 2001 | 24.81 | 26.52 | 22.62 | 100 |
| 2011 | 27.21 | 31.70 | 31.02 | 124 |

*Sources*: Indicators of Regional Development, DES (Various Issues).

followed by Jammu district and Ramban with only 4.16 per cent at the bottom. It indicates that these two cities occupy primate city position having concentration of economic and service activities. Urban population of state is 27.21 per cent as compared to 31.16 per cent at country level as per 2011 census.

Thus demographic characteristics provide an overview of population size, composition, and territorial distribution of population, density and dependency ratio, birth rate, death rate, and natural growth rate and migration and occupational pattern. These indicators help in identifying areas that need policy and programmed interventions, setting near and far-term goals, and deciding priorities, besides understanding them in an integrated structure.

## J&K Economy in Historical Perspective

Generally history of economy is a survey of man's existence and occupation on earth, the ideas, events, and meaning of man's long journey through his birth and development, leading to the progress of civilization, which are basic to any elicitation, indicative of how the past is interpreted and what lessons might be learnt for a clearer comprehension of the thoughts, motivations and actions, the philosophy and forces that operated and influenced him.

Kashmir is perhaps, to possess an authentic account of its history from the very earliest period. This past account of Valley, its culture and traditions, rise, and fall of various Kingdoms, victory and defeats of the people have been noted carefully, yet critically by the sons of its soil. Truly, Kashmiriat literature is very rich in information about Kashmir.

Agriculture was an area of critical concern and agrarian economy of state exhibited all the characteristics of a feudal and stagnant agriculture. The immemorial tradition in Kashmir which treated all land as the property of the ruler and those who cultivated it as his tenants, led to the creation of various intermediaries between the state and the cultivators from ancient times down to the pre-reform period (Ali, 1978). The organization of rural economy during the ancient period was directed towards the sole purpose of collecting revenue from the tenants. However, the best names remembered by the Kashmiris are Lalitaditya (697–738

AD, Karkota Dynasty) and Zain-ul-Abidin (1420–70). Lalitaditya was the best interest of *cultivators*. The most magnificent Muslim ruler, Zain-ul-Abidin was deservedly surnamed Budshah or the great king. The glorious aspect of his rule of about 52 years was promotion of learning, arts and crafts and, above all, tolerance towards the minority communities. He did not use official income for personal ends (J&KGSM, 2012–13).

The revenue administration and organization during medieval Kashmir (1339–1589) was not different from that of earlier Hindu period. The revenue demand during medieval period stood at one-sixth of the produce in the beginning and was later raised to one-third. The system of collection of revenue remained unchanged. During the Mughal period (1586–1753), large chunks of land were granted as Jagirs and Muffis with proprietary rights to those who carried favours with the kings. The 'Jagir' was a free grant of one or more villages from the ruler to the grantee as a reward for some conspicuous service, either military or otherwise. The people still enjoyed peace and orderly government during Mughal period. The Mughal introduced various reforms in the revenue industry and other areas that added progress. The constructions of splendid gardens and of some public works are the hall mark of this period (Bamzai, 2008).

During the Afghan rule (1753–1819), the system of revenue collection did not differ in practice. In this period, a portion of revenue was transferred to Afghan capital in Kabul.

During the Sikh rule (1819–1846) the miseries of the cultivators increased. The grant of land as Jagir and Maufi continued but without proprietary rights and large tracts of fertile land were reserved for royal households termed as 'Khalis', which later assumed the corrupted nomenclature of 'Khalsa', which gradually led to large scale revenue farming between the cultivator and the state. The land-holding systems prevalent between 12th and 19th centuries give rise to a long chain of intermediaries between the state and the actual tillers. There was a Malik Ala, Malik Adna, the occupancy tenant of grade A, the occupancy tenant of grade B, and the Sub-tenant. On the top were the Jagirdar, and Maufidar and the Illaqadar. This resulted in the development of landed aristocracy, absentee landlordism, concentration of land among few, and alienation of land from small and petty owners to bigger landlords and increasing expropriation of the share of peasantry. The peasants who depended on the agricultural economy were at the mercy of the rapacious officials, who enacted the 'last bush of grain from their meagre produce' (Land Committee Report, J&K Govt., 1951–52).

The conquest of Kashmir by the Sikhs in 1819 AD resulted more trouble for the masses as the triumphant army resorted to loot and marauding. Most of the governors gave utmost priority to raising revenues. However, Mehan Singh (Sikh governor, 1834–1841 AD) is known to have toned up the administration by imposing discipline and accountability and by making *food grains* available at subsidized rates. On the defeat of the Sikhs by the British, the latter annexed and then sold Kashmir to the local feudatory Gulab Singh under the *Treaty of Amritsar* for a sum of Rupees 75 lakhs. Gulab Singh consolidated power and hence commenced the Dogra rule in Kashmir (Kalis & Shaheen, 2013).

Maharaja Gulab Singh restored law and order at the initial stage and introduced a system of rationing of rice for the people who did not possess agricultural land, particularly the city dwellers. However, peasants continued to suffer on account of defective system of land revenue and corrupt procedures for its collection. The incidence of land revenue was three times more than the amount demanded in the British districts of Punjab. The plight of the other classes was no better than the peasants. Shawl industry witnessed a general decline because high taxes levied on shawls. Muslims of the State were exorbitantly taxed by the government and subjected to every kind of extortion and oppression. Due to heavy taxes on cultivation no more than about 1/16 of cultivable land was cultivated. Under pressure from the British, the problems of the peasantry received some attention during Maharaja Hari Singh (last ruler) reign in 1926 AD. He granted certain concessions to the peasantry in terms of tenancy rights and a land settlement operation was launched, initially through an expert A. Wingate and, two years later, this task was entrusted to Sir W. R. Lawrence, who accomplished the assignment. The exercise undertaken by him represents a landmark in the land administration of the State (Schofield, 2001).

In the late 1940s, land was the main source of income for the state's citizens; it contributed 60 per cent to the GSDP and employed 85 per cent of the labour force. Although rice was the main crop and the staple food for the state's citizens, the area's abundant forests and animal husbandry provided important sources of income. Handicrafts, including woodworking and wool weaving, had a market not only among the tourists who visited the area but also all-over British India. Thus two sectors—tourism and handicrafts—were important sources of external commerce for the state. These sectors were also the main *foreign exchange* earners for the area and gave Kashmir a reputation for beauty and dexterity. With abundance of water, it was natural that Kashmir would depend on agriculture for most of its income and for the livelihood of most of its population. For the same reason, horticulture was more prevalent in Kashmir (Burki, 2007).

Having gone through a period of extreme exploitation at the hands of the Dogra rulers, who were theoretically autonomous but in practice the stooges of the British imperialism, the population of the state in general and that of the valley in particular was living in the most abject conditions (Naik, 2011).

Furthermore, unlike India, which along with impoverished economy also inherited some useful assets in the form of national transport system and a good capitalistic base and entrepreneurial class (Vaidyanthan, 2005) from the British, the state of J&K inherited nothing but an impoverished economy from the Dogras. During the Dogra rule, an overwhelming majority of the population of the state was dependent on agriculture. But in view of the archaic agrarian structure, the agriculturalists and the agricultural workers in Kashmir were not having a fair deal as they had to carry on their shoulders the burden of absentee landlordism (Gupta, 1967). In 1921, the Census Report noted:

*It would be observed that out of every 10,000 persons 8,173, about 82 per cent, are dependent on the exploitation of animals and vegetation. Or more properly speaking on pasture or agriculture.... Of the agricultural population more than 98 per cent are ordinary cultivators, 1.4 per cent are supported by the raising of farm stock, while the aggregate share of growers of special products and forestry does not exceed .4 per cent. 1,160 persons out of every 10,000, or 11 per cent of the population, were employed in industries of different kinds, the more notable among them being the industries of dress and toilet (30.4 per cent), textiles (23.1 per cent), wood (12.2 per cent), food industries (8 per cent), metals (6.4 per cent) and ceramic (6.1 per cent). For every 10,000 persons only 86 derive their livelihood from transport, which does not come up to 1 per cent of the total population ... Only 3.3 per cent of the total population follow the calling of trade ... Public force absorbs .7 per cent of the population (Army*

*59 per cent, police 41 per cent), while the corresponding share of public Administration works out at 1.08 per cent.*

There were very little changes in the economy of the state in 1941 as the Census Report stated:

> *The Jammu and Kashmir state cannot compare with Great Britain, Bengal, and Bihar; it has a few industries but the more important of these—forest exploitation, sericulture, and fruit growing—are closely allied with agriculture and the state must be described as almost entirely agricultural.*

The economic policies of the state were concerned more with protecting and promoting the interests of the Raj (Dogras) and its collaborators (mostly Hindus) rather than welfare of the general masses (Wani, 2015). The administration's primary preoccupation was to maintain law and order, streamline tax collection, and ensure defence. The Dogra state, therefore, can be said to have represented framework for economic stagnation and social backwardness.

The legacy of such a kind of regressive policy-based on over-taxation, discrimination, and apathy towards the development put the economy of the state in a vicious circle of poverty in 1947 characterized by one of the lowest per capita income and consumption levels among the states of the sub-continent (Malik, 2005). Low-income levels resulted in low levels of savings and capital formation and, therefore, low productivity and low levels of income and this whole vicious circle perpetuated poverty in the state.

It was against these polices of the state that a popular movement was launched under the leadership of Sheikh Mohammad Abdullah to establish a nation-state to put an end to the religious discrimination and economic exploitation. Later on, under the influence of Socialism, Sheikh Mohammad Abdullah advocated the abolition of landlordism and the distribution of land to the tiller.

Therefore, the process and pattern of economic development of post-1947 had been dependent upon its inherited pattern of underdevelopment. There is no denying the fact that the British rule in India was very exploitative, leading to what *Gunder Frank* describes as the *development of underdevelopment* but the magnitude of oppression and exploitation in Kashmir was more propelled by Dogra rulers (Chandra, 2007).

It is worth mentioning here that the programme of the reconstruction of the state economy had been articulated by the political leadership since 1940s in the form of a manifesto called *Naya Kashmir or New Kashmir* in 1944 to emancipate them from the century's exploitation, oppression, backwardness, poverty, and the like (Kanjwal, 2017). The programmes envisaged institutional and agrarian restructuring to liberate and unleash the productive forces from the shackles of parasitic landlordism and also to clear decks for rapid modernization and industrial growth. Absentee landlordism was abolished and the actual tillers were made the owners of land. This interventionist role of the state was not for the welfare of a selected few as had been tradition under Dogra rule but was meant to benefit the whole society. It is therefore, not for nothing that the state at this point of time was looked upon as a benevolent state.

Based on reform agenda contained in the document *Naya Kashmir* formulated by the National Conference in 1944, the peoples' government which took over the reins of power from the Dogras in 1947, launched several measures aimed at ameliorating the conditions of the masses, especially the *peasantry*. The first radical land reform legislation, enacted in 1950, abolished the big landed estates without compensation of any kind, transferring the ownership to the actual tillers of land. Another law enacted by the new government ended the perpetual indebtedness from the rural population. These laws further refurbished by new Agrarian Reforms Act of 1976 responsible for providing an egalitarian base to land ownership (Rekhi, 1993).

In 1948, the attempt towards Jagirdari abolition was made through the enactment of Tenancy (Amendment) Act leading to the emancipation of peasantry by conferring protected tenancy rights in respect of land not exceeding 17 canals Abi or 33 canals Khuski in Kashmir province and 33 canals Abi and 65 canals Khushki in Jammu Division. However, this act was more tenurial-security—oriented rather than having a redistributive bias (Hassan, 2009).

On 13 July 1950, the Govt. under a historic decision of transferring land to the tiller passed the Big Landed Estates Abolition Act. The surplus land (above ceiling) was transferred to the tillers. The tiller was made the full owner of the land transferred to him. As a result of this about 900 land owners were expropriated without payment of compensation from the surplus land (above the ceiling) amounting to about 4.5 lakh acres out of which about 2.3 lakh acres were transferred to the tillers in ownership right free from any encumbrances. The feudal structure of agrarian economy in the mid-1947 era made the peasants miserable victims of serfdom. These reforms reduced rural poverty but could not ensure self-sustained growth of agriculture because of a combination of political and economic factors (Ali, 1978).

In 1950, the state had a meagre per-capita income of Rs. 208 (at 1960–61 prices) and the rate of literacy was just about 5 per cent against all India level of 18.33 per cent. Agriculture the predominant sector of the economy was stagnant and the productivity of the land/worker was very low. Industrial development was almost negligible and the lack of infrastructure had crippled the economy and accentuated the poverty syndrome (Misri & Bhat, 1994).

During the period of independence of India, there were three highways linking the state with the outside world. They were Jhelum Valley Road from Srinagar to Kohala via Baramulla and Domel; Banihal Road from Srinagar to Sialkot via Banihal and Jammu and Abbotabad Road from Domel to Abbotabad via Ramkot. All these highways connected the state with that part of Punjab which had become the part of Pakistan. Even the rivers provided the cheapest mode of transportation for the timber of Kashmiri forests and fast transportation of fruits, vegetables, woollen and silk materials, carpets, and pretty products of skilled Kashmiri artists and artisans to Pakistan (Joseph, 1992).

No doubt, Abdullah was ideologically oriented towards the socialistic principles of the Indian State but the measures he took once in power clearly indicate that he wanted J&K to be an economically independent state. To have a balanced budget, his government preferred to broaden the tax base of the state than to be dependent on external financial assistance. In this regard, his government remained adamant to continue with the custom barriers between J&K and the rest of India and levied taxes on education as well. Through such measures the government no doubt could balance its budget and decrease the deficit, the budget deficit in 1952 had been only 7.11 lakh while as it had been 3.7 crore, 2.8 crore, 2.9 crore, 2.5 crore for the years 1948, 1949, 1950, 1951 respectively, but at the same time the cost of living in the state increased leading to the disenchantment of the people, a situation very well exploited by Ghulam Mohammad Bakshi later on.

Apart from that, Abdullah launched a vigorous campaign in favour of making the state self-sufficient. Immediately after coming to power steps were taken to increase the production of food grains and programmes such as *Grow-More-Food Scheme* was launched under which new lands hitherto uncultivated were brought under cultivation. To secure the supply of food grains to the city people the infamous practice of Mujawaza—whereby peasants were called upon to deliver shali to government granaries in the city, so that it could be distributed to the city population—was reintroduced. Furthermore, to popularize the self-sufficiency, Sheikh even told the people to consume potatoes than to be dependent on imports thus earning him the name of Aaloo Bab.

By 1953 the government of Kashmir was divided within itself, its members pull in different directions and proclaims different policies (Guha, 2008). There is a bit of controversy regarding the cause of the split within the national conference's leadership arose over the autonomy versus integration issue. As Sheikh Abdullah and Mirza Afzal Beg wanting the state government to have at least the powers granted in the Instrument of Accession (Balraj, 1981), while as other National Conference ministers viz. Bakshi Ghulam Mohd, G. M Sadiq, D. P. Dhar, S. L. Sharif favouring greater integration with India. Consequently Abdullah was overthrown and Bakshi was invited to form the government.

After Abdullah's government was sacked, Bakshi Ghulam Mohammed became the prime minister of state with the support of Indian government. In order to quell discontent, the government of India proposed to step up the economic development in the region. The government of India realized that the only way the people of Kashmir could be kept under control and convinced of the merits of closer ties with India, was to provide the region with economic prosperity. Thus, in 1953, the India's Planning Commission advanced a loan of $14.9 million to the state government (Wajahat, 2004). Bakshi adopted a *populist style*, holding a Darbar (court) every Friday, where he used to hear the grievances of public (Ramachandra, 2008). A compulsory procurement of food grains, which had caused great hardship to the people, was abolished. Ration was subsidized to the consumers to the extent of 75 per cent of its cost and monopoly of cooperatives, which had become a symbol of tyranny was broken (Puri, 1981).

On April 1954, the custom barriers between the State and rest of India were abolished. Notwithstanding that the abolition of custom duties decreased the cost of living in the state. The imported commodities from India were cheap and durable and enhanced the choice of the Kashmiri consumers, and greatly helped in reducing the burden of indirect taxation on masses and led to greater investments from India for the improvement of roads and communication to facilitate the exchange of goods, however, it flooded the Kashmiri markets with finished goods, exposed its indigenous industries. This had a long-term impact on the development of indigenous industries in the state as the two key stimuli viz. import-substitution and growth of home market led to the development of industries in post-1947 (Drabu, 2004).

Although, the concept of planned development was introduced in J&K, along with other states of India right from the First Plan in 1951 but planned development in the state in true sense started with the Second Five Year Plan (1956–61). This was so because of the fact that real emphasis towards the attainment of declared goals of development policy like rapid increase in living standards, full employment at adequate wages, reduction inequalities, was given by the introduction of the Second FYP. In the initial period (pre-1954), under the Article 370 of the Indian constitution, taxes, which in other cases were collected by the Union, remained exclusively under the state control and the Income Tax Department of the state remained free from the control of India (Report on Economic Reforms of J&K, 1998). However, the change of government in the state leads drastic change in financial relations with the union.

Through different Acts since 1957, the state entered into financial arrangements with the centre government which brought it at par with other state with respect to financial matters including proportionate allocation of funds from the centre (Anand, 2006). The financial integration of Kashmir with the centre, which Sheikh had resisted and which was gladly accepted by Bakshi, brought great financial aid to the state.

The Second Five Year Plan aimed at securing a coordinated and balanced development of the economy of the state with a view to ensure better standard of living for its people. Unlike the first plan which had a limited character and gave main emphasis on agriculture, the second plan was of a larger dimension. The second state plan made it clear that the plan was designed to satisfy the objectives of opening up of new areas like, large and medium industries and extension of irrigation facilities on a large scale and the development of backward areas. The Third Plan (1961–62 to 1965–66) envisaged vital economic policies for the speedy achievement of a socialist pattern of society (J&K: A Review of Progress, 1969). The development schemes incorporated in the new Plan stressed on state income, power resources, industries, and employment opportunities.

Besides the reorganization of rural economy by enlarging the scope of agriculture the plan gave top most priority to the development of power, setting up of industries and exploitation of untapped mineral wealth of the state (Review of Progress, J&K, 1969). During the Second and Third plan periods, which also coincide with the financial integration of the state with the Indian union, the rate of growth in the State Domestic Product was of the order of 8 per cent. Not surprisingly therefore, this phase (1956–1966) was one of the basic infrastructure building phases in the state. The amount of assistance increased from Rs. 10 crores during the First Plan to 62 crores at the end of the third plan. It is worth noting that the financial assistance received by the state was the highest percentage of assistance received by any other state of the Indian union.

Notwithstanding that the government levied certain taxes for the first time during the Third plan viz. electricity duty (from April 1962), agricultural income tax (from September 1962), and passenger tax (1 July 1963) and increased the scope of sales tax and per capita state tax to increase revenue and decrease the state's dependence on the centre, however, even in 1968–69 the per capita tax in J&K State at Rs. 14 was very low against other states and the state's income through all its tapped sources was far less than its expenditure. Besides there had been a fast increase in expenditure on police, famine relief, food subsidies, and debt services which had reduced the funds available for development. Therefore, the state continued depends on the centre for financial assistance (Bhattacharya, 1994). However, the generous financial assistance especially in the form of loan led to heavy indebtedness of the state and increased its dependence on centre. It was the policy adhocism at the central level which translated into a soft budget constraint for the government. This, in the long run, had proved detrimental and adverse impact on the culture of management of state finances (Ganguly & Bajpal, 1994).

Notwithstanding that with regard to raising the revenue and minimizing the expenditure, the state government had recommended, for the period between 1966 and 1975, that the sales tax should be reviewed and tax rate on items which were not of mass consumption be enhanced and the coverage of tax should also be extended. The land revenue should be made more just and elastic by relating it to productivity and charging different rates according to the size of the holding. The non-developmental expenditure should be kept to the minimum and policy of food subsidy should be reviewed to reduce the burden on the expenditure.

In 1969, while devising the formula for sharing Central Assistance among states the Fifth Finance Commission, acting in line with the *Gadgil Formula,* had accorded special status to J&K along with Assam and Nagaland. Besides historical and political reasons, the bases of declaring the three states as Special Category States were the harsh terrain, backwardness, and social problems prevailing. However, after its inclusion in the Special Category States, the state of J&K was treated differently. The state was not provided with the facility of plan assistance at the rate of 90 per cent in the form of grant-in-aid and 10 per cent in the form of loan, which was bestowed to special category states (Jamwal, 1994).

The development of the state through planning received a new impetus with the introduction of Single Line Administration in 1976 by Sheikh Mohammad Abdullah. Through this process, which was a unique concept of decentralized planning (Review, J&K, 1998), decentralization was brought at the district level and district development boards were constituted for planning at the district level with the twin objective of making planning more reflective of the hopes and aspirations of the common man and ensuring speedy implementation of the programmes. The system of decentralized planning yielded considerable benefits in terms of extending the impact of developmental programmes and in galvanizing public involvement as well as reducing regional disparities.

To make decentralized planning more effective larger freedom was given to the District Development Boards during the Ninth Plan for the fixation of priorities and inclusion of projects having local area relevance. The state's continued dependence on the centre finance transfers had been caused by various factors. Failure to mobilize enough resources within the state had been the foremost cause. Having ratified all post-1953 political changes in the state through the Accord of 1975, Sheikh Abdullah received Indian financial assistance as enthusiastically as Bakshi had (Economic Review of J&K, 1984–85).

However, the central plan assistance to the state did not take care of the resource gap in the non-plan budget up to the Seventh Plan (1985–1990). It was because of this liberal financial assistance which the state received from the centre that the plan expenditure in aggregate and per capita terms since first Five Year plan, had increased over time—the per capita expenditure had gone up from a mere Rs. 34 in the First Plan to Rs. 556 in 1987–88 of Seventh Plan and that the state could formulate developmental plans which besides agriculture gave thrust on the creation of adequate infrastructure like power, transport, and provisions of social and community services in the form of schools, health centres, piped water supply, social welfare centres, etc.

However, one major side effect of the policy of liberal funding was that it failed to give the state an impetus to mobilize its own resources for economic growth. The state continued to be among the poorest states of India and the impact of the plans in terms of developmental indicators had not been significant.

Furthermore, most of the funds which the state received from centre for the economic development of the State were either siphoned off into the pockets of the ruling elite or were spent as Non-Plan Expenditure, important to mention that the central assistance to the state did not take care of the resource gap in the non-plan budget prior to the Seventh plan (1985–1990). It is also worth to mention here that the discriminatory 70:30 formula regarding the devolution of funds between the centre and the state led to the indebtedness of the state to the centre as a result of which about 50 per cent of the state's expenditure began to comprise of debt and interest repayments (Malik, 2005).

Estimates of the State totals based on sample survey showed that in 1953–54 there were 4.76 lakh operational holdings in the rural sector of J&K, out of which 4.05 lakh (85 per cent) were agricultural holdings. The results estimated at state level showed that in 1960–61 there were 5.31 lakh operational holdings over an area 18.75 lakh acres. Although average size of agricultural operational holding appreciably did not decline

Table 1.17  Size, Number and Area Operated in J&K State

| Size of operational holdings (acres) | No. of operational holdings (1000 acres) | Percentage | Area (1000 acres) | Percentage |
|---|---|---|---|---|
| Up to 0.49 | 26 | 4.90 | 7 | 0.370 |
| 0.50–0.99 | 48 | 9.04 | 37 | 1.97 |
| 1.00–2.49 | 173 | 33.52 | 304 | 16.21 |
| 2.50–4.99 | 158 | 29.75 | 545 | 29.07 |
| 5.00–7.49 | 70 | 13.18 | 411 | 21.92 |
| 7.50–9.99 | 25 | 4.71 | 210 | 11.20 |
| 10.00–12.49 | 13 | 2.45 | 137 | 7.31 |
| 12.50–14.99 | 5 | 0.94 | 69 | 3.68 |
| 15.00–19.99 | 5 | 0.94 | 77 | 4.11 |
| 20.00 & above | 3 | 0.57 | 23 | 4.16 |
| Total | 531 | 100 | 1875 | 100 |

Source: Agriculture Census, 1970–71, J&K government, p. 7.

between 1953/54 and 1960/61 yet it remained far below at all India average (Agriculture Census, 1970–71). In 1970–71 holdings below 5 acres constituted 88.60 per cent of total holdings, against 77.31 per cent in 1960 and 73.34 per cent in 1950. The statistics regarding size, number and area under operational holdings during 1960–61 is presented in Table 1.17.

As per *Agriculture Census 2001*, the average size of operational holdings reduced to 0.66 hectares and there are 8.46 lakh holdings below 0.5 hectares size comprising 1.99 lakh hectares operational area, being cultivated (operated) by 3.02 lakh of population. Another category of cultivating households is the size class of operational holding 0.5–1.0 hectare, operating 2.30 lakh hectares of operational area comprising 3.49 lakh. The worst situation emerges when look at sub marginal holdings, that is holdings less than 0.5 hectares size. These holdings accounted 58.64 per cent as per *Agriculture Census 2001* with average size 0.22 hectare comprising about 47 lakh persons. It means 4.7 million rural populations on an average have 4.4 kanal of land or less, far below the subsistence level thus having serious bottleneck to get two square meals from land.

The Eighth *8th Agriculture Census* (2005–06) depicts operational holdings under different size classes. The total number of operational holders has been worked out to be 13.77 lakhs and average size of operational holding was found out to be 0.67 hectare. About 94 per cent of operational holders fall in the category of Marginal and Small farmers. About 5 per cent of operational holders fall in semi-medium category holding, only 1 per cent of the operational holders fall in the Medium category holding and only 0.04 per cent of the operational holders fall in the large category holding.

Till 1965–66, traditional agricultural practices were followed. After 1966 the farmers adopted new agricultural improved practices by using high yielding varieties of seeds (HYV) but limited to certain areas and some crops only as a humble beginning. A main factor responsible for adoption of this technology change was because of improved and assured irrigational facilities with high yielding crops. The benefits of technological changes accrued to only such areas and crops which enjoyed irrigation facilities and its impact on hilly agriculture was very low. Thus agricultural changes were area-specific and crop-specific.

## Development through Decades

The development programmes in the state received a fillip with the introduction of 'Planning' in 1951. The launching of First FYP (1951–56) marked the elimination of age-old backwardness of State. The analysis of the Table 1.18 brings some interesting facts. First, no important changes have taken place in respective plan priorities. Irrigation, power, transport and social services continued to remain areas of focus from 1st to 8th plan. From Eighth Plan onwards, rural development seems to be added objective of the state planning. Second, there has been huge gap between the plan outlay and actual expenditure. This is presented in column No. 4.

Third, gap between actual expenditure and plan outlay indicates that either outlays have not been carefully worked out or actual execution of expenditure has remained faulty for reasons best known to planners and administrators whose activities are influenced by politicians.

The state continued to be the least industrialized among all states. A couple of factors, viz., violence, and paucity of resources, treacherous terrain, infrastructural bottlenecks, and crippling effect of transportation had been responsible for the industrial backwardness. Furthermore, the

Table 1.18 Outlay and Actual Expenditure during Plan Period (FYP) from 1950–51 to 2007–12 for Jammu & Kashmir State (Rs. In Crores)

| Plan Period | FYP Outlay | Actual Expenditure | Gap | Priority Sectors |
|---|---|---|---|---|
| 1951–56-I | 12.74 | 11.52 | 1.22 | Irrigation, Power, Transport, Communication |
| 1956–61-II | 33.92 | 25.94 | 7.98 | Agriculture, Irrigation, Transport & Social Services |
| 1961–66-III | 75.15 | 61.85 | 13.3 | Irrigation, Social Service & Agriculture |
| 1969–74-IV | 158.40 | 162.84 | 4.44 | Irrigation, Power, Social Service, Transport & Communication |
| 1974–79-V | 362.60 | 278.65 | 83.95 | Irrigation, Power & Social Service |
| 1980–85-VI | 900.00 | 998.14 | –98.14 | Social Service, Irrigation, Power & Agriculture |
| 1985–90-VII | 1400.0 | 2006.23 | 606.23 | Social Service, Irrigation, Power & Agriculture |
| 1992–97-VIII | 4000.0 | 4520.07 | –520.07 | Irrigation, Power & Social service |
| 1997–02-IX | 10000.0 | 7524.87 | 2475.13 | Social service, Irrigation, Power, Agriculture & Rural Development |
| 2002–07-X | 14500.0 | 14172.47 | 327.53 | Social service, Irrigation, Power, Agri & Rural Development |
| 2007–12-XI | 25834.0 | 21788.73 | 4045.27 | Power, R&B, Education & Agriculture and Irrigation |
| 2012–17-XII | 43337.3 | 37163.85 | 6173.54 | Agriculture, Infrastructure, Health, Education, Tourism |

Source: State Finance Commission Report, Govt. of J&K/Indicators of Economic Development (J&K), 2015–16 (DES).

absence of forward-looking entrepreneurial elite in the state and dearth of raw material sources within the state acted as an impediment to the industrialization of the state.

Since the beginning of mid-1980s, the price has continuously risen. However, during the last quarter of financial year, 2008–09, the inflation rate started coming down mainly due to declining commodity prices and crude oil prices. The mild slowdown in the economy during 2000s resulted in production cuts over a wide spectrum of industries leading to unemployment. Then it becomes necessary to ease money supply (Economic Surveys, 2001 & 2011).

It supports *Structuralists* claimed that inflation is essential for economic growth, however, against monetarists who believe inflation as detrimental to economic progress. It is noticeable that Growth Rate of State Economy output is positively related to the total inflation rate of State Economy.

## Trend of Food Crop Productivity in Agro-Climatic Zones of J&K, 1981–2011

Agricultural productivity is an important indicator of agricultural development. It depends both on the physical as well as socio-economic factors, viz. climate, soil, irrigation, per capita income, literacy, sex ratio, and occupational structure, etc. Since the productivity data is not available at agro-climatic zone level, therefore the productivity of districts has been used to generate the productivity database for agro-climatic zones by using the 'proportional weight age' method.

As per various reports of *State Finance Commission,* the productivity of all the major crops grown in the state has increased over the period of time and the trend of the major crops grown in different agro-climatic zones shows variation among themselves.

The temperature and precipitation regimes are different in the different parts of the state; therefore different types of crops are grown in different districts. Maize is dominant crop in the districts having more area under mountains like Kupwara, Rajouri, Poonch, Ramban, Doda, Kishtwar, and Udhampur. Rice is dominant crop in all the districts of Kashmir valley except Kupwara and Srinagar. In Jammu province, Jammu district has substantial area under rice cultivation. In Ladakh province, millets, wheat, and orchard cultivation is practiced.

The agricultural productivity varies from one region to another owing to the different soil types, climatic parameters, etc. The productivity of paddy during 2011–12 is highly amounted in IJ (25.76 Q/ha) followed by 3J (22.99 Q/ha), maize is dominant crop in IJ (21.41 Q/ha) followed by 2J (18.97 Q/ha). And the productivity of wheat is maximum concentrated in

L (19.39 Q/ha). Agro-Climatic Zone L is bestowed with the productivity of wheat only, not paddy and maize.

It is observed that productivity of paddy is high in the areas of Jammu, Kathua, Samba districts in Jammu province and in Kashmir province, it is more in Jhelum valley floor (area on both sides of river Jhelum) including the areas of Anantnag, Kulgam, Pulwama, Srinagar, Baramulla, Bandipora, and Kupwara districts.

It is evident that productivity of wheat is high in the Jammu & Ladakh division of the state. Kashmir Province has low to medium levels of productivity. The lowest productivity is found in Jhelum valley floor of Kashmir valley.

The productivity of paddy in the agro-climatic zones of J&K has increased from 9.22 quintals/hectare to 21.97 quintals/hectare, thus implies a total increase of 12.50 quintals/hectare during these twenty-eight years. The productivity has not increased much in the first fifteen years (1980–1995) and due to the use of improved seeds and fertilizers; it has increased at a fairly good rate in the last sixteen years (1995–2011). Three zones out of the total in the state have more productivity increase than state average (12.50 q/ha). The productivity of paddy (1981–2011) in the agro-climatic zones for the State is depicted in Table 1.19.

Table 1.19 Productivity of paddy in ago-climate zones of J&K State, 1981–2011

| Zone | Productivity of paddy (Quintals/hectare) | | | | | | | |
|------|---------|---------|---------|---------|---------|---------|---------|----------------|
|      | 1980–81 | 1985–86 | 1990–91 | 1995–96 | 2000–01 | 2005–06 | 2011–12 | Change (q/ha) |
| 1K   | 8.84    | 9.72    | 10.96   | 12.57   | 14.73   | 16.84   | 21.87   | 13.03 |
| 2K   | 9.96    | 10.96   | 12.37   | 14.18   | 16.62   | 19.00   | 20.58   | 10.62 |
| IJ   | 10.66   | 11.90   | 13.10   | 15.49   | 18.32   | 22.73   | 25.76   | 15.10 |
| 2J   | 8.48    | 10.24   | 11.44   | 13.28   | 15.55   | 17.99   | 21.03   | 12.55 |
| 2'J  | 8.70    | 9.57    | 10.66   | 12.01   | 13.91   | 16.22   | 21.12   | 12.42 |
| 3J   | 9.28    | 10.83   | 12.04   | 14.01   | 16.40   | 19.50   | 22.99   | 13.71 |
| 3'J  | 8.80    | 10.26   | 11.17   | 12.86   | 15.08   | 17.29   | 20.38   | 11.58 |
| 4J   | 9.05    | 11.02   | 11.79   | 13.45   | 15.61   | 17.42   | 20.05   | 11.00 |
| L    | –       | –       | –       | –       | –       | –       | –       | – |
| Mean | 9.22    | 10.56   | 11.69   | 13.48   | 15.78   | 18.37   | 21.72   | 12.50 |

Source: Compiled by using data obtained from Financial Commissioner's office, 2011.

Table 1.20  Productivity of maize in agro-climate zones of J&K State

| Zone | Productivity of maize (Quintals/hectare) | | | | | | | |
|------|---------|---------|---------|---------|---------|---------|---------|--------|
|      | 1980–81 | 1985–86 | 1990–91 | 1995–96 | 2000–01 | 2005–06 | 2011–12 | Change |
| 1K   | 5.71    | 6.08    | 6.88    | 7.88    | 8.94    | 10.26   | 12.9    | 7.19   |
| 2K   | 6.46    | 6.88    | 7.79    | 8.92    | 10.13   | 11.62   | 14.63   | 8.17   |
| IJ   | 11.12   | 12.15   | 13.25   | 14.56   | 15.74   | 17.81   | 21.41   | 10.29  |
| 2J   | 8.1     | 9.18    | 10.45   | 11.93   | 13.54   | 15.36   | 18.97   | 10.87  |
| 2'J  | 8.53    | 9.75    | 10.87   | 12.77   | 14.94   | 17.7    | 17.03   | 8.5    |
| 3J   | 9.39    | 10.47   | 11.63   | 13.01   | 14.43   | 16.42   | 14.9    | 5.51   |
| 3'J  | 8.24    | 9.44    | 10.67   | 12.37   | 14.22   | 16.55   | 12.35   | 4.11   |
| 4J   | 8.86    | 10.09   | 11.30   | 12.52   | 14.08   | 16.51   | 15.61   | 6.75   |
| L    | –       | –       | –       | –       | –       | –       | –       | –      |
| Mean | 8.30    | 9.26    | 10.36   | 11.74   | 13.25   | 15.28   | 15.98   | 7.67   |

*Source*: Compiled by using data obtained from Financial Commissioner's office, 2011.

The highest productivity increase has been observed in zone 1J (15.10 q/ha), followed by 3J (13.71 q/ha), and 1k (13.03 q/ha), while as lowest increase is observed in zone 2k (10.62 q/ha) and 4J (11 q/ha). The productivity of rice is not possible in one zone of the state (zone L) because of the unfavourable geographical conditions for the growth of the crop.

The productivity of maize in all the agro-climatic zones of the state has increased. In absolute values, it has increased from 8.30 quintals/hectare in the year 1980 to 15.98 quintals/hectare 2011, thus implies a total increase of 7.67 quintals/hectare. Like paddy, the productivity has increased at a slower rate in the first 15 years. The productivity of maize in agro-climatic zones is in Table 1.20.

## Brief Description of Agro-Climatic Zones

Since all climatic zones are not feasible for agricultural crop growth because of high altitude. Therefore, they have been designated as 'climatic zones' and not agro-climatic zones. The characteristics of both climatic and agro-climatic zones are highlighted in the below.

(I)    Zone 1K: This zone covers the Jhelum valley floor in Kashmir Valley. Therefore being fertile, it is devoted to rice, maize, and mustard cultivation. It receives adequate precipitation and the temperature is favourable for crop cultivation. The productivity of rice is more in this zone than zone 2K.

(II)     Zone 2K: This zone lies between 1700 and 3000 m and therefore besides rice and maize, orchard cultivation is dominant in this zone. The overall agricultural productivity in this zone is neither too low nor too high. It receives more precipitation but less temperature than zone 1K.

(III)    Zone 3K and 3'K: These two zones lie above 3000 m and therefore crop cultivation is not possible. These zones receive more precipitation especially in the form of snow. These zones cover substantial area of Bandipora, Ganderbal, Anantnag, and Budgam districts of Kashmir valley.

(IV)    Zone 1J: This zone has the lowest altitude (below 500 m) and is basically an extension of Northern plains of India. It is very fertile and is known for 'Basmati rice' cultivation. It receives sufficient rainfall and adequate in isolation, therefore has highest productivity among all the zones.

(V)     Zone 2J: This zone has an altitude of 500–1000 m. It is adjacent to zone 1J and it includes the areas of Kathua and Udhampur. Maize is dominant crop in this zone followed by wheat and rice.

(VI)    Zone 2'J: This zone occupies the areas of Rajouri and Samba districts. It is a productive zone and all the crops grown in this zone have high productivity. This zone receives sufficient rainfall and insolation.

(VII)   Zone 3J: This zone lies between 1000 and 2000 m and occupies the areas of Kathua, Jammu, Rajouri, and Samba districts. It is agriculturally productive and also has substantial area (4131 km2). Wheat, Rice, and Maize are grown in this zone.

(VIII)  Zone 3'J: This zone occupies the areas of Udhampur, Reasi, Poonch, Rajouri, Ramban, and Doda districts. It has an altitude of 1000–1700 m and occupies an area of 7732 km2. It receives maximum annual precipitation than other zones (1592 mm/annum).

(IX)    Zone 4J: This zone lies on higher altitude and therefore receives comparatively less insolation. It includes the areas of Kathua, Doda, Kishtwar, and Poonch districts.

(X)     Zone L: This zone occupies the areas of Leh and Kargil districts. It lies above 3000 m. Millets, Barley, and Wheat is grown. Besides, it is famous for apricot cultivation. It occupies highest area (93531 km2) among all the zones and being cold desert, it receives less precipitation (157 mm/annum). The temperature is also low in this zone with mean maximum of 11.11 C and mean minimum of −2.53 C.

(VII)   Zone 3J: This zone lies between 1000 and 2000 m and occupies the areas of Kathua, Jammu, Rajouri, and Samba districts. It is agriculturally productive and also has substantial area (4131 km2). Wheat, Rice, and Maize are grown in this zone.

(VIII) Zone 3′J: This zone occupies the areas of Udhampur, Reasi, Poonch, Rajouri, Ramban, and Doda districts. It has an altitude of 1000–1700 m and occupies an area of 7732 km2. It receives maximum annual precipitation than other zones (1592 mm/annum).

(IX)    Zone 4J: This zone lies on higher altitude and therefore receives comparatively less insolation. It includes the areas of Kathua, Doda, Kishtwar, and Poonch districts.

(X)     Zone L: This zone occupies the areas of Leh and Kargil districts. It lies above 3000 m. Millets, Barley, and Wheat is grown. Besides, it is famous for apricot cultivation. It occupies highest area (93531 km2) among all the zones and being cold desert, it receives less precipitation (157 mm/annum). The temperature is also low in this zone with mean maximum of 11.11 C and mean minimum of −2.53 C.

(XI)    Zone 3K, 3′K, 5J, 5′J, and 5″J: These five zones lie above 3000 m altitude. Therefore these zones are not suitable for crop cultivation and so have been designated as climatic zones and not agro-climatic zones. Zone 3K and 3′K occupy the parts of Ganderbal, Bandipora, Kupwara, and Budgam districts, while as zones located in Jammu division (5J, 5′J, and 5″J) occupy the parts of Kishtwar and Doda districts.

The productivity of wheat in agro-climatic zones also shows significant increase.

The productivity of wheat has increased from 7.41 quintals/hectare to 17.67 quintals/hectare, thus implies a total increase of 10.26 quintals/hectare. Like in case of paddy and maize, the productivity of wheat has also increased at a slower rate in the first fifteen years (1980–1995) than the

Table 1.21 Productivity of wheat in ago-climate zones of J&K State

| Zone | Productivity of Wheat (Quintals/hectare) | | | | | | | |
|---|---|---|---|---|---|---|---|---|
| | 1980–81 | 1985–86 | 1990–91 | 1995–96 | 2000–01 | 2005–06 | 2011–12 | Change (q/ha) |
| 1K | 5 | 5.62 | 6.44 | 7.46 | 8.45 | 9.82 | 12.37 | 7.37 |
| 2K | 5.67 | 6.37 | 7.31 | 8.46 | 9.58 | 11.12 | 14.01 | 8.34 |
| 1J | 10.51 | 11.83 | 13.36 | 14.72 | 14.97 | 16.43 | 18.91 | 8.40 |
| 2J | 7.01 | 8.04 | 9.78 | 12.04 | 13.64 | 15.45 | 18.87 | 11.86 |
| 2'J | 7.3 | 8.55 | 9.98 | 11.65 | 13.71 | 16.3 | 19.09 | 11.79 |
| 3J | 8.22 | 9.4 | 11.03 | 12.97 | 14.07 | 15.81 | 18.42 | 10.2 |
| 3'J | 7.61 | 8.78 | 10.05 | 11.65 | 13.25 | 15.6 | 19.10 | 11.49 |
| 4J | 7.86 | 9.16 | 10.04 | 11.63 | 12.7 | 15.01 | 18.84 | 10.98 |
| L | 7.5 | 8.59 | 9.77 | 11.30 | 13.51 | 15.72 | 19.39 | 11.89 |
| Mean | 7.41 | 8.48 | 9.75 | 11.32 | 12.65 | 14.59 | 17.67 | 10.26 |

Source: Compiled by using data obtained from Financial Commissioner's office, 2011.

last sixteen years (1995–2011) taken for the study. Regional variations in the increase in productivity are observed across different agro-climatic zones of the study area. The highest increase is recorded in L (11.89 q/ha), followed by 2J (11.86 q/ha), and 2'J (11.79 q/ha), while the lowest is observed in 2k (8.34 q/ha) and 1k (7.37 q/ha).

## Levels of Crop Productivity in Agro-Climatic Zones, 2011

The determination and measurement of spatial variation of agricultural productivity is of vital importance for agricultural planning and development. The crop productivity among different agro-climatic zones of J&K, the productivity of the three crops discussed above has been taken. The agricultural productivity (indicators) of three crops in agro-climate zones is depicted in Table 1.22.

The indices for all the districts have also been calculated by taking state as 100 (for average composite index of 17.69) as given in Table 1.23.

The range of composite indices varied across the agro-climatic zones from the minimum value of 36 in 'Zone L' including the areas of Leh and Kargil to the maximum of 123 in 'Zone 1J' including the areas of Jammu,

**Table 1.22**  Agricultural productivity indicators in agro-climatic zones

| Zone | Paddy ($X_1$) | Wheat ($X_2$) | Maize ($X_3$) |
|------|------|------|------|
| 1K | 21.87 | 12.37 | 12.9 |
| 2K | 20.58 | 14.01 | 14.63 |
| IJ | 25.76 | 18.91 | 21.41 |
| 2J | 21.03 | 18.87 | 18.62 |
| 2'J | 21.12 | 19.09 | 17.03 |
| 3J | 22.99 | 18.42 | 14.9 |
| 3'J | 20.38 | 19.10 | 12.35 |
| 4J | 20.05 | 18.84 | 15.61 |
| L | 0 | 19.39 | 0 |
| Total | 173.78 | 159.01 | 127.45 |
| Mean | 21.72 | 17.67 | 15.93 |

*Source*: Compiled by using Tables 1.20, 1.21, 1.22, 2011–12.

**Table 1.23**  Composite Index of Agricultural Development in J&K

| Zone | Composite Index | Indices |
|------|------|------|
| IK | 15.71 | 88 |
| 2K | 16.40 | 92 |
| IJ | 21.96 | 123 |
| 2J | 19.46 | 109 |
| 2'J | 19.10 | 107 |
| 3J | 18.75 | 105 |
| 3'J | 17.32 | 97 |
| 4J | 18.03 | 101 |
| L | 6.42 | 36 |
| Average | 18.39 | 103 |

*Source*: Compiled from by using Table 1.23.

Samba etc. which indicates that the former is highly advanced in the agricultural productivity and the latter is highly disadvantaged.

The zones which perform well in agricultural productivity are IJ (indices value between 110 and 130). The other zones (2J, 2'J, 3J, and 4J)

Table 1.24  Ranking of Zones in respect of Agricultural productivity

| Index Value | Above 110 | 100 to 110 | 90 to100 | Below 90 | Total |
|---|---|---|---|---|---|
| Category | High | Medium | Low | Very Low | |
| Name of Zones | IJ, | 2J, 2'J, 3J, 4J | 2K, 3'J | IK, L | |
| No. of Zones | 01 | 04 | 02 | 02 | 09 |
| Percentage area to zones total | 11.1 | 44.4 | 22.2 | 22.2 | 100 |

*Source*: Calculated.

are comparatively less developed and have the indices value below 100 to 110. The composite indices of agricultural productivity of different agro-climatic zones in the state are grouped into four categories which are produced in Table 1.24.

Kashmir was an economic paradise before 1980s. Present people are deeply rooted in the past history of violence stated since 1980. It stood stumb block for the overall development of state, thus wrecked state economy fully.

The age-old economic ties of the people living in the state, particularly on its borders, with those living on the other side of the frontiers had been cut off, thereby shattering the entire economic structure which was so labouriously and diligently built through centuries (Techno-Economic Survey of J&K, 1969). With the closure of the highways for trade after 1947, cost of living increased. Blocking the historical routes of the state and cutting off the centuries, old cultural and trade connections with the neighbouring countries retarded the economic development of the state in general and some of the hilly areas in particular (Development Strategies for J&K, 1960, ORF).

The disastrous fallout of the fifty years of mismanagement propelled more by the inception of violence started 1989. Due to high political instability right from 1989, all sectors of economy were distorted. The serious unemployment and economic downturn during the early phase of militancy, a large number of unemployed youths who belong to extremely poor sections of society joined anti-nation movement and also forced migration of Kashmiri Hindu and pundits took place. The instability and lack of any conclusive resolution have left the population of Kashmir divided and uncertain about their future resulted impoverishment through the channels of reduction of the capital, income and employment, physical destruction of agricultural resources, reduced investment, and mass displacement of human resources (Islam, 2014). In addition to falling within 'grey zone', death, curfew and other mobility restrictions have added fuel to the fire. Thus, every sphere of the State economy is under the eclipse of non-economic activities (Singh, 2004).

The armed conflict resulted loss of number of human resources. More commonly the widows become economically dependent on the labour of their children with the result child labour trend increased in the state (Rather, 2013).

The economic wheel of the State is stagnant and it has far-reaching consequence if it is not handled with care right now. It is the need of the hour to reinstate political stability, peace, and communal harmony for bringing about reconstruction of the State (Sehgal, 2011). The Government should without delay concentrate on infrastructural development and bringing unemployed youth (idle brains) in the loop of economic development. Further militancy and militarization (occupied large productive land area) has ruined the state and reconstruction of economic sector and education sector are the need of the hour.

# 2

# State of Economic Growth and Development

The pillars of any state rest on the building blocks of Economy, Environment, Education, Employment, and Healthcare. Although each block is important for the stability and growth of a civilization but 'Economy' is the corner stone on which the prosperity of a state rests.

J&K is an Indian state that has its own distinct and peculiar economic ethos. The state has a predominant place as it shares the international boundary with Pakistan and China. It is bestowed with rich natural resources. It is enriched with the boundless beauty of snow-clad mountains, large natural lakes, forests, rivers, and springs. It comprises three main natural regions, namely, Jammu, Kashmir, and Ladakh. However, for administrative purposes, the state is divided into two main divisions, Kashmir with 12 districts (including two districts of Ladakh region) and Jammu with 10 districts.

At the time of the birth of India and Pakistan, the state of J&K with a population of four million people, most of it concentrated in the fertile valley of the Jhelum River of the Indus River system, was one of the least developed regions in the Indian sub-continent (Bhargava, 1969). The economy of the state was overwhelmingly rural and agricultural in character. Nearly 90 per cent of people lived in villages and derived their livelihood from agricultural and related pursuits using traditional techniques. The extreme backwardness of the state was reflected by the abysmal mass poverty, deprivation, hunger, disease, and ignorance. The electricity generation capacity was less than 5MW, communications were poorly developed in most parts of the state and the average life expectancy was only about 27 years (Misri & Bhat, 1994).

With a view to present development performance of the state after Independence, Kashmir economy had a cataclysmic start from Post 1947.

*Jammu & Kashmir.* Bilal Ahmad Khan, Oxford University Press. © Oxford University Press 2022.
DOI: 10.1093/oso/9780192849656.003.0002

The state embarked upon its development process by the enactment of Big Landed Estates Act 1949–1950, a radical land redistribution measure which abolished as many as 9 thousand Jagirs and Muafis. The 4.5 lakhs acres of land so expropriated was redistributed to tenants and landless. Land ceiling was fixed at 22.75 acres. It was followed by little or negligible social disturbance. Despite this, no compensation was paid to landlords. This measure set the stage for new economy. In the given circumstances, the land reforms proved sufficient to the economic condition of the countryside with the hitherto tenants in a position to own land and cultivate it for themselves (Jamwal, 1994).

However, the reforms though unprecedented in their nature and scale were not only pursued for their own sake but were also underpinned by an ambitious economic vision. *Naya Kashmir*, a vision statement of Sheikh Muhammad Abdullah, laid down more or less a comprehensive plan for a wholesome economic development of the state (Copland, 1991). But the dismissal of Sheikh Abdullah's legitimately elected government in 1953 by the centre changed all that. The consequent uncertainty which lingers even now created an adhocist political culture animated more by vested interest than a commitment to the development of state. Such a scenario after some time also frittered away the salutary potential of the land reforms. While the radical land redistribution measure had a massive political will at its back.

However, the land reforms in rural Kashmir down the decades have only shown diminishing returns. Most of the arable land was economically unviable. The average size of land-holdings has declined from 1.7 hectares in 1949–50 to 0.5 hectares in 1997–98. Almost 90 per cent of arable land constitutes marginal and sub-marginal holdings. This has reduced the productivity from agriculture to a mere subsistence level. Subsequent developmental strategies failed to the steady agricultural decline (Jasbir, 2004).

In fact, post land reforms, the development process in the state went astray. The successive state governments preferred market-led strategy of growth as against development-led strategy. As the market-led strategy ignored the growth of primary sector and put premium on the expansion of tertiary sector. This meant the provision of employment to educated group, yet unskilled youth became useless tool. This strategy more or less artificially withheld state's economy. A situation was created whereby the state witness falling economic avenues, lack of capital investment opportunities, and economic leakage effect and supply gap in primary and secondary sectors (Rekhi, 1993). An adhocist reliance on tertiary sector saw the massive public investment go into unproductive ventures particularly public administration which kept it bloating by the day; there was a corresponding decline in economic growth.

Tertiary sector being urban in nature, the policy thrust on it also distorted the priorities in rural sector. With Agriculture and allied sectors in decline and no agro-based industries to take over, government employment was the only livelihood option even for the rural youth. And it remains so even now. There was no effort to convert state agriculture into viable commercial farm enterprise, no structural transformation of horticulture, and allied sectors of agriculture to encourage intra-farm migration of labour for gainful employment. As a result, the growth potential of farm sector remained unexploited which led to supply gap on food front and according to experts, low multiplier effect on income and employment generating front. This also caused acute dependence of state for inputs and products from outside.

Since the J&K State is lagging behind in diversified economic structure, as such the state economy is mostly dependent on Agriculture sector. Situation is not any better in primary sector where the proportion of net area sown to the total cropped area, average yield per hectare of land and production of food grains has been stagnant through 80s and much of the 90s. And from the last fifteen years it has been declining. This has created a situation where the imports constitute 80 per cent of the SDP which makes massive leakage effect leading to present crisis (JK Digest, 2011–12).

Amongst the allied Sectors of Agriculture, Live stock is an important component of primary sector. It contributes 17 per cent to the GSDP of state according (Annual Report, 2000–01, Department of Agriculture, J&K Govt.). The state is highest consumer of mutton and milk in India. J&K has the highest live stock population in the country, even though we are importing 45 per cent of live stock from rest of the country. The cattle and poultry rearing provide gainful employment to small and marginal farmers.

Live stock has a prominent role to play in industrialization of the state. The live stock is the best source of raw material for Tanneries and leather Industry. They are a source of raw material to many industries and at the same time provide market to an industrial product. Hides and Skins, wool and bones are found in sufficient quantities in the state which constitute the main raw material for many such industries. All efforts are being made to achieve the all round development of Animal Husbandry in the state particularly in sheep, dairy, and poultry farming (Annual Report, 1999–2000, AHD, J&K).

A good beginning has been made to the Poultry Farming in the state. However, they need to be encouraged by the Government by providing adequate financial support and technical know-how. This would also help in solving the unemployment problem to a great extent.

Prior to the turbulent period, the J&K economy was primarily based on agriculture and the service sector was dominated only by tourism. Tourism was identified as the engine of growth and development. However, militant activities since 1989 onwards, there was a colossal set-back of it. History bears witness to the fact that whenever and wherever militancy or political instability found roots, the economy of that region became a major causality (Bookman, 1991).

While the feasibility of heavy industry in the state was thought to have geographical limitations, there was little effort, to develop the alterna-tive Valley-friendly industry. The state's economic history offers plenty of evidence to underline this neglect and its fallout. While in 1980–81, the contribution of industry (Secondary) sector was 13 per cent of state domestic product and gone down to 6 per cent in 2000–01 (Economic Survey, 2001–02, DES).

Thus state is unable to generate resources on its own and depends considerably on central aid. Down the years, this dependence has only doubled as the Table 2.1 below amply demonstrates. While the tax and non-tax revenue has sharply declined as a percentage of total resources that of central grant-in-aid has correspondingly increased.

Even the state has been bestowed by nature with suitable climate for enormous fruits. The opportunities were investigated in the state for ex-ploiting vast potential of fruits under individual, joint venture and spon-sored efforts. The area under fruits growing has been found 2.68 lakh hectares in 2005–06 that accelerated to 3.38 lakh hectares in 2016–17 and the production has increased from 14.13 lakh MTS in 2005–06 to 22.23 lakh MTS in 2016–17, recording an increase of 23.58 per cent. The Area,

**Table 2.1** Tax and non-tax revenue and Grant-in-aid, Percent

| Year | Tax & non-tax revenue of J&K to total revenue | Grant-in-aid to total resources |
|---|---|---|
| 1973–74 | 49.75 | 51.25 |
| 1977–78 | 43.98 | 56.02 |
| 1986–87 | 30.74 | 69.26 |
| 1997–98 | 18.76 | 81.24 |

*Sources*: State Finance Commission (Various Reports).

Production, and Productivity of fruits (All fruits) for the whole State of J&K from 2005–06 to 2016–17 is depicted in Table 2.2.

The inception of violence since 1989 converted state economy into fragile economy. As a result of prolonged conflict till now, the state's economy has been one of the slowest growing regional economies in South Asia. That is why it is among the poorer states of India. In 2001, it was the 6th poorest state in India in terms of Per Capita Income.

Insurgency has been a major factor over low productivity in agriculture and industrial sector. It leads poor industrial infrastructure along with the poor investment that has left the industrial sector in its infant stage which impeded employment and income generation. There has not been a suitable strategy for the potential sectors to achieve higher economic growth. Lack of good governance and sound fiscal management has also been responsible for poor economic growth of the state (GK, 24 September 2007).

Thus conflict and instability in the State have been a major hindrance to the region's development and progress and remains far from satisfactory. There is a vast array of literature on the same theme and the role of people in the middle of the two great regional powers of Pakistan and India (Bose, 1999).

## Analysis of Development Potential

Economic growth in J&K has been severely stifled due to security concerns. As a result, there are virtually no engines of job creation and resources are used inefficiently and without long-term vision. Additionally, the lack of domestic industry has made the state heavily dependent upon central government financing. Moreover, J&K has seen little in the way of foreign investment (KSG, 1997). While the state receives significant amounts of aid from the Indian government, most of that funding is used towards the state's immense bureaucracy, one plagued by corruption.

However, state does possess significant domestic resources that provide opportunities for economic development. Specifically, the agriculture, tourism, and infrastructure sectors hold significant development potential. Therefore, the benefits of successful projects focused on developing agricultural capacity will have a broad reach. Agriculture is a historically viable and sustainable industry in the region. Consequently, projects can focus on modernizing the industry instead of trying to incubate a new,

**Table 2.2** Area, Production and Productivity of All fruits, 2005–06/16–17

| Year | Fruit | Area (in Het) | Production in Lakhs MTS | Productivity |
|---|---|---|---|---|
| 2005–06 | Fresh | 1.75 | 12.89 | 7.36 |
| | Dry | 0.93 | 1.24 | 1.33 |
| | Total | 2.68 | 14.13 | 5.27 |
| 2006–07 | Fresh | 1.85 | 13.77 | 7.43 |
| | Dry | 0.99 | 1.31 | 1.33 |
| | Total | 2.84 | 15.08 | 5.31 |
| 2009–10 | Fresh | 2.10 | 15.35 | 7.31 |
| | Dry | 1.05 | 1.78 | 1.70 |
| | Total | 3.15 | 17.13 | 5.44 |
| 2010–11 | Fresh | 2.17 | 20.46 | 9.43 |
| | Dry | 1.08 | 1.76 | 1.63 |
| | Total | 3.25 | 22.22 | 6.84 |
| 2015–16 | Fresh | 2.42 | 22.18 | 9.16 |
| | Dry | 1.12 | 2.76 | 2.87 |
| | Total | 3.56 | 24.94 | 7.38 |
| 2016–17 | Fresh | 2.42 | 19.59 | 8.09 |
| | Dry | 0.97 | 2.76 | 2.84 |
| | Total | 3.38 | 22.35 | 6.59 |

*Source*: Digests of Statistics, Directorate of Economics and Statistics, J&K Government (Various Issues).

untested industry. The mountainous geography within State presents a challenge to the modernization of transportation. Regardless, much of region remains environmentally appropriate for the agricultural projects underway (Jones, Corey, Bartosz, & Tahir, 2010).

The major inputs (land and labour) required to build up the industry are abundant in the State. Government has developed much of the human capital needed for the agricultural industry to flourish. Projects highlighting infrastructure, modernization, and the market aspect of the agriculture industry offer the most potential to alter economic circumstances in the near term and on a large scale (Agriculture Dept, 2010, Govt. of J&K).

The 2006 Task Force on Development of J&K identified tourism as one of the main engines of growth in the region. The development of the tourist industry can have a significant impact on the overall growth of the state because of its ability to create direct and indirect employment, as well as growth in allied industries. Tourism will likely contribute to the growth of secondary sectors such as handicrafts, which have historically benefitted to the state from visitors. By generating new employment and creating sources of income, especially for unemployed youth, tourism can undermine the sources of separatist recruitment. In 1998, unemployment in J&K stood at 700,000 (JK Economic Survey, 2002, DSE). As tourism is widely recognized as a major mechanism of employment generation and holds significant potential for alleviating youth unemployment, thereby eroding separatist support.

Landlocked and distant from major markets of India, J&K faces high transportation costs, making it harder for the state to compensate for the drawbacks of the small size of its domestic market. While a weakness in both public and private sector capacity is a key concern for the state, the geographical spread of the state adds a further dimension to the challenge, as internal distances are quite large and the population highly decentralized. Deficiencies in the institutional capacity of J&K reduce the state's ability to participate fully in trade activities, both of which harm its economy.

J&K possesses significant potential in the area of energy production. The state's waterways have the capacity to generate 16,480 megawatts of hydroelectric power (Digest, DES, 2011-12), nearly equivalent to the total generating capability of the United States (U.S. Energy Information

Agency, 2010). If this is efficiently harnessed, the state could become a major energy producer in the region, supplying electric power to northern India, Pakistan, and Central Asia.

## Absolute Level of Development

Although J&K is far from achieving independent economic viability, the rise in the region's absolute development level carries the potential for increasing separatist sentiment. The economic growth in J&K may be used by those favouring secession as an economic argument to promote the ability of the state to survive independently. On the other hand, a decrease in economic growth has been found to be strongly associated with greater likelihood for conflict (Miguel, Satyanath, & Sergenti, 2003). Consequently, the effect of absolute development in J&K will depend on the overall strategy employed in addressing the specific risk and opportunity areas within the context of social, political, and economic environments.

Successful agricultural development will lead to increased income for a large portion of J&K. This can lead to a perceptible rise in the level of overall development in the state, particularly in rural areas where the income from farming has not been strong. This improvement in the absolute level of development may increase secessionist sentiment as residents perceive the region is more viable as a free-standing entity (Report of ADS, 2010).

Meaningful growth of the tourism sector will necessarily influence expansion in allied sectors, leading to an overall rise in state income. This will strengthen state's economic viability. However, the likelihood that the resulting absolute growth will contribute to secessionism will probably remain low because current projects are firmly tied to larger national development plans and depend on national funding. In addition, the extent to which tourism depends on regional peace and stability further undermines the feasibility and success of separatist conflict (Tourism Department, J&K, 2010).

Improvements to the state's transportation, communication, and power infrastructure will lead to increased income in the region by facilitating increased productivity. Improved road and rail will increase the accessibility of tourist destinations and market access to Kashmiri goods. In this way, infrastructure can be a catalyst, enhancing the effect of improvements in the agriculture and tourism sectors. As such, infrastructure development must be coupled with development in major industries such as agriculture and tourism that can take advantage of the increased capacity (Schaffer, 2005).

## Relative Level of Development

When viewed in the context of J&K, relative level of development is principally a function of the degree to which benefits from economic development accrue disproportionately to any particular district or social group. Development that creates interregional disparity in income through resource draining or exploitative strategies effectively cancels out any positive effects on the region as a whole.

The economic underdevelopment of the state, coupled with perceived political discrimination, tends to fuel secessionist sentiments when the affected population is not ethnically representative of the nation as a whole (Lewis, Mitra, & Alison, 1996). This happens to be the case in J&K, where Muslims represent two-thirds of the population and exhibited the highest levels of separatist sentiment and insurgent violence, with the result economic activity has been most disrupted. Jammu, on the other hand, enjoys better location and transport infrastructure. Residents of the Kashmir Valley complain that central development programs tend to disproportionately benefit Jammu (Schaffer, 2005). Economic projects in the state must be chosen not on the basis of their convenience or ease of implementation, but rather on their potential to produce equitable development across all districts and social groups. Failure to do so will exacerbate existing inequity continuing to fuel separatist sentiment.

As income from agriculture rises, so will average income levels across the state. Urban dwellers will further increase their incomes, which are already high relative to the state as a whole. More importantly, rural dwellers, which have low incomes relative to all of state, will see their incomes climb closer to the national average. Equalizing rural income, relative to the rest of India, will reduce feelings of economic injustice.

The extent to which tourism development is equitably pursued among all three regions will determine its effect on minimizing ethno-religious grievances between Muslims and Hindus. The positive effect of tourism development on allied sectors will contribute to the overall rise in state income, thereby helping to decrease income inequality with respect to the rest of India (Tourism Dept., J&K, 2007).

Infrastructure development will enhance the effects of agriculture and tourism projects by increasing efficiency and improving market access. An additional factor for consideration is the potential impact of power generation infrastructure for the J&K as a whole. The potential for sustainable hydropower generation is exceptionally large. However, one must consider the feasibility of exploiting all available resources and the time necessary to implement such projects. It is unlikely that the region will produce sufficient electric power that it could become a net power exporter in the near future. Additionally, treaty complications with Pakistan for water use rights complicate fully exploiting the region's hydro resources, particularly if the benefits are conferred principally to India-controlled J&K (Digest (DES), 2011–12).

## Trade Dependency

An independent J&K cannot be economically viable in its current state. However, the less that the state is integrated into the national economy, the higher the likelihood for secessionist sentiment to persist. If the state and central authorities continue to be perceived as ineffective or unwilling to invest in local development, secessionist sentiment will continue to fester and the risk of conflict will likely increase. Therefore, effective development measures would encourage domestic trade and investment linkages to substantially deepen economic integration with the rest of India.

Much of the developments in the agricultural sector come from increased access to export markets (via India). This makes trade more dependent on nation. Increased trade dependency reduces residents' desire to secede (Kraska, 2003).

Tourism as a service sector commodity presents significant export potential that ongoing and future development plans aim to address. However, tourism is distinct in that it moves consumers to the 'product' rather than transporting the product to consumers. It is thus intricately tied to other industries such as agriculture, land, and labour. Therefore, the tourist industry's trade dependence significantly is influenced by the level of dependence in other sectors of the economy (JK Economic Survey, 2012).

Improvements to the state's transportation and communication infrastructure will facilitate deeper economic integration with the rest of India by allowing Kashmiri goods to flow out and tourists to flow in. While there is the potential that these infrastructure improvements will open Kashmir to the global economy, direct trade with international partners is unlikely to become large relative to trade with India (Shekhawat, 2008).

## Net Capital Flows

J&K is one of the largest recipients of grants from the central government, placing the state in a firmly positive net capital flow position, and minimizing the associated risk of a rise in secessionist activity. This is unlikely to change in the foreseeable future as current development plans envision a further rise in investments across economic sectors. Central and state authorities also seek to expand private and foreign investment sources. In turn, the State is among the lowest contributors of PCY tax to the central government. As a result, the state's present net outflow position does not increase the risk of secessionism. It is crucial, however, that profits realized under the current development schemes be reinvested back in the local economy in order to avoid public perception of economic exploitation, which would likely lead to rise in secessionist sentiment (Report of TFD, 2006, Retrieved, 2010).

J&K has a very favourable net capital flow position relative to India as a whole. Government put more money into the region than they withdraw in taxes. Increased trade dependency may involve a slight rise in outflow, as some agricultural profits will be drawn by firms outside J&K (Report of TFD, 2010). However, it seems unlikely this outflow will be substantial enough to overcome the large inflow of national development support. As long as they are widely perceived, continued positive net capital flows will reduce the desire of Kashmiri residents to secede.

Violence has prevented meaningful development and left the infrastructure in shambles. As such, substantial investment is needed to expand and modernize the industry. Because of this, tourism will likely be a source of a significant capital flow into the state. Boosting investment, therefore, carries the potential of significantly increasing net inflows, thereby likely reducing insurgency. Attracting foreign tourism and investment is crucial in this regard, as tourists from abroad will bring in needed foreign currency.

Infrastructure development projects in J&K had required significant capital investment from the Indian government and continue to require funding for the foreseeable future. As such, the Railway Link throughout whole valley, from several years for completion continues to draw funding from the central government. Other projects such as roads and telecommunications infrastructure completed over a shorter time period (Shekhawat, 2008).

By increasing transportation costs, the risk of economic leakage increases. This loss of funds may create the perception that foreign businesses are profiting at the expense of local stakeholders. This perception may arise despite absolute gains from trade in goods and services if residents of J&K State perceive a net loss in capital. This perceived loss will reduce the positive capital flows. Development of electric power generation infrastructure may produce similar effects if profits accrue mainly to national utilities located outside the state.

## Economic Decentralization

J&K occupies a semi-autonomous position within India. This boosts the perception and practicality of its viability as an independent entity and, in turn, contributes to a rise in secessionist sentiment. The higher degree of decentralization in J&K relative to the rest of India, however, is offset by the high level of economic integration and trade dependence with the national economy. Current development plans call for the expansion of private sector and small business ventures, which will contribute to increased decentralization of the local economy. However, this effect will likely be curbed by J&K's continued reliance on Indian markets and trade networks and may even decrease with the deepening of the state's economic integration with the rest of India. The bulk of agriculture development schemes, while planned and funded at the national level, are implemented by state institutions. Any secessionist sentiment fuelled by this decentralization of economic power will be tempered by the heavy financial reliance on the national government, insofar as this reliance is popularly perceived.

Although central and state authorities collaborate in creating development strategies, including a greater focus on private-sector investment and state-level implementation, overall investment, and coordination is conducted predominantly at the national level. Consequently, as long as state development authorities continue to depend on central funding, the risk of heightened violence resulting from economic decentralization will remain low. The development of the state's infrastructure is highly dependent upon central support for the duration of project and beyond, related to initial construction and later maintenance (Rao, 2009).

J&K relies almost entirely on central funding while generating virtually no resources of its own. The hostile environment has severely discouraged private investment and enterprise. By necessity, successful development projects require funding and central coordination from the Indian government, creating critical linkages between local and national institutions. Current Indian development programs in J&K stand to increase absolute levels of development reduce economic decentralization, increase net capital inflows, and increase trade dependence on India. While increased absolute levels of development carry the possibility of increased secessionism and achieve a level of development sufficiently high to contemplate self-sufficiency which is extremely low. The effect on relative levels of development is significantly more ambiguous, as residents may not recognize an improvement in their economic position relative to the rest of the country.

It would, therefore, be necessary to put the economy back on the rails to enable the average person to get employment opportunities. This would require giving fillip to the economic activities that have traditionally been the mainstay of the State's economy and continue to hold significant potential for growth and employment. Such activities include Agriculture (including Horticulture), Handicrafts, and Livestock on modern lines. It would be equally necessary to ensure diversification of the State economy, especially expanding the industrial base by generally

have a traditional bent of mind. Diversification of agricultural activities is the need of the hour to keep up with the changed circumstances (Report from DAC, 2007, retrieved 2010).

The potential of Horticulture in J&K State is high, given the rich diversity in its flora and fauna and varied agro-climatic situation. The state enjoys monopoly in certain fruits, vegetables, and medicinal plants and there is an immense scope for increasing the production of other horticulture products that are marketed in rich and export markets. It is important that the limiting factors in both production and marketing of fresh produce are addressed speedily and linkages between farmers and buyers are established by developing agricultural and horticultural mandies at faster pace and on modern and scientific lines. This would not only reduce supply chain costs but would also help the farmers with an assured market for their produce. Technological improvements are necessary to bring about lower costs in processing as well as reducing wastages in fruits.

J&K has unexploited capacity to produce products which have value demand and ready for attractive markets both in India and Overseas (e.g. bio aromatics, medical herbs, organic vegetables, etc.). To enable exploitation of these opportunities, major programmes are needed to educate farmers to change traditional production habits and grow market rewarded crops.

Potential for bringing additional area under Walnut is enormous. As per preliminary estimates (Indicators of Regional Dev. 2011–12 (Part-I), DES) about 0.50 lakh hectares are available on which walnut cultivation can be undertaken successfully. This will help to create green cover in hilly areas and conserve soil from erosion, besides, proving high value wood for wood carving industry, as well as, walnuts for export purposes.

The food processing and horticulture industries are intimately related to areas of infrastructure that include processing facilities such as cold chain, refrigerator facilities, and transport by both rail and road to destination markets as well as market infrastructure for farmers to sell their produce on remunerative prices. This when addressed in totality would bring about a lower cost, high value delivering chain that can change the face of horticulture in the state. There is need to improve packing and standardization of the state's horticulture produce.

The three biggest employment generators in the region-tourism, horticulture and handicraft are facing their own challenges. While the handicrafts are facing a serious threat from cheap machine-made imitations and counterfeits which has affected the livelihood of around 2.5 lakh artisans of state. Tourism has been hit by prolonged and continuous shutdowns (GK, 17 October 2016).

The two sectors namely handicrafts and horticulture has rescued the state's economy in the absence of tourism in the past two and half decades. The income and exports from handicrafts alone have been Rs. 1151 crore and Rs. 1600 crore in the financial year 2016–17. Currently horticulture and handicrafts are hemmed in not only by an assortment of domestic problems; they also face severe pressures and competition from a globalizing economic regime. According to G. M. Ganai, former secretary Fruit Growers and Dealers Association, said 'free trade under new WTO regime as a result of which fruits from a number of countries have posed a serious market challenge to Kashmir fruits' (Report from Dept. of Horticulture, J&K, 2012). The state Govt. must promote handicrafts industries by increasing shopping arcade in their existing properties and provide space for handicrafts industry to display their products.

The State of J&K is rich in hydel power resources. The state power development corporation has estimated a total hydel power potential of 20000 MW and identified about 16000 MW for the four rivers in the state- Chenab (10853.81 MW), Jhelum (3141.3 MW), Indus (1598.7 MW), and Ravi (417.00 MW) (JK Economic Survey, 2009–10).

Despite the fact that the state could be among the frontline states owing to huge hydel power potential but it is presently facing an acute shortage of energy resources as the current generation is only 1658.59 MW whereas the current demand on account of domestic, industrial, agricultural and other demands is estimated about 2000 MW. This acute deficiency in energy sector has impeded not only the industrial development but also the other ancillary sectors. If the power sector is fully developed, the state would certainly attain the status of power exporting states (Indicators of Economic Development, DES 2015–16).

What is needed, therefore, is the reconstruction of the enabling conditions for a functioning peacetime economy. Mere growth of economy cannot bring social justice unless it is coupled with employment generating opportunities for deprived and marginalized sections of the society. More poverty alleviation and developmental schemes should be in operated in the State with central assistance in order to curb and tackle the prevailing situation in the state.

## Changing Structure and Contribution of Various Economic Sectors

The Sector or activity-wise composition of NSDP gives an idea of the relative position and contribution of a particular sector in the economy that facilitates to provide inputs to economists, policymakers planners, etc. for formulation of plans for the overall economic development of the State. It is analysed primary sector played a leading role in NSDP and start to dwindle since 1980. However, contribution of tertiary sector particularly increased.

Judged in terms of NSDP, services sector is emerging as an important growth driver and the manufacturing sector is relatively stagnant while agricultural productivity has decreased significantly. It is a point of concern that the combined contribution from primary and secondary sectors is becoming less than the lone contribution from service sector which is a very unhealthy condition for sustaining growth in the long run. Consideration the scope of expansion in manufacturing sector and service sector, it is the only agriculture that can hold us back (GK, 29 January 2013).

## Regression Linear Type

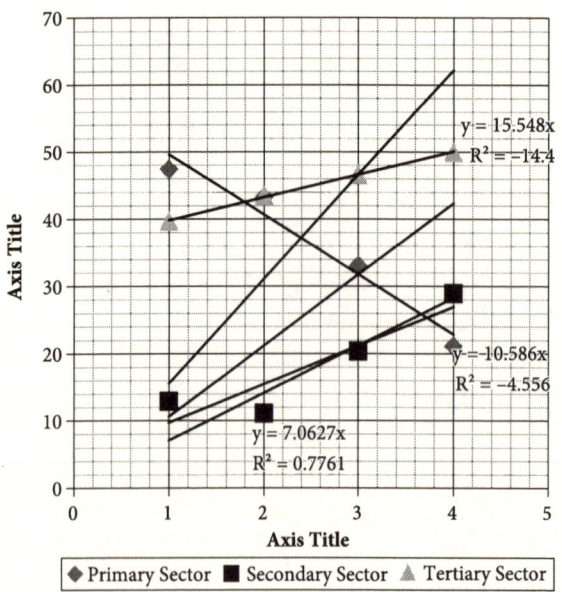

However, urbanization pressure has directly impacted the size of land holdings (average holding size 0.67 hectares against 1.23 hectares in India as per latest *agriculture census, 2015–16* and area under cultivation (8 per cent cultivable area and net area sown constitutes only 30 per cent of the reporting area).

## Performance of Primary and Non-Primary Sectors

By examining the sectoral shares of primary and non-primary sectors in NSDP in terms of percentage, at current prices, the share of primary sector was 47.29 per cent in 1980–81, decreased to 21.10 per cent in 2010–11, showing a decrease of almost 26 percentage points while as at constant prices (at 1993–94 prices), in 1980–81, the percentage share of primary sector was 47.40 per cent which decreased to 21.98 per cent in 2010–11, showing a decrease of almost 25 per cent points. At current prices, in 1980–81 the percentage share of non-primary sector was 52.71 per cent which increased to 78.90 per cent in 2010–11, showing an increase of almost 26 per cent while as at constant prices (1993–94 prices), in 1980–81, the percentage share of non-primary sector was 52.60 per cent which increased to 78.02 per cent in 2010–11, showing an increase of 25.42 percentage points. The share of Primary Sectors and Non-Primary Sectors in NSDP to state economy from 1981 to 2011 is shown in Table 2.4.

In terms of Kuznets analysis the relative share of manufacturing has to increase in the long run there by demonstrating industrialization taking place in the economy. But disaggregating the data of J&K economy, the relative share of industry is accounted for, by construction to a greater degree, that is, by about 19.82 per cent and 2.65 per cent accounted for manufacturing sector and its ancillary (Table 2.3). In comparison to other northern growing states, J&K is greatly dependent. Most of the construction materials and much of the labour in construction industry are imported. Therefore, the investment opportunities and gainful economic pursuits particularly in terms of employment generation are not realized in the state.

The J&K economy product contribution of the agricultural sector *(A-sector)* has been very limited because of stagnant non-agricultural sector *(non-A sector)*. Market contribution has also been low because

**Table 2.3** Distribution of Net State Domestic Product (Industry of Origin) at Current Prices and Constant Prices (1993–94) (Per cent)

| Sector wise (NSDP) | | 1980–81 | 1990–91 | 2000–01 | 2011–11 |
|---|---|---|---|---|---|
| **Primary Sector (Agriculture)** | | **47.40** | **43.29** | **33.01** | **21.10** |
| I | Agriculture including livestock | 37.63 | 35.70 | 29.47 | 15.70 |
| II | Forestry & Logging | 8.96 | 6.97 | 2.68 | 4.61 |
| III | Fishing | 0.45 | 0.56 | 0.72 | 0.51 |
| IV | Mining & Quarrying | 0.36 | 0.06 | 0.14 | 0.28 |
| **Secondary Sector (Industry)** | | **12.90** | **13.90** | **20.34** | **28.94** |
| I | Manufacturing (registered Sector) | 1.34 | 2.13 | 1.12 | 2.65 |
| II | Manufacturing (Unregistered Sector) | 3.31 | 3.41 | 2.21 | 3.82 |
| III | Construction | 7.65 | 9.96 | 11.21 | 19.82 |
| IV | Electricity, gas & water supply | 0.60 | 2.46 | 5.80 | 2.65 |
| **Tertiary Sector (Services)** | | **39.70** | **43.49** | **46.65** | **49.95** |
| I | Transport, Storage and Communication | 0.82 | 0.37 | 8.20 | 7.97 |
| II | Trade, hotels & Restaurants | 17.16 | 16.48 | 8.20 | 7.97 |
| III | Banking and Insurance | 1.63 | 2.33 | 4.37 | 3.71 |
| IV | Real estates, Ownership of dwellings and Business services | 9.23 | 3.63 | 5.81 | 3.26 |
| V | Public Administration | 4.93 | 12.62 | 14.65 | 18.99 |
| VI | Other Service | 5.93 | 8.07 | 13.63 | 16.21 |

*Source*: Directorate of Economics & Statistics (Various Issues).

**Table 2.4** Share of PS and NPSs in NSDP to State Economy, 1981–2011, (Percent)

| Year | Primary Sector | | Non-Primary Sector | | NSDP | |
|---|---|---|---|---|---|---|
| | Constant Prices | Current Prices | Constant Prices | Current Prices | Constant Prices | Current Prices |
| 1980–81 | 47.40 | 47.29 | 52.60 | 52.71 | 100 | 100 |
| 1985–86 | 44.84 | 41.19 | 55.16 | 58.81 | 100 | 100 |
| 1990–91 | 38.47 | 43.29 | 61.53 | 56.71 | 100 | 100 |
| 1995–96 | 39.58 | 38.06 | 60.42 | 61.94 | 100 | 100 |
| 2000–01 | 32.58 | 33.01 | 67.42 | 66.99 | 100 | 100 |
| 2005–06 | 30.70 | 29.03 | 69.30 | 70.97 | 100 | 100 |
| 2010–11 | 21.98 | 21.10 | 78.02 | 78.90 | 100 | 100 |

*Sources*: Directorate of Economics and Statistics, J&K Government (Various Issues)

most of the factor inputs required by rural population are imported like tractors, fertilizers, pesticides, and other agricultural implements.

Factor contribution has remained relatively much higher than product and market contribution because increases in rural incomes, because of growth of agricultural and tertiary sectors, have contributed significantly to capital formation which Kuznet terms as factor contribution. Further, agricultural sub-sectors like horticulture have contributed towards the foreign exchange earnings of the state which is not explicitly identified by Kuznets but is implicit in his market contribution. In order to show the contribution of agriculture to NSDP (Net State Domestic Product), the following expressions have been used.

$P = P_a + P_n$ ...... (1) Whereas $P$ = total national product $P_a$ = agricultural net product,

$P_n$ = non-agricultural net product

$\delta P = P_a + P_n$ ..... (2)

Write $r_a$ for $P_a/P_a$, $r_n$ for $P_n/P_n$:

$\delta P = P_a r_a + P_n r_n$ ...... (3)

$P_a r_a = \delta P - P_n r_n$ ....... (4)

$P_a r_a / \delta P = 1 - P_a r_a / \delta P$ ....... (5)

Substituting for $\delta P$ on the RHS of Equation (5) from Equation (3):

$P_a r_a / \delta P = 1 - P_n r_n / P_a r_a + P_n r_n$

$= P_a r_a + P_n r_n - P_n r_n / P_a r_a + P_n r_n$

$= P_a r_a / P_a r_a + P_n r_n$

$= 1 / (P_a r_a + P_n r_n)/ P_a r_a$

$= 1 / 1 + P_n r_n / P_a r_a$ ............... (6)

Kuznets formula expressing an inverse relationship between agriculture's share of GDP growth ($P_a r_a/\delta P$) and the product of the ratio of sectoral shares of GDP ($P_n/P_a$) and the ratio of sectoral growth rates ($r_n/r_a$) is given by Equation (6).

On the basis of these equations, relevant estimates are present in Table 2.5.

The above table clearly confirms various types of correlations explained by Kuznets Model of Structural transformation from primary to non-primary sector. The various types of correlations are as:

The percentage share of primary sector in NSDP was 47 per cent where as the growth rate of non-primary sector was 4.14 per cent in

**Table 2.5** Agriculture's contribution to Economic Growth Rate in J&K, at (1993-94 prices)

| $P_a$ | | $P_n$ | | $r_a$ | | $r_n$ | | $P_n/P_a$ | | $r_n/r_a$ | | $P_a/r_a$ | | $\delta P/P$ | |
|---|---|---|---|---|---|---|---|---|---|---|---|---|---|---|---|
| 1981 (TE) | 2011 (TE) | 1981 (TE) | 2011 (TE) | 1981–95 | 1996–2011 | 1981–95 | 1996–2011 | 1981 | 2011 | 1981 | 2011 | 1981 | 2011 | 1981 | 2011 |
| 47 | 22 | 53 | 78 | 2.41 | 3.50 | 4.14 | 9.48 | 1.13 | 3.55 | 1.72 | 2.71 | 1.94 | 9.62 | 2.27 | 1.54 |

*Source*: Digests of Statistics, Directorate of Economics and Statistics, J&K Government (Various issue)

*Note*: TE: Triennium Average; $P_a$ = A-sector (Primary Sector) share of NSDP; $P_n$ = Non-A sector (Non-Primary Sector) share of NSDP; $r_a$ = Average annual growth rate of A-sector product; $r_n$ = Average annual growth of non-A sector product;

$P_a/r_a$ = Ratio of A-sector to NSDP growth (derive from Pa, Pn, ra, rn using Kuznets formula)

$\delta P/P$ = Average annual growth rate of NSDP

1981 period. In 2011, period percentage share of NSDP decreased to 22 per cent in primary sector while as the growth rate of the non-primary sector increased to 9.48 per cent in the same time period. Therefore, shift of percentage share from primary to non-primary sector leads to increase in the growth rate of non-primary sector which is a viable shift for overall economy.

The growth rate of primary sector and the growth rate of non-primary sector are directly related to each other. The growth rate of primary sector was 2.41 per cent in 1981 where as the growth rate of non-primary sector was 4.41 per cent in the same time period. The growth rate increased to 3.5 per cent of primary sector in 2011 while the growth rate of the non-primary sector increased to 9.48 per cent in the same time period. Therefore, the ratio of non-primary percentage share to primary has increased from 1.13 to 3.55 where as the ratio of growth rate of non-primary to primary sectors has increased from 1.72 to 2.71. The Table again confirms the Kuznets model of inverse relation between $P_a/r_a$ and $\delta P/P$.

Therefore, from the above discussion it becomes clear that the structural change from primary to non-primary sector is viable as it increases the growth rate of both the sectors. However, the growth rate of primary sector has not improved so much, that is, it has not crossed 5 per cent growth rate mark during the entire period. This is really a matter of concern for J&K state economy.

## Crisis in Growth

J&K economy is facing crisis in the agriculture and industrial sector as these sectors are showing a dismal performance. The agricultural sector is showing a declining trend from 1960 to 61 onwards and industrial sector is showing a constant trend which amounts to stagnation in the classic sense. The dismal performance of these sectors is mainly due to lack of clear cut strategy. Most of the expenditure incurred on agriculture in the state, increased over the plan period, has been on minor irrigation.

Moreover the declining trend of primary sector can be attributed to the stagnation in food grain production from 1980–81 to 2010–11.

The state of J&K has not even become self-sufficient in the production of agricultural commodities, both cereal and non-cereal. The production of total food grains stood at 15,325 thousand quintals in the year 2003–04. While as in the succeeding year, the figure stood at 15,027 thousand quintals means a decrease by 298 thousand quintals and further decreased to 15,025 thousand quintals during 2005–06. During 2010–11, import figure of food grains were accorded at 553.5 thousand metric tons. The second factor responsible for the slow growth of primary sector especially agriculture is rapid growth of marginal holdings. These small holdings are mostly sub divided and fragmented, and are not found in one complete block and hence un-economic. A delayed breakthrough in agriculture is mainly attributed to small holdings that defied the introduction of modern farm practices (Digest, 2011–12, DES).

Thus agriculture sector is emerging as un-viable economic enterprise in changing structure of the state economy. Since performance of agriculture forms the basis of growth and development of an economy as it has *multiplier effects* across the economy. Unfavourable climatic conditions and lack of irrigation in some areas is the stumbling block. Modern technology and equipments are put in use to increase the agricultural productivity but there seems yet long distance to be covered in this behalf. Thus, agriculture being the main component of primary sector and with half of the state's population deriving their income from agriculture and absorb huge chunk of population.

An important aspect responsible for underdevelopment of the state economy is the overdependence on imports to meet the growing needs of the population. The state is suffering from very large trade deficit. The steady increase in the import and export in terms of value of taxable goods is presented in the following Table 2.6.

The export-import ratio was 0.40 in 1990–91. For subsequent periods the estimates have been low the aforesaid estimates as 0.22 in 1994–95 then to 0.04 and 0.31 in 2001 and 2004–05, respectively. It is only 2010–11 that the figure showed marginal improvement and has raised to 0.55.

In absolute terms the trade deficit of the state went up from 746.35 to 9783.78 in 2010–11 except in the year 2000–01 when the figure is showing the negative figure (−1.56). Exports from state include

Table 2.6  Value and Ration of Exports & Import, ( in crores)

| Year | Value of taxable goods Imported | Value of taxable goods Exported | Export Import Ratio (E/I) | Trade Deficit |
|---|---|---|---|---|
| 1990–91 | 1253.75 | 507.40 | 0.40 | 746.35 |
| 1994–95 | 2536.53 | 560.84 | 0.22 | 1975.69 |
| 2000–01 | 938.24 | 939.80 | 0.24 | –1.56 |
| 2004–05 | 8173.64 | 2509.10 | 0.31 | 5664.54 |
| 2010–11 | 21986.26 | 12202.48 | 0.55 | 9783.78 |

Source: Commissioner Office (Srinagar), Dept of commercial Taxes, J&K Government.

handicraft products, horticulture products, skin, and hides and turpentine and wood in raw form only in the absence of necessary industrial base. The reason behind the above analysis is that the state has failed to expand its productive capacity particularly in secondary sector. However, the import and export of the state have increased since the last two decades which is mainly attributed to the development in means of transport communication, besides banking, and insurance.

The impact of tourism is extremely ambivalent. On the one hand, tourism plays an important and certainly positive role in the economic development, cultural exchange, and further promotes international relations of state. On the other hand, many hopes that were placed on tourism as an engine of economic development have been disappointed and strained due to violence. So, tourism needs pertinent care on sound efficacies. It is demonstrated that the socio-cultural significance of tourism, measured in terms of employment is very large.

To sum up, it is observed that the industrial setup prior to 1947 was practically non-existent in J&K. Agriculture was the principal sector contributing towards the economy but being feudal in nature, it hardly contributed towards the development of the state economy. After independence, due importance had been given to industrial and other sectors. However, still agriculture maintains its dominance. Even government on the industrial front despite announced various measures for boosting industrial growth could not promote industrial growth pretend ferocities surfaced since 1989. Furthermore, the weak infrastructure has hindered in the exploration of such resources.

## LOC Trade

India believes in maintaining friendly relations with global world especially with neighbouring countries including Pakistan. For maintaining cordial relation with Pakistan, a number of initiatives Confidence Building Measures (CBMs) have been taken by Govt. of India which includes Line of Control (LOC) Trade in J&K State. Trade is in the interest of people of two neighbouring countries or borders for peace and prosperity. Owing to proximity and socio-cultural and ethnic relations, the economic linkage and dependability develop automatically for the mutual benefit of the people of borders. Such trading activities have been traditionally going on in most of the border areas of the neighbouring countries of the world. Various socio-economic conditions physical, political, and environmental aspects of the neighbouring countries or borders, however, govern or decide the intensity, volume, and nature of the cross-country or cross-border trade.

India's trade links with its neighbouring countries are centuries old. The history of trade with China and Central Asia could be traced back from the ancient Silk Road route since the Roman times. Trade through Nathla Pass accounted for 80 per cent of total cross border trade between China and India in early 1900s. Trade with the East Asian nations through the sea route in the east has a glorious history.

Since partition of India, the events and policy trends have led to distances and created differences between India and Pakistan. Nevertheless in terms of history, culture, language, and religions, both countries have number of common features. Number of initiatives has been taken to initiate peace process that could help resolve and address the political conflict between India and Pakistan besides normalizing bilateral relations and economic cooperation between the two nations for their mutual development and growth.

J&K being at the terminal end of the country, along with poor connectivity, remoteness and other disadvantages, is one of the sensitive states. Opening of borders and bringing about economic integration with various regions of the state was very essential for stability, peace, and prosperity.

For achieving these objectives, India and Pakistan have developed mutually agreed Confidence Building Measures (CBM)—structures and agreements from the days of their independence. The present LOC trade is also the result of a series of CBMs during the past few years. The Srinagar—Muzaffarabad (April 2005) and Rowalkote-Poonch (June 2006) bus services and ultimately the cross border trade was realization of the dreams and aspirations of the people of the divided J&K and created goodwill between the two countries.

The historic decision to start trade across the LoC was the outcome of a high-level meeting between the Prime Minister of India and the President of Pakistan in April 2005. Further discussions were held on the subject during the Technical-level talks between the two countries at New Delhi on 2–3 May, 2006 as a part of Confidence Building Measures (CBMs). At that meeting, it was agreed that the Cross LoC trade would be by way of truck services; the list of items for trade would be identified; and the exchange of delegations between the Chambers of Commerce on both sides would be facilitated.

Meanwhile, the process of holding Round Table Conferences on Kashmir was initiated by the Hon'ble Prime Minister of India in 2006. One of the five Working Groups constituted during the second Round Table Conference was the Working Group on strengthening of relations across LoC. This Working Group recommended increasing Cross LoC movement and interaction among people on both sides, including commencement of Cross LoC Trade.

An Oversight and Monitoring Committee (OMC) was set up under the chairmanship of the Union Home Secretary to study the recommendations made by various Working Groups for its implementation in respect of Cross-LOC Trade. The Ministry of External Affairs (MEA) pursued the main recommendations with the Government of Pakistan, whereas the Ministry of Home Affairs (MHA) pursued the issue of creation of the requisite infrastructure at the crossing points in J&K.

In the meeting of the Inter-Ministerial Committee and the State Administration held at Srinagar on June 2008, it was decided to develop Land Customs Stations (now Trade Facilitation Centres) for Uri-Muzaffarabad Trade Route at Salamabad & for Poonch-Rawalkote Trade Route at Chakkan-da-Bagh. The State Govt. was

**Table 2.7** Quantity and Value of Imports and Exports

| Year | Export to Pak | | Import from Pak | |
|------|------------------|------------------|------------------|---------------------------|
| | Quantity (Qtls) | Value INR Crore | Quantity (Qtls) | Value Pak currency (cr.) |
| 2011–12 | 465272.41 | 320.19 | 368535.17 | 531.24 |
| 2012–13 | 768061.86 | 371.67 | 790245.70 | 657.79 |
| 2013–14 | 508024.90 | 244.80 | 247160.96 | 377.35 |

*Note*: The trade is barter in nature and the value figures are based on valuation figures provided by traders.
*Source*: Economic Survey, 2013–14, DES.

asked to identify suitable land for the purpose after getting the specifications and requirements of the Customs and other Central Agencies. Accordingly, land was identified and acquired by the State Government at both the places. Temporary infrastructure was put in place at Salamabad and the bare minimum permanent infrastructure was put in place at Chakkan-da-Bagh out of the resources of the State government in consultation with Central Government. The following table depicts the quantity and value of Imports & Exports between the two countries in the year 2011–12, 2012–13, and 2013–14, ending November 2013:

## Infrastructure at Trade Facilitation Centres (TFCS)

Infrastructure (Phase-I) created at Salamabad, Uri, & Chakkan-da-bagh, Poonch at a cost of Rs. 895.72 lakhs & Rs. 995.00 lakhs respectively under SRE and ASIDE funding. DPRs under (Phase-II) at an estimated cost of Rs. 585.00 lakhs for Salamabad, Uri, & Rs. 1040.70 lakhs for Chakkan-da-Bagh, Poonch submitted to MHA, for approval/release of funds.

The basket of goods traded consists of agricultural products and few handicraft and handloom products. The significant part of LoC trade is that the static and dynamic benefits of trade are so enormous and so diversified that both the trading partners involved are benefited, over and above the fulfilment of the peoples' aspirations. The LoC trade will open new markets for the export of more items which will go a long way in the development process of the state. Besides the trade route provides an alternative of Srinagar Jammu highway, which remains closed off and on during winters, for the supply of essential commodities.

## Banking Facilities

A presentation was made by the representative of the RBI on the proposed banking mechanism in the Joint Working Group Meeting. The Indian side made a lot of effort to persuade the Pakistani delegation on this issue in view of the enormous increase in the volume of trade.

The trade involves two sovereign countries Governments of India and Pakistan and since the Cross LOC Trade is not an international trade, there are certain issues which remain to be sorted out by mutual agreement on both the sides and such matters are being vigorously persuaded at the State level with the Government of India. The state government has constituted a high level committee for regularly attending to the issues which are coming in the way of LoC trade for making it more purposeful and successful. The LoC Trade will go a long way in improving the relationship between the two neighbouring countries and will definitely pave way for the success of SAFTA.

Thus Trans LOC trade between India and Pakistan via Kashmir has assumed special significance in the context of normalization of relations of the two countries followed by a better understanding of the issue of J&K. Line of control trade areas are Pak-occupied Kashmir, Uri, Kargil, and Poonch. This development will have a healthy impact on the J&K particularly Kashmir, which specialize in the manufacture of handicrafts, including carpets, Peppier machine, wood carving, and embroidery items and also gifted with the production of world famous exotic apples and dry fruit like nuts apricots and almonds. The Trans LOC trade will greatly help find an attractive market for Rs. 1600.00 crores worth of handicraft products and Rs. 1200.00 crore worth of fresh and dry fruit business being produced by both small and big artisans as well as orchardists (J&K economy performance analysis, 2007–08).

Poonch-Rawalkot economic zone in 2006 noted more than 27 crores trade was done between India and Pakistan. The Trans LOC trade is likely to give a major fillip to the tourism industry in the state because the people across the Loc will be curious to see the places and the people in Kashmir which is world famous for its enchanting ecology and environment. Most of the Kashmiri Products are going to Namakmandi, a famous market in Peshawar which centres to the Central Asia such as Uzbekistan, Tajikistan, Afghanistan, Iran, China, Azad Kashmir, and Pakistan (*The Hindu*, dated 18 November 2008).

# 3

# Evolution of Labour
# Since Independence

Before partition, Jammu and Kashmir, with a geographical area of 222,870 sq. km, was the largest princely state of British India. But this large area was inhabited with only 39 towns and 8903 villages. The total population in 1947 was estimated at 40 lakh, compared to 1.39 Crore in 2017. Agriculture and allied activities have been the mainstay of the people of Jammu & Kashmir. The demand for labour in the state was therefore easily met by state's domestic rural and tribal workforce across the year.

Though in the beginning, the labourers had no importance, but with the growth of various industries of the State, the labour class became an important part of the society and statistics of more or less accurate nature were made available in various reports published from time to time (Census of India, 1921).

Industry provided employment to a large number of agricultural families. During the first quarter of the last century the two silk factories of Srinagar and Jammu alone absorbed 56 per cent of the total number of labourers engaged in textile industries. Of this number, 1461 were skilled workmen and the rest unskilled. Besides, about 5000 families got part-time employments in the silk-worm rearing operations.

With the passage of time, this number increased and towards the end of our period of study, there were about two lakh and fifty thousand people in the villages who found part-time employment in the silk-worm rearing operations. Moreover, four thousand labourers in the cities depended entirely, for their living on silk reeling, seed production, and silk weaving during the period. This does not include fairly large number of men, who were involved indirectly in the various operations of the industry, such as labourers engaged casually on mulberry nurseries, watching of mulberry plantations, carrying the loads, and also those working in the companies who insured the goods of the industry (Census of India, 1941).

*Jammu & Kashmir.* Bilal Ahmad Khan, Oxford University Press. © Oxford University Press 2022.
DOI: 10.1093/oso/9780192849656.003.0003

Mostly widows, with a sprinkling of destitute, old married women and young girls, before they attained the usual age of marriage comprised the strength of this labour community. According to the Census Report of 1921, two-thirds of the strength of this labour community was Muslims of lower ranks and their number was twenty, under fourteen years of age mostly engaged in sorting out of cocoons.

Most of the conventions sanctioned by the International Labour Organization were adopted by the Government of India. It must, however, be said to the credit of the Jammu and Kashmir Government that attempts were made to move with the spirit of the time, by having some sort of minimum age limit fixed for the employment of labour in the factories. It was during the second quarter of the last century that the age limit was fixed by the management of the factories at 11 years and subsequently raised to 12.

As some operations connected with the industry were such that they attracted child labour. A word of explanation seems necessary in this connection. Various operations involved in the industry called for technical skill. Such training was not imported in any organized institutions, established for the purpose in the State as is done today. It was acquired by habitual association and contact in actual working conditions with those who had already acquired the skill. The new recruits were generally taken in for the simplest operations which needed least amount of technical skill, such as cooking of cocoons, the cleaning of wastes and knotting of broken ends of the silk thread, and finally, the reeling of raw silk and all subsequent processes. The old labourers, thus, found it convenient to associate their little children or brothers or relatives with themselves for learning tie art, obviously for economic reasons. This led to the involvement of child labour in the industry in the State (Wazir, 1996–97).

During the first half of the last century, the labour legislation for the betterment of industrial labourers was still in a backward state in India. As a result of the influences of the International Labour Organization the matters were improving more or less satisfactorily in British India. They had there a Factory Act which was being steadily improved and brought in line with advanced legislation in other countries. The State of Jammu and Kashmir was also trying to follow the example set by British India. Towards the end of last century, the State Legislature passed the Factory Act and workmen's compensation Act more or less on the same lines as those obtaining in British India. However, what was wanted regarding formal state legislation through the normal constitutional procedure was to some extent made up in the State by executive orders caused by the peculiar organization of the industry on the monopolistic basis. These orders were passed by the State Council of Ministers to grant bonus to the labourers; thereby, making the co-sharers with the State in profits.

During the first four decades after the organization of the industry, nothing was done on a large scale to provide social amenities to the labour community. As already referred to, the comprehensive enquiry made into the conditions of the industry in 1942, because of which a scheme of reorganization was proposed and the same, after being considered by a special committee appointed for the purpose, was sanctioned by the government (Reorganization Report of 1942). Some very interesting recommendations for providing social amenities to the labourers and ameliorating, in many respects, the general condition of the labourers in the factories concerned are given as follows:

1. Providing a Maternity Bonus of Rs. 15/- per birth bearing in mind that there were only fifty female labourers in Srinagar Silk Factory and seventy-five in the Jammu Silk Factory.
2. Providing a Sickness Allowance in case of serious illness, to be duly attested to by the competent medical authority, the allowance was to be up to 10 days wage of the class to which the labour concerned belonged at the time of his illness.
3. Providing a Contributory Provident Fund for those labourers who had a continuous service of at least five years, the labourer contributing 6 per cent of his wage and the Government contributing an equal amount the total with simple Interest at the same rate as in vogue in case of permanent employee to be payable when the labourer attained the age of 65 years or was otherwise incapable of work. This was to be a sort of pension for the labourers to fall back upon in their old age.
4. Establishment of a social centre for the workers in the factory at Srinagar as had already been established at Jammu factory. The centre was to have arrangements for adult education, fading room, and a library in order to prevent lapses into illiteracy. Arrangements of lectures on subjects of common interest to the labourers such

as the advantage of personal hygiene and sanitation, first aid to the injured, precautions against the epidemics, and so on. The expenditure on these items was partly to be financed by the labourers themselves and Government was to provide only the necessary accommodation for housing the Reading Room and the library.

5. Establishing an Accident Fund to provide compensation for work to those who got incapacitated permanently or temporarily through an accident while discharging their functions.

6. Providing the facilities of accommodation on spot to certain vendors who were to supply articles of granted purity under the supervision of the Department. This had already been tried on a small scale, with great success in Jammu.

7. Establishing Medical Dispensaries at the two factories, one in Srinagar to have a whole-time doctor of the Sub-Assistant Surgeon grade and the other in Jammu on a part-time basis with necessary stocks of medicines, etc.

Some of these recommendations were straightaway accepted by the Government and action was taken to implement them. The most important recommendation which the Government accepted was, to sanction a temporary measure of bonus 25 per cent of wages in order to improve the efficiency of the labourers and to attract new recruits to the industry. This step, as a matter of fact, did a lot of good to the labour community.

A few years before the end of last century, the State launched a campaign to drive away illiteracy from the State, especially among the labourers. A serious attempt seems to have been made by the management of the industry to impart training to all the illiterate members of the staff and labourers in all the branches of the industry at the headquarters. Practically hundred per cent of the employees and operatives (including the female sorters) in Jammu factory were declared literate after the prescribed test conducted by the State Education Department. This was a record that any concern will be legitimately proud of. The problem of avoiding lapses into illiteracy was also tackled along with the campaign against illiteracy (Wazir, 199697).

It may be mentioned here that the part played by the labourers themselves in ensuring the success of the scheme by attending classes regularly, taking advariage of the library, and even contributing funds to a large extent for financing the scheme deserves the highest praise. The members of the staff too acquitted themselves creditably by playing the role of honorary teachers and taking the classes outside the legitimate working hours of the factory, and their contribution to the funds required for this purpose. Indeed, the whole movement and the results achieved was an instructive lesson in what honest and genuine cooperation among various groups, which composed the personnel of an industry, achieved for the common good of all concerned.

The political movement of Kashmir, though initially mobilized people based on their religious identity, evolved to include a strong economic content, in the later years. By the beginning of the decade of 1940, the movement had come under the leftist influence, and the economic concerns started characterizing its political discourse. Under the leadership of India Marxists, particularly K. M. Asraf and B. P. L. Bedi, an indigenous leftist leadership had evolved in Kashmir. This leadership was involved in giving an intellectual direction to the youth through a 'study circle' propagating 'the philosophy of Marxism and communism' (Chandra, 1985). The leftist influence was also seen in the trade union politics, especially the Mazdoor Sabha that was launched in 1937 and was comprised of the existing organizations like the Kashmir Motor Drivers Association, the Carpet Weavers Association, and the Tonga Drivers Association, among others. With the organization of Mazdoor Sabha, grievances of workers were brought into the public domain. The government-run silk factory workers, for instance, became very active and launched various activities, including strikes and demonstrations. The Kissan Sabha was organized around the same time, though it was not as active as the Mazdoor Sabha.

The mobilization of the workers and peasants through trade union politics changed the political language of Kashmir. It became common to see red banners and flags, particularly in the city of Srinagar. With the demonstrating workers condemning their economic exploitation and demanding economic justice, a new rights-based discourse was being introduced in Kashmir, which was rapidly substituting the discourse based on religious overtones.

The left intervention helped to give a progressive direction to the movement. The entry of leftists in Kashmir in a big way coincided with the conversion of the Muslim Conference into the National Conference. By 1943, there had emerged a big group of CPI progressives in the National

Conference who could influence its further strategy of struggle in a decisive mannerly. The included chiefly the leaders of workers and peasants, intellectuals and political workers of National conference (Chandra, 1985). Among the prominent leaders of National Conference who came under the influence of leftist ideology and politics included leaders like Ghulam Mohammad Sadiq, D. P. Dhar, Mir Qasim, and G. R. Ranzo. Most of them held a very influential position within the party. The group became active in giving a leftist direction to the political movement in Kashmir.

It was during this time that an ideological structure of National Conference was also chalked out and a strong economic content was incorporated in the movement politics. The New Kashmir Manifesto, the blueprint of the Conference, was a document that was set in a future constitution of the state, but also for the social-economic restructuring of the state. Linked with the process of boarding the political movement, this manifesto was to reflect the shift in the political discourse from religious to a class-based one.

Fighting the long-standing poverty of the peasants and artisans and unmitigated helplessness of workers was the major goal of the New Kashmir manifesto. This was to be achieved through a complete reorganization of the agrarian structure and eliminating its parasitical and feudal components, on the one hand, and empowering the peasantry, artisans and other working classes, on the other. Hence, the manifesto was a complete plan for restructuring the economy. Among other things, it called for planned development of the economy to ensure a rapid rate of economic growth along with increasing social justice. In terms of agricultural policy, it listed its basic aim as fair distribution of land and elimination of parasites, middleman, and others who do not contribute to its productivity. It also talked of compulsory work for all residents of the state, right to unemployment insurance, right to rest, right to education, minimum wages, and so on. Among the crucial parts of manifesto were specific charters for peasants, workers, and women.

The charter of peasant's rights sought to empower the peasants by seeking to dismantle the feudal basis of agriculture. As per this charter, every peasant was to have the right to possess land for tilling and the land owned by absentee landlords was to be handed over to the peasants. It sought to abolish beggar and all feudal impositions, compulsory offerings, and gifts to feudal lords. It also sought to free the peasant from the burden of loans and debts. The charter of the rights of labourers meanwhile provided for right of employment, right to freedom from exploitation, right to have a standard of living much above the bare existence, and right to equality of wages. Rights to pension, hygienic residence, free treatment, and right to education were also included in the list of rights of labourers.

Soon after assuming power, the National conference government started working on the economic goals laid down in the New Kashmir Manifesto. It particularly focused on land reforms. These reforms took place in three phases. In the first phase, that is in April 1948, the privileges enjoyed by jagirdars, muafidars, and mukkarrees were abolished. This decision affected 396 jigirdars and 2347 mukkaridars (*The Hindustan Times*, 17 July 1953). In the second phase of land reforms that took place in October the same year, State Tenancy Act of 1924 was amended and relief was given to large number of tenants. Referring to the logic of these reforms, Aslam notes that, 'It gave priority to the reorganization of agriculture on the modern and rational basis, through the abolition of landlordism, securing the land to the tiller and the formation of cooperation association'. However, it was in 1950 in the third phase of reforms that the abolition of Big Landed Estates Act of 1950 was passed. As per this act, a ceiling on the holding of land was placed at 22.75 acres. The act also provided for transfer of surplus land to tillers who were cultivation on the land. The tillers were to be given the land with no payment. This was the most sweeping reform that substantially changed the pattern of landholding in the state.

Although land reforms were in pursuance of the political movement led by the National Conference and that they benefitted a large number of underprivileged and oppressed peasants, these came in for criticism within the state. Much of this criticism was launched by the depressed land-owning class on the ground that they were not treated at par with their counterparts in the rest of India and were not paid any compensation for losing their land. It was this resentment that led them to oppose the very logic of Article 370.

Irrespective of these problems, the progressive nature of the land reforms has been widely acknowledged. These have been hailed as some of the most radical and most effective land reform legislations in India changed drastically the agricultural and social structure of Kashmir

(Korbel, 1966). The feudal system was abolished, landlordism disappeared, and the thousands of peasants living in virtual slavery became the landholders. It was because of the land reforms that the political transition in Kashmir could be attained very smoothly.

However, it is not only from the perspective of immediate implications, but also from the long-term perspective, the implications of land reforms for the society in Jammu and Kashmir have been widely acknowledged. Haseeb Drabu (2013) has linked the land reforms of early post-accession period with the better human development indicators at present, especially among rural masses of the state. He argues that in Jammu and Kashmir the households living below the poverty line are just 3 per cent as against 26 per cent at the all India level.

The state economy of post-1953 period was quite distorted. Neither the agrarian nor the industrial sector could strengthen itself. The failure to pursue a follow-up of the land reforms of the pre-1953 period led to the overall economic stagnation. Land reforms had certainly benefitted the peasantry and had helped them to rise above the miserable condition of poverty, but they could not rise above their subsistence level. Though most of the tillers became the owners of the land, yet the size of the landholding was so small that it affected its overall productivity. The economy of the state, on the whole, has remained a backward economy, which has been dependent on the loans, grants, and packages from the centre. To quote the State Development Report of the Planning Commission of India (Planning Commission of India, 2003), 'The state ranks among one of the bottom-line states with respect to socio-economic development indicators.' It further noted that inadequate infrastructure has hampered the growth of productive sector.

The post-1953 period has been witnessed not only to the emergence of the middle—class Kashmiris, but also a very affluent class. Much of this class is comprised of those who benefitted from the money coming from the centre including the bureaucrats, politicians, trades, contractors, engineers, among others.

Commenting on the emergence of the nouveau riche class of Kashmiris and the acquisition of their fortunes through dubious means, Punjabi (1992) noted, 'The acquisition of wealth and its vulgar display became the prominent feature of social life in Kashmir'. The wide gulf between those who monopolized the fruits of prosperity and those who remained deprived and untouched by development schemes and funds brought about slowly a creeping feeling of dissatisfaction. This feeling was further intensified by generally prevailing corruption and unscrupulousness. Meanwhile, there remained the problem of unemployment. While the number of middle-class educated Kasmiris had increased, there were not sufficient avenues from them to be suitably employed. Noting the unemployment of the educated youth, the State Development Report thus notes, 'Work opportunities, however, have not kept pace with the increasing population. The problem of unemployment gains more importance because of increasing unemployment of the educated in the state. Almost 70 per cent of the population is directly or indirectly dependent on agriculture and allied activities which continue to be a subsistence sector. In the absence of industrial growth and neglible scope for absorption in the private sector, many have been rendered unemployment and have joined the ranks of job seekers'.

(Planning Commission, 2003)

Government service and other salaried jobs were normally taken up by a small portion of comparatively educated Kashmiri Pundits. Majority of population comprising of Muslims were more involved in skill-driven arts and crafts. The prolific growth in home-based artisan enterprises in cities and towns provided source of livelihood and employment to generations after generations. The dignity of labour was associated with craft and both men and women were actively involved in these home-based businesses throughout the year. Utilization of labour at different layers was therefore smoothly distributed among, urban, rural, skilled, unskilled, educated, and uneducated classes. With change in time and growth in population, the demographic changes in the state resulted in a paradigm shift with unfavourable repercussions. Dignity of labour in farming, sheep rearing, handicrafts, etc. is a thing of past. This has tilted the scale in such a fashion that we are slowly and gradually getting buried under a pile of unemployed youth.

Although J&K Govt. has established an institutional mechanism for planning and management of state's labour force and also for implementation of various legislations through various institutions like State Labour Department, Provident Fund Organization, State Insurance

Corporation (ESIC) and Jammu and Kashmir Building and Other Construction Welfare Board, however, the situation on ground is very grim. A very unorganized and of-control situation has aroused wherein locals are starving for work and outsiders are getting absorbed with ever-increasing pace. The reasons are manifold ranging from changing perception towards dignity of labour to mismatch between skill requirements by markets and those imparted by our vocational education system (GK, July 4, 2017).

Although there are numerous central and state govt. legislations, which are supposedly being enforced for safety and protection of labour rights, however, what is equally important is providing direction to the unorganized sector with a long-term objective of reducing unemployment. There is an immediate need to adopt globally used policies of labour economics in order to recognize the dynamics and functions of the labour markets. Labour economics can assist in understanding the pattern of income, employment, and wages by regulating employee–employer exchanges. There is no doubt that Jammu & Kashmir has a very serious unemployment problem, which is only growing bigger. The need to understand and reform our labour issues is therefore of utmost importance.

# 4

# Occupational Pattern and Levels of Workforce

The United Nation Development Programme has warned that India need to generate 28 Crore jobs before 2050 to absorb all the new entrants into the workforce. Probably, its flagship programme 'Make in India', may lead to creation of jobs but the State of J&K has a different scenario as far as jobs are concerned. Technological Advances leads 'Automation' generates jobs in one sector but complicate the job prospects in all other fields. As a result, the employment may see a decline in manufacturing sector. The absence of 'Industrial Platform' leaves little chance of generation of jobs.

Development-and-Unemployment Syndrome is gripping in many economies except the few who are able to stride along with technological advances. There is a law 'Okun's Law' which reflects the relationship between unemployment and GDP growth, that is, unemployment rises by 1 per cent, the GDP growth rate will be impacted by 2 per cent or it will be 2 per cent lower than the potential of the country. No Govt. in this world can sustain a jobless growth for a long period of time.

The dependence on material is easily understandable but the paradox of employment is a grave matter of concern largely due to the economic distress and mismatch of the opportunities. As per the statistics from 1981 to 2011 the occupational pattern of the State too has shifted from primary sector, which decreased from 63.88 per cent to 41.48 per cent and secondary sector, which decreased from 14.25 per cent to 3.99 per cent, trending towards the increase of employment in tertiary sector, that is the service sector from 21.87 per cent to 54.33 per cent. The shift from primary to tertiary is without undergoing the development in the secondary sector, which in fact provides the maximum opportunities for creation of jobs on a larger scale. It highlights lopsided path of economic development on one hand and agricultural or industrial backwardness on the other (Seth, 2018).

*Jammu & Kashmir*. Bilal Ahmad Khan, Oxford University Press. © Oxford University Press 2022.
DOI: 10.1093/oso/9780192849656.003.0004

The primary sector, which is categorically associated with agriculture, has limitations as far as the topography of our state is concerned; arable land being too limited unlike Punjab. Hence, the possibility of employment generation in this sector can be ruled out. As far as the secondary sector which is associated with manufacturing, which can in turn be boosted by industrial setup, too is not being given the due consideration because of the strategic instabilities looming all the time around. It also takes a back seat, no doubt it being the biggest contributor to the employment front. Nonetheless, we are left with only one sector which can be looked after is the tertiary sector. The fact that, the development of tertiary sector, in the absence of the primary and the secondary, is a lop sided development but herein as far as our State is concerned, the only way to boost employment is the tertiary sector which can act as a life-saving drug to check the 'Brain Drain' of the native youth.

This is definitely going to give an opportunity to the younger talented youth from institutes like IIM, IIT, NIT, and many more educational institutes of the State, who are otherwise compelled to leave the State in search of 'Greener Pastures'; the brains which could have been instrumental in the development of the native land. Moreover, the limitations in the growth of primary and secondary sector, that is, the topography and the geographical location has no meaning as far as the blooming of the tertiary Sector is concerned; it being primarily 'internet dependent', which in itself has no bounds.

To ensure sustainable development, the 'Talent Gap', explained as the anomaly of 'Rising Unemployment' and 'Falling Growth' needs to be cupped which can only be addressed if the 'Tertiary Sector' is given the prime focus. If ever this demographic advantage is not exploited; the same is going to add to the 'Dependency Ratio' in future in our country too like US, China, and Japan. The advantage of 'Demographic Dividend' being boasted by the Prime Minister Narendra Modi will turn into another disaster, that is, the 'Demographic Disaster', to be handled in future along with the other Disasters in the Disaster Management Policies of the Country.

The most lugubrious that the state of J&K confronting is prolonged civil strife and unrest for more than three decades. The government took stock of the performance in major developmental programmes and highlights the policy initiatives. However, the drawbacks and disadvantages of the enduring unrest caused due to conflict have put the state in general and the valley in particular to tremendous economic and welfare hardships. As a result, there are virtually no engines of job creation and resources are used inefficiently and productive sources converted into unproductive factors (JK Digest, 2011–2012).

The J&K state has been a continuous victim by violence and has been quite unfortunate with regard to political instability right from 1980. This prolonged cycle of unrest became the stumbling block for economic development and turned it into shambles. The state is a bone of contention between India and Pakistan and three wars have been fought between these two countries over this region and both have their own perspectives regarding the cause and course of conflict however, the people of Kashmir particularly youth are suffering the most and plunged into grief. Growth and development get retarded to a large extent. Due to serious unemployment and economic downturn during the early turbulent phase of 90s, a large number of youth joined militancy and also forced migration of Kashmiri Hindu and pundits took place to a large extent. Thus whole pattern of employment in the J&K State get distorted (Khan, 2016).

Even before the turbulent period J&K economy has experienced a fairly high progress in terms for creation of job opportunities. There were major economic activities prevailing in the state. However, ferocity that spilled over since 1989 hit all the sectors badly. Subsequently strength of economic stability as well as employment opportunities eroded. The state revived to some extent depends upon the normalcy produced in the state. For instance, peace process (Initiation of a Dialogue Process) was held in 2004 then recovery took place (Lovass et al., 2014). The two countries agreed that constructive dialogue would promote progress towards common objective of peace and economic development for the future generation. The development took place in short period of time, which is, in 2–3 consecutive years after dialogue. However, the susceptibility of agreement was not perpetual. The overall analysis of composite dialogue shows that it was a *zero sum game* and both sides have not achieved desired goals in the prolonged life.

Kashmir being a conflict ridden zone has far less opportunities for employment than rest of the other states. With an underdeveloped industrial sector and the inability of government to create enough jobs, there seems to be no immediate solution (Habibullah, 2009). Lack of avenues to engage youth in meaningful ways will always drive youth towards the miscreants in this society. In the absence of healthy sources of entertainment and competitive sports, they are inevitably going to be on the streets, either as mob or harmlessly wasting away their lives. Young populations across the world are generally seen as drivers of socio-economic growth, but in Kashmir, the youth bulge is a problem.

The brunt of violence resulted negligible investments with business marred by uncertainties. The Economic development is the first causality due to lack of 'enduring peace'. Conflict creates macroeconomic instability and crisis volatility. The major costs of macroeconomic instability are significant in terms of welfare loss, increase in inequality, poverty, and decline in long term growth. J&K economy is experiencing abnormal volatility but *crisis volatility*. Crisis volatility is an extreme shock exceeding certain cut off points. The continued lockdown or curfews in the state due to unrest are the instance of Crisis volatility (JK Economy Survey, 2016–17).

The increasing population and unemployment are becomes a matter of concern over the years despite planned development. The number of educated unemployment is increasing and continue to inflate year after year. However, the avenues of employment generation have not increased proportionately. High incidence of unemployment among the youth and the educated has emerged as an area of concern in the State. It reached at alarming dimensions which is ever increasing every passing year with thousands of educated and uneducated youth getting added to the list of unemployment largely due to economic distress and mismatch (Nengoo, 2015). The state has earned a distinction to have the highest number of unemployment rate in entire North India. As per the Annual EUS Report (2014) released by Labour Bureau under Union Ministry of Labour and Employment, J&K has the highest unemployment rate of 10 per cent in North India. It is pathetic to see highly educated persons belong to extremely poor sections aspiring for a low grade job in the uncertain and unrest circumstances.

Unemployment has become a lethal weapon now. The serious blockade has been the inability of youth to go abroad particularly in the Gulf Region for job. Kashmiri young is hardly getting passport and takes more than 2 years to get a passport card. It is abhorrent that government is unable to stop Kashmiri youth crossing over the LoC and returning with guns to create havoc but is reluctant to give passports to genuine persons trying to get some gainful employment abroad Normally in other parts of India a passport can be issued on the certificate given by any government officer.

Besides, critical climate also became obstacle to major and minor construction. Economic apotheosis activities are confined to a few months of summer. Almost 90 per cent skilled and unskilled labour migrates from Bihar, UP, West Bengal, etc. to Kashmir Valley for a few months of summer season.

The government adroitly must think about a long-term plan for unemployment youth. It has to devise a policy to channelize youth bulge constructively. Government should aware about the growing rate of unemployment sitting idle have a disastrous impact during the time to come in the conflict zone.

It cannot be tackled by slogans and ad hoc measures. It requires a definite and clear policy with a time bound blueprint to tackle various possible avenues of employment. The government needs to realize the explosive dimensions of the problem. The frustration of the youth is increasing rapidly which apart from increasing their alienation is converting them into a readymade material for destructive exploitation

## Trends of Workforce at All India Level

The size of employment in any country depends to a great extent on the level of development. Therefore, when a country makes progress and its production expands the employment opportunities grow. In India, during the past three decades production has increased in all the sectors of economy. In response to these developments the absolute level of employment has not grown. During the planning period, unemployment in absolute terms has increased at national level. This has happened because during the first decades of planning, trend rate of growth was considerably lower than the targeted rate. Therefore, jobs in adequate number were not created. Economic growth by itself does not solve the problem of unemployment. *Prabhat Patnaik* has succinctly remarked, 'A higher arithmetical figure of growth rate is neither a necessary nor a sufficient condition for alleviation of unemployment.' In fact, there exists a real conflict between the objectives of economic growth and employment in the early phase of economic development. Examining this issue in the existing Indian context, Prabhat Patnaik has very correctly argued, 'While growth per se means nothing for unemployment, this growth fetishism can be exploited by finance capital to wrest concessions to the detriment of employment objective.'

B. Hazari and J. Krishnamurthy have brought out the conflict between growth and employment inherent in the Mahalanobis strategy which guided India's development efforts for about two decades. Basic assumption of economic planning in India was that growth would automatically solve the unemployment problem. However, this was not to be so. Until the FYP 1978–83 was formulated, this conflict was not recognized by the government. Since the adoption of neo-liberal economic policies in India since 1991, the government's obsession with the high rate of economic growth has made it completely oblivious to possible conflict between economic growth and the employment. Hence, in recent years, growth in India has been mostly 'Jobless'. This is substantiated by the fact that during 1990s and 2000s, unemployment has increased (Mishra & Puri, 2008).

Among the different demographic aspects, occupational pattern of a country plays an important role in analysing the population. Occupational distribution of a country's population provides the information regarding the radiance of occupation and main source of livelihood. It also indicates the main source of production of GNP. Besides it throws light on the extent of labour force and population engaged in different sectors of economy. It has got practical importance too while framing the economic policy of the country with a view to provide gain full employment. In developing countries like India where economic policies have been adopted to achieve the objectives of optimum utilization of resources, occupational pattern is an integral part of the policy or economic planning (Indian Economy, Misra & Puri, 2008).

The change in modern developmental includes a relocation of workers from agriculture towards non-agricultural production and sectoral shift is often reflected in a migration rural to urban areas since most of industries are often geographically concentrated in and around urban areas. Currently market differences exist in occupational structures of countries, in LDCs of Asia and Africa a sizable proportion of labour force is engaged in agriculture and other activities, whereas in Western Europe and North America, only a small percentage of labourers seek employment in this sector (Roy, 2008).

While India taking into account where the market for manufactured commodities is limited and less than 18 per cent of its working force is employed in this sector. However in developed countries there are extensive markets for industrial products. Industries have been set up on a big scale which provides employment to majority of labour force. With the rise of PCY, trade grows and transport, communications and banking facilities expand in response to increase demand for their services. Consequently, the proportion of labour force in the tertiary sector increases. At present, in the U.S.A nearly two-thirds of the working populations are absorbed in this sector. In contrast, underdeveloped countries having one-fifth of its labour force absorbed in tertiary sector (Uma, 2013–14).

Today, India is counted among the most important emerging economies of the world but employment conditions in the country still remain poor. Even today the large proportion of workers engaged in agriculture (49 per cent) contributes a mere 14 per cent to the GDP. In contrast, the service sector contributes 58 per cent of GDP barely absorbs 27 per cent of the employment and the share of manufacturing in both employments (13 per cent) and GDP (16 per cent) is much lower than in South-East Asian countries. India's 520 million workers account for about one-sixth of total workforce of the world. In terms of size, it is next only to China, which accounts for nearly one-fourth of world's workforce. India has rather a low proportion of workers to total population, mainly due to low participation of women in work. It has a very low sex ratio in its labour force around 28 per cent as compared to 40 per cent in the world. Most of the workers have very low education and skill levels—only about 52 per cent of the workers are educated as compared to 77 per cent in the world as a whole (Papola, Alakh, & Sharma, 2006).

Broadly, an economy is classified into primary sector, secondary sector and tertiary sector. Generally, productivity in tertiary sector is very high. Hence, transfer of population primary industries to secondary and eventually to tertiary activities is considered a reliable index of economic progress. Colin Clark in his book *Conditions of Economic Progress* argues that there is a close *relationship* between developments of an economy on the one hand and occupational Structure on the other and economic progress is generally associated with certain distinct necessary and predicable changes in occupational structure.

## Labour Force Growth in India, 1981–2011

The size of labour force depends on all economically active population including the unemployed. During the three decades period 1970–2011, labour force in India increased erratically more than double. It may be noted that the average rate of growth of labour force was 2.96 per cent per annum during the 1980s. It declined to 2.37 during 1990s but reversed subsequently to 2.78 in 2001 and 2.69 per cent per annum in 2011.

## Sectoral Employment Shares in India, 1983–2010

Majority of Indian workers were engaged in agriculture and allied activities. With economic development, agriculture is expected to decline in importance in terms of its share in employment and output. Proportion of agriculture in total employment has declined over the years: from 74 per cent in 1972–73 to 68 per cent in 68 per cent in 1983, 60 per cent in 1993–94, and to 57 per cent in 2004–05. It has declined further to 51 per cent in 2009–10. But the decline in the employment share of agriculture has been much slower than in its share in GDP from agriculture. Thus, while share of agriculture in GDP declined from 41 per cent in 1972–73

**Table 4.1** Growth of Labour force in India, 1981–2011.

| Year | Labour Force (in crore) | Average Annual Growth Rate |
|------|-------------------------|----------------------------|
| 1981 | 24.20 | 2.96 |
| 1991 | 30.60 | 2.37 |
| 2001 | 40.22 | 2.78 |
| 2011 | 48.17 | 2.69 |

*Source*: Tata Service Ltd, Statistical Outline of India, Excluding Assam and J&K.

to 15 per cent in 2009–10. That employment declined from 74 per cent to 51 per cent. Rate of decline in GDP share has been faster during 1993–94 to 2009–10, from 30 per cent to 15 per cent, while the rate of decline in employment share has been relatively slow, from 64 per cent to 51 per cent. The sectoral share of employment during the reference period is depicted in Table 4.2.

The decline in employment share of agriculture has been mostly compensated by an increase in the share of secondary sector in the pre-reform period but since the economic reforms the tertiary sector has been the main gainer of the shift in employment. Yet, increase in its employment share has not been commensurate with the increase in its share of GDP during 1993–94/2009–10. The share of secondary sector in employment has increased at a relatively faster rate while its share in GDP has remained constant at about one-fourth of the total. Within the secondary sector construction has sharply increased its share in employment. Manufacturing increased its share both in employment and GDP. In the tertiary sector, trade experienced fast increase in its share in employment and smaller increases in its share in GDP in the post-reform period but saw only a small increase in its employment. Financial services registered a fast increase both in its employment and GDP share, though its share in employment is small (2.25) and GDP (15.64). Community, social and personal services used in the tertiary sector, saw a marginal decline in the pre-reform period and is now the smallest in GDP, though it continues to be second largest, after trade, in terms of employment.

The asymmetry in the rate of change in employment and GDP shares of different sectors has serious implications in terms of differences in earnings and income between different sectors. In 1972–73, agriculture employed 74 per cent workers and produced 41 per cent of GDP. Per worker productivity and income in agriculture was significantly lower than non-agricultural activities even then ratio being 1:3.6. In 2009–10, the ratio has gone up to 1:6. Thus there has been a large decline in the relative earnings of agricultural workers. That is partly because agricultural growth has been consistently much lower than that in the non-agricultural sectors. Agriculture has grown at an average rate of 2–3 per cent per annum as against 5–6.5 per cent growth in the non-agricultural sector during the period under consideration. But even if agriculture grew at a rate of about 4 per cent per annum, as envisaged in Eleven FYP, it cannot

**Table 4.2** Sectoral share of employment (UPSS) in India (Percent)

| Sector | 1983–84 | | 1993–94 | | 2004–05 | | 2009–10 | |
|---|---|---|---|---|---|---|---|---|
| | Employ | Output | Emp | Output | Emp | Output | Emplo | Output |
| **Primary Sector** | 68.59 | 37.15 | 63.98 | 30.01 | 56.30 | 20.20 | 51.30 | 15.23 |
| Mining & Quarrying | 0.61 | 2.25 | 0.69 | 2.51 | 0.56 | 2.20 | 0.64 | 1.74 |
| Manufacturing | 10.63 | 14.52 | 10.63 | 14.46 | 12.27 | 12.15 | 11.50 | 15.41 |
| Utilities | 0.28 | 1.71 | 0.40 | 2.43 | 0.27 | 2.29 | 0.28 | 1.10 |
| Construction | 2.24 | 5.81 | 3.24 | 5.76 | 5.69 | 6.62 | 9.60 | 6.67 |
| **Secondary Sector** | 13.78 | 24.30 | 14.96 | 25.15 | 18.78 | 26.24 | 22.02 | 25.92 |
| Trade & Hostelling | 6.35 | 11.51 | 7.59 | 12.18 | 10.89 | 15.54 | 11.38 | 15.53 |
| Transport & Comm. | 2.49 | 5.99 | 2.87 | 6.62 | 4.08 | 10.25 | 4.48 | 14.00 |
| Finance, Insur, Real est. & bus Services | 0.83 | 8.31 | 0.97 | 12.17 | 1.71 | 13.53 | 2.25 | 15.64 |
| Community, social & personal services | 7.96 | 12.75 | 9.64 | 13.86 | 8.24 | 14.25 | 8.57 | 13.67 |
| **Tertiary Sector** | 17.63 | 38.56 | 21.07 | 44.84 | 24.92 | 53.56 | 26.67 | 58.84 |
| All Non Agricultural | 31.41 | 62.85 | 31.02 | 69.99 | 43.7 | 79.80 | 48.70 | 84.77 |
| Total | 100 | 100 | 100 | 100 | 100 | 100 | 100 | 100 |

*Source:* Estimates based on various rounds of NSSO data on Employment and Unemployment.

employ many more persons productively. In other words, new jobs that are required to be created are not to be in agriculture, they have to come from the non-agricultural sectors. In a 25–30 years perspective, employment structure must be envisioned as consisting of about 30–35 per cent in agriculture and 70–75 per cent in non-agricultural activities. It would imply that all the new employment opportunities will be located in non-agriculture activities in the coming years.

## Occupational Distribution of Workforce in India, 1981–2011

The occupational distribution of workforce by the sectoral distribution has been changed since 1981, particularly in the decade 1991–2011. Large proportion of labour force employed in the agricultural sector reflects the predominance of agriculture in the economy. The occupational distribution of workforce in India since 1981 in terms of per cent is reflected in Table 4.3.

We notice that since 1980 there was a significant decline in the relative importance of agriculture. According to the 1981 census, agricultural and

**Table 4.3** Occupational Distribution of working force in India (Percent)

| Occupational | 1981 | 1991 | 2001 | 2011 |
|---|---|---|---|---|
| Agricultural and allied activities | 68.7 | 66.9 | 56.7 | 49.04 |
| Mining & Quarrying | 0.6 | 0.6 | 0.6 | 0.5 |
| **Total Primary Sector** | 69.3 | 67.4 | 57.3 | 49.09 |
| Household other than HH industry | 11.3 | 9.4 | 13.9 | 12.6 |
| Construction | 1.6 | 1.9 | 3.7 | 5.57 |
| **Total Secondary Sector** | 12.9 | 12.1 | 17.6 | 18.2 |
| Trade and Commerce | 6.3 | 7.1 | 9.4 | 12.62 |
| Transport, storage & communication | 2.7 | 2.8 | 4.0 | 4.61 |
| Other Services | 8.8 | 10.5 | 11.8 | 12.51 |
| **Total Tertiary Sector** | 17.8 | 20.4 | 25.2 | 32.71 |
| Total | 100 | 100 | 100 | 100 |

*Source*: Various Issues, Census of India, Govt. of India

allied activities accounts 68.7 per cent of labour force, secondary sector accounted 12.9 and tertiary sector accounts 17.8 per cent. Thus, there is a significant rise in the percentage of labour force employed in the manufacturing and tertiary sector. The tertiary sector in India accounts more improvement. Tertiary sector got high priority, 17.8 per cent to 32.71 per cent during 1980–2011. This indicates significant improvement of the tertiary sector.

## Growth and Elasticity of Employment in India, 1983–2010

Aggregate employment has grown at an average annual rate of two per cent in India during the past four decades. However, a large part of this growth of employment simply indicates growth in labour force. It has seen a declining trend decade after decade. It was 2.44 per cent during 1972–73/1983, 2.02 per cent during next 10 year period, 1.84 during 1993–94/2004–05, 1.50 during 1999–2000/2009/10, and 0.22 per cent during 2004–05/2009/10 (NSSO Rounds).

Between these decadal periods, some fluctuations were noted in shorter periods of 5 years. The most favourable interpretation of this upturn in employment growth in post-2000 period is that the teething troubles of economic reforms led to slow growth of employment initially were over by 2000 and globalization started having its beneficial effect on employment with the state of millennium.

The fact that GDP growth was no better—was in fact lower during 2000–2005 than during 1994–2000, that most employment growth recorded during the later period was in the informal sector of which a large part was as self-employment in agriculture, and organized sector employment, in fact, saw an absolute decline, however, raise doubts about the high employment growth during 2000–2005 being demand-led and productive. A virtual stagnation in employment during 2004–05/2009–10 as revealed by the latest round of NSSO survey casts further doubt on the veracity of 2004–05 estimates. This has been largely due to sharp fall in women workforce participation rate due to increase in schooling etc.

The long-term trend of decline in the rate of employment growth is, however, a fact that cannot be ignored. What is particularly intriguing

**Table 4.4** Growth & Elasticity of Employment in India (UPSS), Percent

| Sector | 1983/1993–94 | | 1993–94/2004–05 | | 1999–2000/2009–10 | | 2004–05/2009–10 | |
|---|---|---|---|---|---|---|---|---|
| | Emp | Elast | Emp | Elast | Emp | Elast | Emp | Elast |
| **Primary Sector** | 1.35 | 0.49 | 0.67 | 0.26 | −0.13 | −0.05 | −1.63 | −0.53 |
| Mining & Quarrying | 3.24 | 0.53 | −0.08 | −0.02 | 2.70 | 0.61 | 3.00 | 0.73 |
| Manufacturing | 2.00 | 0.41 | 3.17 | 0.47 | 1.95 | 0.25 | −1.06 | −0.11 |
| Utilities | 5.58 | 0.64 | −1.86 | −0.32 | 2.11 | 0.37 | 1.02 | 0.14 |
| Construction | 5.67 | 1.16 | 7.19 | 0.94 | 9.72 | 1.06 | 11.29 | 1.22 |
| **Secondary Sector** | 2.82 | 0.53 | 3.97 | 0.59 | 4.64 | 0.60 | 3.46 | 0.39 |
| Trade, Hostelling etc. | 3.77 | 0.67 | 5.24 | 0.61 | 2.54 | 0.30 | 1.10 | 0.12 |
| Transport & Com. etc. | 3.39 | 0.56 | 5.16 | 0.49 | 3.68 | 0.25 | 2.14 | 0.13 |
| Finance, Ins., Real est. & bus. Services | 3.58 | 0.39 | 7.23 | 0.99 | 7.68 | 0.81 | 5.77 | 0.47 |
| Community, social & personal services | 3.91 | 0.67 | 0.40 | 0.06 | 1.85 | 0.28 | 0.99 | 0.12 |
| **Tertiary Sector** | 3.77 | 0.57 | 3.41 | 0.43 | 2.83 | 0.30 | 1.59 | 0.14 |
| All Non-Agricultural | 3.36 | 0.55 | 3.64 | 0.48 | 3.61 | 0.41 | 2.41 | 0.23 |
| Total | 2.02 | 0.41 | 1.84 | 0.29 | 1.50 | 0.20 | 0.22 | 0.02 |

*Source*: Various rounds of NSSO data on Employment and Unemployment.

is that this decline has accompanied acceleration in the rate of employment. Thus when GDP grew at 4.7 per cent per annum during 1972–73 to 1983, employment growth was 2.4 per cent, GDP growth increased to 5 per cent but employment growth declined to 2.0 per cent during 1983/1993–94, during 1993–94/2004–05 GDP growth accelerated to 6.3 per cent but employment growth further declined to 1.8 per cent and during 2004–05/2009–10, when GDP growth was as high as 9 per cent employment grew at an insignificant rate of 0.22 per cent. The declining trend in the employment content of growth is quite clearly seen in terms of the values of employment elasticity in the table. It was 0.52 during 1972–73/1983, declined to 0.41 in the next 10-year period and further to 0.29 during 1993–94/2004–05. During 2004–05/2009–10, it declined to almost zero.

The employment growth rates have of course varied across various sectors and activities. In secondary sector, consisting of mining, manufacturing, electricity, water, and gas and construction, the growth has been relatively high, in fact the highest among the three sectors during the long period 1972–73 to 2009–10. It has declined over the period with some fluctuation over the shorter period, but has shown a significant increase during 1994–2005. Even during 2004–05/2009–10, when overall employment has virtually stagnated, it has grown at around 3.5 per cent in the secondary sector. Employment growth in the tertiary sector has also been relatively high but has consistently declined over some periods. Growth of employment in the primary sector, as expected, has been the lowest and seen the sharpest decline, in fact, turned negative. Slow and declining growth of employment in agriculture is a result both of the slow and declining rate of GDP growth and a decline in the employment elasticity. In the secondary sector, a high employment growth despite moderate rates of GDP growth has been possible due to high and rising employment elasticity. But in the tertiary sector, even a high GDP growth has not been able to maintain a high growth in employment due to a steep decline in employment elasticity.

Within the secondary or industry sector, construction experienced a relatively high and increasing rate of employment growth. It was as high as over 7 per cent during 1994–2005, almost similar to its GDP growth.

It has recorded 11 per cent employment growth during 2004–05/ 2009–10, when total employment has virtually stagnated. Employment growth in manufacturing has also been moderately high and after declining during 1983/1993–94 over the earlier 10 years period, it registered an increase in the next period, 1994–2005 then again dwindled during 2004–05/2009–10. Employment elasticity in manufacturing has been relatively high except during 2005–2010 when it has, in fact, been negative.

In the service sector, trade and transport have shown the best employment performance, both registering a growth of over 5 per cent during 1994–2005, after having seen a decline in growth rate, sharper in transport than in trade, during 1983–94, over 1973–83. Financial services have recorded the highest increase in employment over the longer period 1983–2005 except during 1983/1993–94. Even during 2004–05/2009–10, this sub-sector of services has registered an employment growth of about 6 per cent, while trade and transport sub-sector experienced only about 1–2 per cent growth in employment. Thus, it appears that all sub-sectors of tertiary sector with the possible exception of community, social, and personal services have shown reasonably high potential for employment generation.

It must be noted that in most sub-sectors of services, while GDP has seen a high and increasing growth rate, employment growth has been on a decline rate. Employment elasticity has, therefore, declined sharply from 0.81 during 1972–73/1983 to 0.30 during 1999–2000/2009–10 in trade from 0.91 to 0.25 in transport from 0.71 to 0.28 in community, social and personal services, although in financial services it increased during 1993–94/2009–10.

Thus, as a whole, it can be concluded that employment content of growth has declined over time. Of course, it has varied across sectors. Primary sector, consisting of mainly agriculture, has witnessed least employment growth which in itself is not worrisome as this sector is home to large bulk of surplus labour. The sub-sectors of tertiary sector such as financial services are linked to globalization have witnessed faster growth of employment. However, manufacturing sector which has significant *multiplier effects* with other sectors has not registered high growth of employment due primarily to low growth of output.

## State-Wise Classification of Workers
## in India, 2011

In a country like India with vast potential and diversity, the creation of an integrated workforce solution targets multiple areas to the stable employment growth. India is a big country both in terms of area and population. Apparently, it looks that workforce trends are quite different in different states. State-level analysis brings comparison of workforce trend in terms of gender and area wise. Working population classified into main and marginal workforce. We examined the total workers out of total population in respect of gender and geographical area of 2011 census. In 2011, there were 481 million working population in India, the second largest after China. Among all states in India Utter Pradesh is leading one having large proportion of workforce and followed by Maharashtra. Utter Pradesh (658.1 lakh) (13.67 per cent All India Level) holds the top rank in total workforce and Manipur State having lowest (1.1 lakh) proportion of workforce amongst all states. In case of male working population, Utter Pradesh stood at first rank in India followed by Maharashtra. Similarly in the case of female working population, Maharashtra stood at first rank in India followed by Utter Pradesh which then followed by West Bengal. Among all the states, workforce participation rate of females in the rural sector was highest in Himachal Pradesh and in the urban sector it was highest in Mizoram. Utter Pradesh and Bihar having the highest workforce population in rural areas amongst other States.

While considering J&K State at national level, it possess 43.2 lakh total working population which accounts 0.89 per cent at All India level. J&K State holds of 26.4 lakh main workers and 16.7 lakh of marginal workers that contributes 0.71 per cent of main workers and 1.34 per cent of marginal workers at All India Level. The State of J&K have 31.9 lakh male working population and out which 23 lakh are significantly main workers. Furthermore, 11.2 lakh female working population and out of which only 3.3 lakh are main workers in J&K State. It is further investigated from the below captioned categories of workers (Table 4.5) that J&K possessed large proportion of workers in rural areas and small in urban areas. The State-wise classifications of workers (Census, 2011) are reflected in Table 4.5.

**Table 4.5** State wise Classification of Workers (Census 2011) *in lakhs*

| | | Working Pop | Main Workers | Marginal Workers | Male Working | Male Main Workers | Female Working | Female Main Workers |
|---|---|---|---|---|---|---|---|---|
| All India | T | 4817.4 | 3624.4 | 1192.9 | 3318.6 | 2731.4 | 1498.7 | 892.9 |
| | R | 3485.9 | 2457.4 | 1028.4 | 2267.6 | 1780.3 | 1218.3 | 677.1 |
| | U | 1331.4 | 1166.9 | 164.4 | 1051.0 | 951.1 | 280.4 | 215.8 |
| J&K | T | 43.2 | 26.4 | 16.7 | 31.9 | 23.0 | 11.2 | 3.3 |
| | R | 31.1 | 16.6 | 14.4 | 22.1 | 14.5 | 9.0 | 2.1 |
| | U | 12.0 | 9.7 | 2.3 | 9.8 | 8.5 | 2.2 | 1.2 |
| Him. Pradesh | T | 35.5 | 20.6 | 14.9 | 20.4 | 14.3 | 15.1 | 6.2 |
| | R | 32.8 | 18.2 | 14.6 | 18.3 | 12.4 | 14.5 | 5.7 |
| | U | 2.7 | 2.4 | 0.3 | 2.0 | 1.9 | 0.6 | 0.4 |
| Punjab | T | 98.9 | 84.5 | 14.4 | 80.7 | 72.6 | 18.2 | 11.8 |
| | R | 61.7 | 51.0 | 10.7 | 49.9 | 44.1 | 11.8 | 6.8 |
| | U | 37.1 | 33.4 | 3.7 | 30.7 | 28.4 | 6.3 | 4.9 |
| Chandigarh | T | 4.0 | 3.8 | 0.18 | 3.2 | 3.1 | 0.7 | 0.6 |
| | R | 0.1 | 0.11 | 0.006 | 0.1 | 0.1 | 0.001 | 0.01 |
| | U | 3.9 | 3.7 | 0.17 | 3.1 | 3.0 | 0.7 | 0.6 |
| Uttarakhand | T | 38.7 | 28.7 | 10.0 | 25.5 | 20.7 | 13.2 | 7.9 |
| | R | 28.8 | 19.9 | 8.8 | 17.2 | 13.2 | 11.5 | 6.7 |
| | U | 9.8 | 8.7 | 1.1 | 8.2 | 7.4 | 1.6 | 1.2 |
| Haryana | T | 89.1 | 70.1 | 19.0 | 68.0 | 58.6 | 21.0 | 11.5 |
| | R | 60.0 | 44.3 | 15.6 | 43.9 | 36.7 | 16.1 | 7.6 |
| | U | 29.1 | 25.7 | 3.3 | 24.1 | 21.8 | 4.9 | 3.9 |

*(continued)*

Table 4.5 Continued

| | | Working Pop | Main Workers | Marginal Workers | Male Working | Male Main Workers | Female Working | Female Main Workers |
|---|---|---|---|---|---|---|---|---|
| Delhi | T | 55.8 | 53.0 | 2.7 | 47.6 | 45.6 | 8.2 | 7.4 |
| | R | 1.3 | 1.1 | 0.1 | 1.1 | 1.0 | 0.1 | 0.1 |
| | U | 54.5 | 51.8 | 2.6 | 46.5 | 44.5 | 8.0 | 7.3 |
| Rajasthan | T | 298.8 | 210.5 | 88.2 | 182.9 | 152.4 | 115.8 | 58.1 |
| | R | 243.8 | 161.7 | 82.1 | 137.7 | 110.6 | 106.0 | 51.0 |
| | U | 55.0 | 48.8 | 6.1 | 45.2 | 41.7 | 9.7 | 7.1 |
| UP | T | 658.1 | 446.3 | 211.7 | 498.4 | 374.2 | 159.6 | 72.1 |
| | R | 519.5 | 335.3 | 184.1 | 383.5 | 278.1 | 135.9 | 57.2 |
| | U | 138.6 | 110.9 | 27.6 | 114.9 | 96.0 | 23.6 | 14.8 |
| Bihar | T | 347.2 | 213.5 | 133.6 | 252.2 | 172.7 | 95.0 | 40.8 |
| | R | 313.5 | 187.2 | 126.3 | 224.3 | 149.8 | 89.2 | 37.3 |
| | U | 33.6 | 26.3 | 7.2 | 27.8 | 22.8 | 5.7 | 3.5 |
| Sikkim | T | 3.0 | 2.3 | 0.7 | 1.9 | 1.6 | 1.1 | .06 |
| | R | 2.4 | 1.7 | 0.7 | 1.4 | 1.1 | 0.9 | 0.5 |
| | U | 0.6 | 0.5 | .007 | 0.4 | 0.4 | 0.1 | 0.1 |
| Arunachal Pradesh | T | 5.8 | 4.7 | 1.0 | 3.5 | 3.0 | 2.3 | 1.7 |
| | R | 4.7 | 3.7 | 0.9 | 2.6 | 2.2 | 2.0 | 1.5 |
| | U | 1.1 | 1.0 | 0.1 | 0.8 | 0.7 | 0.31 | 0.2 |
| Nagaland | T | 9.7 | 7.4 | 2.3 | 5.4 | 4.4 | 4.2 | 2.9 |
| | R | 7.6 | 5.6 | 1.9 | 4.0 | 3.1 | 3.5 | 2.5 |
| | U | 2.1 | 1.7 | 0.4 | 1.4 | 1.2 | 0.7 | 0.4 |

| | | | | | | | | |
|---|---|---|---|---|---|---|---|---|
| Manipur | T | 1.1 | 8.5 | 3.0 | 6.6 | 5.5 | 4.9 | 3.0 |
| | R | 0.81 | 5.9 | 2.1 | 4.6 | 3.8 | 3.5 | 2.1 |
| | U | 0.34 | 2.6 | 0.8 | 2.0 | 1.7 | 1.4 | 0.9 |
| Mizoram | T | 4.8 | 4.1 | 0.7 | 2.9 | 2.6 | 1.9 | 1.5 |
| | R | 2.5 | 2.1 | 0.3 | 1.4 | 1.3 | 1.0 | 0.8 |
| | U | 2.3 | 1.9 | 0.3 | 1.4 | 1.2 | 0.8 | 0.6 |
| Tripura | T | 14.6 | 10.7 | 3.9 | 10.4 | 8.8 | 4.2 | 1.8 |
| | R | 11.1 | 7.7 | 3.3 | 7.6 | 6.3 | 3.4 | 1.3 |
| | U | 3.5 | 3.0 | 0.5 | 2.7 | 2.5 | 0.7 | 0.4 |
| Meghalaya | T | 11.8 | 9.2 | 2.6 | 7.0 | 5.8 | 4.8 | 0.3 |
| | R | 9.7 | 7.3 | 2.4 | 5.6 | 4.5 | 4.1 | 2.7 |
| | U | 2.1 | 1.9 | 0.2 | 1.4 | 1.3 | 0.7 | 0.6 |
| Assam | T | 119.6 | 86.8 | 32.8 | 85.4 | 70.3 | 34.2 | 16.5 |
| | R | 103.6 | 73.1 | 30.5 | 72.5 | 58.8 | 31.1 | 14.3 |
| | U | 16.0 | 13.7 | 2.2 | 12.8 | 11.5 | 3.1 | 2.2 |
| W B | T | 347.5 | 256.8 | 90.6 | 267.1 | 216.7 | 80.4 | 40.0 |
| | R | 240.8 | 164.8 | 75.9 | 182.1 | 140.1 | 58.7 | 24.6 |
| | U | 106.7 | 91.9 | 14.7 | 85.0 | 76.5 | 21.6 | 15.3 |
| Jharkhand | T | 130.9 | 68.1 | 62.7 | 84.2 | 52.3 | 46.7 | 15.8 |
| | R | 107.7 | 48.8 | 58.9 | 648.4 | 35.6 | 42.9 | 13.2 |
| | U | 23.2 | 19.3 | 3.8 | 19.4 | 16.7 | 3.8 | 2.6 |
| Odisha | T | 175.4 | 107.0 | 68.3 | 119.0 | 87.9 | 56.3 | 19.1 |
| | R | 151.0 | 86.2 | 64.7 | 99.4 | 70.4 | 51.6 | 15.7 |
| | U | 24.3 | 20.8 | 3.5 | 19.6 | 17.4 | 4.7 | 3.3 |

*(continued)*

Table 4.5 Continued

| | | Working Pop | Main Workers | Marginal Workers | Male Working | Male Main Workers | Female Working | Female Main Workers |
|---|---|---|---|---|---|---|---|---|
| Chhattisgarh | T | 121.8 | 82.4 | 39.3 | 71.3 | 55.9 | 50.4 | 26.4 |
| | R | 100.6 | 63.6 | 36.9 | 55.2 | 41.1 | 45.4 | 22.5 |
| | U | 21.1 | 18.7 | 2.4 | 16.1 | 14.8 | 5.0 | 3.9 |
| Madhya Pradesh | T | 315.7 | 227.0 | 88.7 | 201.4 | 163.6 | 114.2 | 63.4 |
| | R | 247.1 | 167.2 | 79.8 | 147.4 | 114.8 | 99.7 | 52.4 |
| | U | 68.5 | 59.7 | 8.8 | 54.0 | 48.7 | 14.5 | 10.9 |
| Gujarat | T | 247.6 | 203.6 | 44.0 | 180.0 | 165.6 | 67.6 | 37.9 |
| | R | 155.7 | 118.7 | 36.9 | 101.7 | 91.4 | 53.9 | 27.3 |
| | U | 91.9 | 84.8 | 7.1 | 78.2 | 74.2 | 13.6 | 10.6 |
| Daman & Diu | T | 1.2 | 1.1 | 0.04 | 1.0 | 1.0 | 0.1 | 0.1 |
| | R | 0.2 | 0.2 | 0.01 | 0.18 | 0.2 | 0.04 | 0.03 |
| | U | 0.97 | 0.9 | 0.03 | 0.82 | 0.8 | 0.09 | 0.08 |
| Dadra & Nagar Haveli | T | 1.5 | 1.3 | 0.2 | 1.1 | 1.0 | 0.3 | 0.2 |
| | R | 0.8 | 0.6 | 0.24 | 0.5 | 0.4 | 0.28 | 0.13 |
| | U | 0.7 | 0.6 | 0.04 | 0.6 | 0.6 | 0.09 | 0.07 |
| Maharashtra | T | 494.2 | 437.6 | 56.6 | 326.1 | 299.8 | 168.1 | 137.7 |
| | R | 306.5 | 265.1 | 41.4 | 178.8 | 161.8 | 127.6 | 103.2 |
| | U | 187.7 | 172.5 | 15.2 | 147.2 | 138.0 | 40.4 | 34.5 |
| Andhra Pradesh | T | 394.2 | 330.3 | 63.8 | 241.8 | 214.6 | 152.3 | 11.5 |
| | R | 290.5 | 241.4 | 49.0 | 164.9 | 145.8 | 125.5 | 95.5 |
| | U | 103.7 | 88.9 | 14.7 | 76.8 | 68.7 | 26.8 | 20.2 |

| | | | | | | | | |
|---|---|---|---|---|---|---|---|---|
| Karnataka | T | 278.7 | 233.9 | 44.7 | 182.7 | 163.4 | 96.0 | 70.4 |
| | R | 185.0 | 150.6 | 34.4 | 113.1 | 100.0 | 71.9 | 50.5 |
| | U | 93.7 | 83.3 | 10.3 | 69.5 | 63.4 | 24.1 | 19.8 |
| Goa | T | 5.7 | 4.7 | 1.0 | 4.1 | 3.5 | 1.5 | 1.19 |
| | R | 2.1 | 1.6 | 0.5 | 1.5 | 1.2 | 0.6 | 0.42 |
| | U | 3.6 | 3.1 | 0.5 | 2.6 | 2.3 | 0.9 | 0.76 |
| Lakshad Weep | T | 0.18 | 0.10 | 0.07 | 0.15 | 0.091 | 0.034 | 0.016 |
| | R | 0.04 | 0.02 | 0.024 | 0.037 | 0.02 | 0.018 | 0.003 |
| | U | 0.14 | 0.8 | 0.055 | 0.115 | 0.07 | 0.025 | 0.013 |
| Kerala | T | 116.1 | 93.2 | 22.8 | 84.5 | 71.7 | 31.6 | 21.4 |
| | R | 63.4 | 49.3 | 14.1 | 45.0 | 37.4 | 18.3 | 11.8 |
| | U | 52.7 | 43.9 | 8.7 | 39.4 | 34.3 | 13.3 | 9.6 |
| Tamil Nadu | T | 328.8 | 279.4 | 49.4 | 214.3 | 189.6 | 114.4 | 89.8 |
| | R | 188.6 | 153.3 | 35.2 | 112.1 | 95.5 | 76.4 | 57.8 |
| | U | 140.2 | 126.0 | 14.2 | 102.2 | 94.0 | 38.0 | 31.9 |
| Puducherry | T | 4.4 | 3.9 | 0.45 | 3.3 | 3.0 | 1.12 | 0.93 |
| | R | 1.4 | 1.2 | 0.25 | 1.05 | 0.91 | 0.42 | 0.31 |
| | U | 2.9 | 2.7 | 0.19 | 2.2 | 2.1 | 0.69 | 0.62 |
| Andaman & Nicobar | T | 1.5 | 1.2 | 0.26 | 1.20 | 1.03 | 0.31 | 0.22 |
| | R | 0.94 | 0.72 | 0.22 | 0.74 | 0.60 | 0.19 | 0.11 |
| | U | 0.58 | 0.5 | 0.004 | 0.46 | 0.43 | 0.11 | 0.10 |

*Source:* Registrar General of India.

*Note:* **First,** India excludes population of that portion of which are under illegal occupation of Pakistan and China. **Second,** the Population of India and Manipur are excluding Mao. Mara, Palmate and Purl sub-division of Seagate district in Manipur.

## Trends of Workforce in J&K State, 1981

At the 1981 census, a worker was defined as a person who had participated in any economically productive work during the last one year preceding the date of enumeration. According to this definition, workers include full-time workers, secondary workers and even such workers whose contribution to any economically productive work could even be considered insignificant. The workers were further classified into main and marginal workers. Main workers were determined on the basis of their having worked for the most part of the year, that is, 6 months or 183 days or more. Marginal workers on the other hand were those workers who participated in any economically productive work for less than 6 months preceding the date of enumeration. For example, if a housewife, who mainly attended her household duties, assisted in cultivation or knitted a sweater in lieu of compensation was categorized as a marginal worker. *Adoption of the concept of 'marginal workers' is a special feature of 1981 census.* Persons who did not participate in any kind of work were treated as non-workers.

Workers were further classified into four broad industrial categories viz.; cultivators, agricultural labourers, household industry (a list of a few typical industries that can be conducted on the household industry basis is appended at the end of this volume), and other workers. The other workers include workers in forestry, hunting, fishing, mining, and quarrying, manufacturing and repairs, electricity, gas and water, construction, whole-sale and retail trade, restaurants, hotels, transport, storage and communications, financing, insurance, community and social and personal services, and all public sector and local self-government employees. Thus a slight departure has been made in the presentation of 1981 data in the PCA from the 1971 census format in as much as instead of nine categories as in 1971. The main workers have been classified into four categories only. This has been done on the recommendations of the Planning Commission and Central Statistical Organization. The following statement gives percentage distribution of population of each sex into workers, marginal workers and non-workers in the State/Districts in 1981 along with the classification of main workers into four categories of the reference to the broad industrial categories of 1971 census.

Table 4.6 Distribution of workers by categories and sex, 1981 (Percent)

| State/District | Sex | Total Pop | Total workers | Main workers | Main workers | | | | Margin workers | Non workers |
|---|---|---|---|---|---|---|---|---|---|---|
| | | | | | Cultivators | Agri Lab. | HH Indus | Other worker | | |
| J&K | P | 100 | 44.26 | 30.37 | 17.27 | 1.06 | 1.61 | 10.43 | 13.89 | 55.74 |
| | M | 100 | 55.81 | 52.20 | 29.33 | 1.89 | 2.48 | 18.50 | 3.61 | 44.19 |
| | F | 100 | 31.31 | 5.91 | 3.75 | 0.13 | 0.63 | 1.40 | 25.40 | 68.69 |
| Anantnag | P | 100 | 42.44 | 31.67 | 20.80 | 0.88 | 1.42 | 8.57 | 10.77 | 57.56 |
| | M | 100 | 55.91 | 53.15 | 34.06 | 1.59 | 2.23 | 15.27 | 2.76 | 44.09 |
| | F | 100 | 27.27 | 7.49 | 5.86 | 0.10 | 0.51 | 1.02 | 19.78 | 72.73 |
| Pulwama | P | 100 | 50.70 | 29.04 | 19.03 | 0.59 | 1.48 | 7.94 | 21.66 | 49.30 |
| | M | 100 | 56.53 | 52.74 | 34.69 | 1.12 | 2.48 | 14.45 | 3.79 | 43.47 |
| | F | 100 | 44.19 | 2.60 | 1.56 | 0.01 | 0.36 | 0.67 | 41.59 | 55.81 |
| Srinagar | P | 100 | 34.90 | 30.12 | 5.02 | 0.81 | 4.40 | 19.89 | 4.78 | 65.10 |
| | M | 100 | 52.62 | 51.84 | 8.58 | 1.41 | 6.94 | 34.91 | 0.78 | 47.38 |
| | F | 100 | 14.60 | 5.25 | 0.95 | 0.12 | 1.48 | 2.70 | 9.35 | 85.40 |
| Badgam | P | 100 | 48.73 | 32.81 | 18.29 | 0.87 | 4.61 | 9.04 | 15.92 | 51.27 |
| | M | 100 | 58.65 | 56.58 | 32.36 | 1.62 | 6.75 | 15.85 | 2.07 | 41.35 |
| | F | 100 | 37.46 | 5.78 | 2.28 | 0.03 | 2.17 | 1.30 | 31.68 | 62.54 |
| Baramula | P | 100 | 45.44 | 31.43 | 18.09 | 1.21 | 2.60 | 9.53 | 14.01 | 54.56 |
| | M | 100 | 56.66 | 53.73 | 30.84 | 2.24 | 3.72 | 16.93 | 2.93 | 43.34 |
| | F | 100 | 32.56 | 5.81 | 3.44 | 0.04 | 1.31 | 1.02 | 26.75 | 67.44 |

(continued)

Table 4.6 Continued

| State/District | Sex | Total Pop | Total workers | Main workers | Main workers | | | | Margin workers | Non workers |
|---|---|---|---|---|---|---|---|---|---|---|
| | | | | | Cultivators | Agri Lab. | HH Indus | Other worker | | |
| Kupwara | P | 100 | 48.86 | 30.37 | 22.18 | 2.09 | 0.68 | 5.42 | 18.49 | 51.14 |
| | M | 100 | 56.93 | 53.47 | 39.00 | 3.80 | 0.94 | 9.73 | 3.46 | 43.07 |
| | F | 100 | 39.46 | 3.47 | 2.58 | 0.09 | 0.39 | 0.41 | 35.99 | 60.54 |
| Kargil | P | 100 | 54.94 | 45.33 | 33.65 | 1.47 | 0.12 | 10.09 | 9.61 | 45.06 |
| | M | 100 | 59.53 | 55.05 | 34.42 | 2.57 | 0.11 | 17.95 | 4.48 | 40.47 |
| | F | 100 | 49.57 | 33.94 | 32.74 | 0.19 | 0.13 | 0.88 | 15.63 | 50.43 |
| Leh | P | 100 | 50.39 | 43.55 | 25.47 | 3.20 | 0.37 | 14.51 | 6.84 | 49.61 |
| | M | 100 | 59.46 | 57.13 | 29.67 | 3.29 | 0.21 | 23.96 | 2.33 | 40.54 |
| | F | 100 | 40.15 | 28.22 | 20.73 | 3.11 | 0.54 | 3.84 | 11.93 | 59.85 |
| Doda | P | 100 | 43.36 | 33.48 | 25.30 | 0.89 | 0.61 | 6.68 | 9.88 | 56.64 |
| | M | 100 | 55.52 | 51.29 | 37.03 | 1.61 | 1.00 | 11.65 | 4.23 | 44.48 |
| | F | 100 | 29.90 | 13.77 | 12.32 | 0.07 | 0.19 | 1.18 | 16.13 | 70.10 |
| Udham Pur | P | 100 | 54.58 | 31.62 | 21.90 | 0.25 | 0.38 | 9.09 | 22.96 | 45.42 |
| | M | 100 | 62.04 | 55.19 | 38.10 | 0.44 | 0.59 | 16.06 | 6.85 | 37.97 |
| | F | 100 | 46.35 | 5.62 | 4.02 | 0.03 | 0.16 | 1.41 | 40.73 | 53.65 |

| | | | | | | | | | | |
|---|---|---|---|---|---|---|---|---|---|---|
| Kathua | P | 100 | 43.40 | 28.82 | 17.43 | 1.63 | 0.63 | 9.13 | 14.58 | 56.60 |
| | M | 100 | 55.34 | 50.62 | 30.49 | 2.97 | 1.05 | 16.11 | 4.72 | 44.66 |
| | F | 100 | 30.37 | 5.05 | 3.19 | 0.18 | 0.16 | 1.52 | 25.32 | 69.63 |
| Jammu | P | 100 | 39.43 | 26.66 | 11.20 | 1.46 | 0.41 | 13.59 | 12.77 | 60.57 |
| | M | 100 | 52.64 | 48.48 | 20.90 | 2.60 | 0.68 | 24.30 | 4.16 | 47.36 |
| | F | 100 | 25.02 | 2.86 | 0.63 | 0.21 | 0.11 | 1.91 | 22.16 | 74.98 |
| Rajauri | P | 100 | 44.98 | 27.59 | 20.22 | 0.36 | 0.41 | 6.60 | 17.39 | 55.02 |
| | M | 100 | 55.18 | 49.81 | 36.70 | 0.66 | 0.65 | 11.80 | 5.37 | 44.82 |
| | F | 100 | 33.73 | 3.08 | 2.04 | 0.03 | 0.14 | 0.87 | 30.65 | 66.27 |
| Punch | P | 100 | 46.54 | 27.72 | 20.45 | 1.12 | 0.52 | 5.63 | 18.82 | 53.46 |
| | M | 100 | 56.04 | 50.32 | 37.32 | 2.07 | 0.83 | 10.10 | 5.72 | 43.96 |
| | F | 100 | 35.86 | 2.31 | 1.47 | 0.05 | 0.19 | 0.60 | 33.55 | 64.14 |

*Sources*: Compiled from Census of India.

Upon close scrutiny on data, that total workers (including marginal workers) constitute 44.26 per cent of the total population of which 30.37 per cent are main workers and 13.89 per cent are marginal workers in the state. The remaining 55.74 per cent are the non-workers. The distribution in respect of four categories reveals that cultivators constitute 17.27 per cent while 10.43 per cent are claimed by the category of other workers. Agricultural labourers and household industry respectively make up 1.06 per cent and 1.61 per cent only. As regards the male population 55.81 per cent have been returned as workers of whom 52.20 per cent are main workers and only 3.61 per cent are marginal workers. In the case of female population, however, only 31.31 per cent are workers amongst whom only 5.91 per cent are main workers while 25.40 per cent are marginal workers. As much as 68.69 per cent of the female populations are just non-workers.

The sharp contrast in the proportion of main workers, marginal workers and non-workers among males and females is thus vividly noticeable. The proportion of main workers among males is disproportionally higher than that among females. On the other hand, the proportion of marginal workers and non-workers among females is relatively much higher than among males.

Down at the district level, the proportion of main workers is much higher than the state average of 30.37 in Kargil (45.33) and Leh (43.55). It is also slightly higher in Doda (33.48), Badgam (32.81), Anantnag (31.68), Udhampur (31.62), and Baramula (31.43). Similarly, the proportion of marginal workers is higher than the State average of 13.89 in Udhampur (22.96), Pulwama (21.66), Punch (18.82), Kupwara (18.49), Rajauri (17.39), Badgam (15.92), Kathua (14.58), and Baramula (14.01). Jammu district has returned the lowest proportion of main workers while Srinagar has returned the lowest proportion of marginal workers. The highest proportion of non-workers has been returned by Srinagar (65.10) followed closely by Jammu (60.57). Kargil on the other hand has returned the lowest proportion of non-workers (40.06).

Category-wise classification of main workers shows that the proportion of cultivators is the lowest in Srinagar (5.02) which can directly be attributed to the fact that the district has the smallest rural component. The corresponding proportion is highest in Kargil (33.65). The proportion of cultivators is higher than the state average of 17.27 in other districts also, except in Jammu, where again because of the relatively larger urban component, this proportion is 11.20 per cent only.

Agricultural labourers account a low proportion of 1.06 per cent at state level. The proportion is slightly higher than state average in Leh (3.20), Kargil (1.47), Kathua (1.63), Jammu (1.46), Baramula (1.21), and Punch (1.12). Other districts have lower proportion of agricultural labourers.

The proportion of workers engaged in the HH industry sector is no better (1.61 per cent) at State level. However the position is relatively better in case of Badgam (4.61), Srinagar (4.40), and Baramula (2.60).

The proportion of other-workers ranges 19.89 per cent in case of Srinagar district and 5.42 per cent in case of Kupwara while state average is 10.43. Apart from Srinagar, where this proportion is the highest, the only other districts having returned higher proportion of other workers than the state average are Leh (14.5) and Jammu (13.59).

As between the two sexes, the main workers among the females constitute a very small proportion in comparison to mine workers among males while the proportion of marginal workers among the females is comparatively much higher both at State and district level. Among the district, however, Leh (Ladakh) has returned the highest proportion of males main workers (57.13), while Jammu has claimed the lowest proportion (48.48). The disparity between the proportion of male and female main workers is widest in Badgam (50.80) and Udhampur (49.57), while this disparity is, much narrower in Kargil (21.11) and Leh (Ladakh) (28.91). The percentage distribution of marginal workers in different districts ranges between 6.85 in Udhampur and 0.78 in Srinagar in case of males, while in the case of females it ranges between 40.73 in Udhampur and 9.35 in case of Srinagar.

While the disparity between the proportions of males and females participating in marginal workers is wide in all the districts, the highest gap is observed in Pulwama (37.80) while lowest gap is discernible in Leh (9.60) followed closely by Kargil (11.15).

The sex-wise percentage distribution of non-workers in various districts again shows a wide disparity between males and females, ranging between 38.02 in case of Srinagar and 9.96 in case of Kargil. The differential in the participation of male and female main workers into cultivators, agricultural labourers, household industry and other workers distributed in the various districts is also very significant. While the proportion of male cultivators' ranges between 39.0 in Kupwara and 8.58 in Srinagar. The corresponding female proportion ranges between 32.74 in Kargil and 0.63 in Jammu. The disparity in the proportion of males and females working as agricultural labourers is also very wide, among all the districts, except Leh where these proportions closely correspond to each other. The sex differential in favour of males is discernible in the proportion of workers engaged in the household industry sector also in all districts except Leh and Kargil where it is adverse to males, although the proportions are practically negligible for either sex. The sex differential is preponderantly in favour of males in the proportion of other workers in all districts without any exception.

The disparity in percentage distribution of male and female non-workers ranges between 38.02 in case of Srinagar and 9.96 in case of Kargil.

The table indicated below provides information relating to distribution of 1000 persons, males and females of total, rural and urban areas among the main workers, marginal workers, and non-workers by broad industrial categories of workers.

The table *(Distribution of 1000 persons, males, and females of total, rural and urban areas)* in the above table reveals a wide disparity both between rural and urban areas and also between males and females among main workers, the marginal workers and non-workers. While for the rural population of the State, the proportion of main workers is 307.60, that of marginal workers 169.65 and that of non-workers 522.75, the corresponding proportions in respect of the urban population stands at 289.22, 23.44, and 687.34 respectively. The differentials in the distribution of marginal workers and non-workers among females are no less marked. While the proportion of female marginal workers in rural areas is 309.67, the corresponding proportion in the urban areas stands at 42.72 only. Even in respect of female main-workers the urban proportion is only 51.11 per 1000 as against the rural proportion of 61.16. The proportion of female non-workers in the urban areas is correspondingly higher in the rural areas. Likewise the proportion of marginal workers among males is higher in the rural areas than in the urban areas with correspondingly lower proportion of non-workers among males in the rural areas than in the urban areas. While the overall proportion of rural main

**Table 4.7** Distribution of workers by sex, Census—1981 (Per 1000 persons)

| Districts | Total Workers | | | Main workers | | | Marginal workers | | | Non-workers | |
|---|---|---|---|---|---|---|---|---|---|---|---|
| | Persons | Male | Female | P | M | F | P | M | F | P | F |
| J & K | 442.60 | 558.11 | 313.11 | 303.71 | 521.97 | 59.06 | 138.87 | 36.14 | 254.01 | 557.70 |
| Anantnag | 424.43 | 559.14 | 272.66 | 316.76 | 531.48 | 74.85 | 107.67 | 27.66 | 197.81 | 575.57 |
| Pulwama | 506.98 | 565.30 | 441.92 | 290.43 | 527.44 | 25.98 | 216.55 | 37.86 | 415.94 | 493.02 |
| Srinagar | 348.99 | 526.18 | 146.02 | 301.23 | 518.39 | 52.47 | 47.76 | 7.79 | 93.55 | 651.01 |
| Badgam | 487.33 | 586.47 | 374.62 | 328.09 | 565.78 | 57.86 | 157.24 | 20.69 | 316.76 | 512.67 |
| Baramula | 454.45 | 566.58 | 325.62 | 314.29 | 537.27 | 58.10 | 140.16 | 29.31 | 267.52 | 545.55 |
| Kupwara | 488.60 | 569.29 | 394.61 | 303.73 | 534.67 | 34.66 | 184.87 | 34.61 | 359.95 | 511.40 |
| Kargil | 549.45 | 595.33 | 495.67 | 453.30 | 550.51 | 339.37 | 96.15 | 44.82 | 156.30 | 450.55 |
| Leh | 503.88 | 594.60 | 401.53 | 435.47 | 571.29 | 282.24 | 68.41 | 23.31 | 119.29 | 496.12 |
| Doda | 433.60 | 555.23 | 299.03 | 334.76 | 512.91 | 137.67 | 98.84 | 42.32 | 161.36 | 566.40 |
| Udhampur | 545.81 | 620.42 | 463.48 | 316.22 | 551.87 | 56.21 | 229.59 | 68.55 | 407.27 | 454.19 |
| Kathua | 434.00 | 553.43 | 303.74 | 288.25 | 506.20 | 50.53 | 145.75 | 47.23 | 253.21 | 566.00 |
| Jammu | 394.26 | 526.45 | 250.21 | 266.56 | 484.87 | 28.64 | 127.70 | 41.58 | 221.57 | 605.74 |
| Rajauri | 449.81 | 551.76 | 337.32 | 275.88 | 498.04 | 30.77 | 173.93 | 53.72 | 306.55 | 550.19 |
| Punch | 465.41 | 560.43 | 358.55 | 277.22 | 503.19 | 23.09 | 188.19 | 57.24 | 335.46 | 534.59 |

(continued)

**Table 4.7** Continued

| Districts | Total Workers | | | Main workers | | | Marginal workers | | | Non-workers |
|---|---|---|---|---|---|---|---|---|---|---|
| | Persons | Male | Female | P | M | F | P | M | F | P |
| **Rural** | | | | | | | | | | |
| J & K | 477.25 | 572.67 | 370.83 | 307.60 | 528.56 | 61.16 | 169.65 | 44.11 | 309.67 | 522.75 |
| Anantnag | 436.03 | 563.77 | 292.02 | 319.35 | 534.12 | 77.25 | 116.68 | 29.65 | 214.77 | 563.97 |
| Pulwama | 518.98 | 568.89 | 463.26 | 291.03 | 529.10 | 25.21 | 227.95 | 39.79 | 438.05 | 481.02 |
| Srinagar | 523.22 | 598.73 | 437.74 | 332.37 | 569.08 | 64.41 | 190.85 | 29.65 | 373.33 | 476.78 |
| Badgam | 514.41 | 602.12 | 414.87 | 335.43 | 579.19 | 58.77 | 178.98 | 22.93 | 356.10 | 485.59 |
| Baramula | 474.58 | 576.40 | 357.60 | 317.72 | 543.81 | 57.98 | 156.86 | 32.59 | 299.62 | 525.42 |
| Kupwara | 488.66 | 569.43 | 394.70 | 303.09 | 535.06 | 34.72 | 184.76 | 34.28 | 359.98 | 511.34 |
| Kargil | 550.95 | 595.99 | 498.51 | 455.84 | 551.26 | 344.74 | 95.11 | 44.73 | 153.77 | 449.05 |
| Leh | 504.11 | 587.39 | 412.71 | 432.72 | 560.99 | 291.96 | 71.39 | 26.40 | 120.75 | 495.89 |
| Doda | 440.81 | 558.80 | 310.84 | 337.56 | 514.57 | 142.58 | 103.25 | 44.23 | 168.26 | 559.19 |
| Udhampur | 571.07 | 532.57 | 503.37 | 318.76 | 557.48 | 55.99 | 252.31 | 75.09 | 447.38 | 428.93 |
| Kathua | 451.60 | 560.70 | 332.97 | 289.31 | 508.47 | 51.01 | 162.29 | 52.23 | 281.96 | 548.40 |
| Jammu | 436.58 | 544.62 | 320.52 | 263.42 | 488.53 | 21.62 | 173.16 | 56.09 | 298.90 | 563.42 |
| Rajauri | 455.27 | 553.14 | 347.88 | 274.12 | 497.01 | 29.54 | 181.15 | 56.13 | 318.34 | 544.73 |
| Punch | 478.32 | 567.72 | 377.75 | 278.80 | 507.90 | 21.05 | 199.52 | 59.82 | 356.70 | 521.68 |

**Urban**

| | 312.66 | 504.12 | 93.83 | 289.22 | 497.54 | 51.11 | 23.44 | 6.58 | 42.72 | 687.34 |
|---|---|---|---|---|---|---|---|---|---|---|
| J & K | | | | | | | | | | |
| Anantnag | 327.70 | 520.39 | 111.76 | 295.11 | 509.41 | 54.94 | 32.59 | 10.98 | 56.82 | 672.30 |
| Pulwama | 385.37 | 528.79 | 226.48 | 284.35 | 510.54 | 33.76 | 101.02 | 18.25 | 192.72 | 614.63 |
| Srinagar | 306.79 | 508.72 | 74.79 | 293.70 | 506.20 | 49.56 | 13.09 | 2.52 | 25.23 | 693.21 |
| Badgam | 322.71 | 491.87 | 128.39 | 283.49 | 484.77 | 52.27 | 39.22 | 7.10 | 76.12 | 677.29 |
| Baramula | 324.29 | 503.07 | 118.72 | 292.15 | 495.01 | 58.89 | 32.14 | 8.06 | 59.83 | 675.71 |
| Kupwara | 486.89 | 567.17 | 391.41 | 298.20 | 521.76 | 32.32 | 188.69 | 45.41 | 359.09 | 513.11 |
| Kargil | 522.82 | 584.25 | 441.81 | 408.28 | 537.89 | 237.34 | 114.54 | 46.36 | 204.47 | 477.18 |
| Leh | 502.29 | 639.31 | 315.25 | 454.23 | 635.14 | 207.27 | 48.06 | 4.17 | 107.98 | 497.71 |
| Doda | 318.98 | 500.44 | 103.77 | 290.30 | 487.41 | 56.53 | 28.68 | 13.03 | 47.24 | 681.02 |
| Udhampur | 306.08 | 506.46 | 80.10 | 292.04 | 499.26 | 58.35 | 14.04 | 7.20 | 21.75 | 693.93 |
| Kathua | 296.95 | 497.52 | 72.73 | 280.02 | 488.68 | 46.76 | 16.93 | 8.84 | 25.97 | 703.05 |
| Jammu | 293.83 | 484.31 | 78.98 | 274.01 | 476.40 | 45.73 | 19.82 | 7.91 | 33.25 | 706.17 |
| Rajauri | 350.85 | 528.02 | 135.26 | 307.65 | 515.82 | 54.33 | 43.20 | 12.20 | 80.93 | 649.15 |
| Punch | 274.01 | 452.07 | 75.01 | 253.76 | 433.08 | 53.34 | 20.25 | 18.99 | 21.67 | 725.99 |

*Source:* Census 1981

Table 4.8  Categories of Main Workers, 1981 Census (Per 1000)

| | Cultivators | | | Agricultural Labourers | | | Household Industry | | | Other workers | | |
| --- | --- | --- | --- | --- | --- | --- | --- | --- | --- | --- | --- | --- |
| | P | M | F | P | M | F | P | M | F | P | M | F |
| J & K | 172.68 | 293.3 | 37.51 | 10.61 | 18.92 | 1.29 | 16.09 | 24.84 | 6.28 | 104.35 | 184.96 | 13.98 |
| Anantnag | 208.0 | 340.6 | 58.59 | 8.86 | 15.89 | 0.94 | 14.21 | 22.26 | 5.13 | 85.69 | 152.71 | 10.19 |
| Pulwama | 190.32 | 346.9 | 15.56 | 5.95 | 11.18 | 0.11 | 14.79 | 24.78 | 3.64 | 79.37 | 144.52 | 6.67 |
| Srinagar | 50.24 | 85.81 | 9.48 | 8.06 | 14.09 | 1.16 | 43.97 | 69.44 | 14.80 | 198.96 | 349.0 | 27.03 |
| Badgam | 182.85 | 323.6 | 22.83 | 8.73 | 16.16 | 0.29 | 46.11 | 67.52 | 21.76 | 90.40 | 158.50 | 12.98 |
| Baramul | 180.93 | 308.5 | 34.40 | 12.13 | 22.4 | 0.38 | 25.97 | 37.16 | 13.12 | 95.26 | 169.29 | 10.20 |
| Kupwara | 221.78 | 389.9 | 25.80 | 20.8 | 38.01 | 0.89 | 6.85 | 9.36 | 3.92 | 54.22 | 97.29 | 4.05 |
| Kargil | 336.47 | 344.21 | 327.4 | 14.74 | 25.67 | 1.94 | 1.20 | 1.12 | 1.28 | 100.89 | 179.51 | 8.76 |
| Leh | 254.68 | 296.71 | 207.27 | 32.04 | 32.9 | 31.12 | 3.66 | 2.07 | 5.45 | 145.09 | 239.7 | 38.4 |
| Doda | 252.99 | 370.32 | 123.19 | 8.86 | 16.11 | 0.83 | 6.14 | 9.95 | 1.92 | 66.77 | 116.53 | 11.73 |
| Udhamp | 218.99 | 381.05 | 40.19 | 2.46 | 4.40 | 0.32 | 3.85 | 5.86 | 1.63 | 90.92 | 160.56 | 14.07 |
| Kathua | 174.31 | 304.9 | 31.87 | 16.34 | 29.7 | 1.82 | 6.27 | 10.55 | 1.60 | 91.33 | 161.09 | 15.24 |
| Jammu | 112.02 | 209.0 | 6.34 | 14.56 | 26.0 | 2.07 | 4.12 | 6.86 | 1.12 | 135.86 | 242.99 | 19.11 |
| Rajauri | 202.20 | 366.9 | 20.41 | 3.57 | 6.55 | 0.28 | 4.07 | 6.51 | 1.38 | 66.04 | 118.02 | 8.70 |
| Punch | 204.47 | 373.26 | 14.65 | 11.20 | 20.7 | 0.55 | 5.27 | 8.27 | 1.89 | 56.28 | 100.99 | 6.00 |

**Main workers**

| RURAL | Cultivators | | | Agricultural Labourers | | | Household Industry | | | Other workers | | |
|---|---|---|---|---|---|---|---|---|---|---|---|---|
| | P | M | F | P | M | F | P | M | F | P | M | F |
| J & K | 212.47 | 361.69 | 46.03 | 11.63 | 20.74 | 1.47 | 13.72 | 21.02 | 5.59 | 69.78 | 125.11 | 8.07 |
| Anantnag | 226.4 | 370.57 | 63.87 | 9.40 | 16.83 | 1.02 | 13.58 | 21.24 | 4.94 | 69.98 | 125.48 | 7.42 |
| Pulwama | 202.29 | 368.5 | 16.78 | 5.69 | 10.69 | 0.10 | 14.22 | 24.04 | 3.24 | 68.83 | 125.94 | 5.09 |
| Srinagar | 207.91 | 357.62 | 38.43 | 18.86 | 31.38 | 4.69 | 35.9 | 55.49 | 13.8 | 69.63 | 124.59 | 7.41 |
| Badgam | 205.0 | 364.12 | 24.48 | 8.91 | 16.48 | 0.31 | 50.0 | 73.36 | 23.5 | 71.49 | 125.23 | 10.50 |
| Baramul | 202.45 | 346.5 | 37.02 | 12.22 | 22.5 | 0.39 | 28.13 | 40.48 | 13.94 | 74.92 | 134.37 | 6.63 |
| Kupwara | 225.55 | 396.7 | 26.27 | 20.9 | 38.1 | 0.90 | 6.76 | 9.21 | 3.90 | 50.69 | 91.09 | 3.65 |
| Kargil | 350.3 | 361.63 | 337.0 | 15.37 | 27.08 | 1.73 | 0.93 | 1.16 | 0.66 | 89.26 | 161.39 | 5.30 |
| Leh | 282.6 | 333.19 | 226.0 | 33.0 | 34.0 | 31.99 | 3.27 | 1.89 | 4.78 | 113.84 | 191.89 | 28.2 |
| Doda | 267.47 | 391.91 | 130.40 | 8.84 | 16.11 | 0.84 | 6.41 | 10.44 | 1.96 | 54.84 | 96.11 | 9.38 |
| Udhampu | 240.92 | 419.89 | 43.90 | 2.54 | 4.54 | 0.34 | 4.17 | 6.43 | 1.70 | 71.13 | 126.62 | 10.05 |
| Kathua | 191.32 | 334.5 | 35.63 | 15.86 | 28.91 | 1.68 | 6.60 | 11.28 | 1.51 | 75.53 | 133.78 | 12.19 |
| Jammu | 153.00 | 287.54 | 8.49 | 18.32 | 32.87 | 2.68 | 5.16 | 8.85 | 1.20 | 86.94 | 159.27 | 9.25 |
| Rajauri | 210.67 | 383.14 | 21.42 | 3.48 | 6.39 | 0.29 | 4.24 | 6.83 | 1.39 | 55.73 | 100.65 | 6.44 |
| Punch | 215.52 | 393.18 | 15.63 | 11.17 | 20.6 | 0.57 | 5.39 | 8.58 | 1.81 | 46.72 | 85.55 | 3.04 |

(continued)

Table 4.8 Continued

| URBAN | Main workers | | | | | | | | | | | |
|---|---|---|---|---|---|---|---|---|---|---|---|---|
| | Cultivators | | | Agricultural Labourers | | | Household Industry | | | Other workers | | |
| | P | M | F | P | M | F | P | M | F | P | M | F |
| J & K | 23.45 | 39.47 | 5.13 | 6.80 | 12.21 | 0.61 | 24.97 | 39.00 | 8.93 | 234.00 | 406.86 | 36.44 |
| Anantnag | 54.61 | 90.22 | 14.70 | 4.35 | 7.97 | 0.30 | 19.46 | 30.88 | 6.66 | 216.69 | 380.34 | 33.28 |
| Pulwama | 69.08 | 128.49 | 3.25 | 8.57 | 16.15 | 0.18 | 20.62 | 32.25 | 7.73 | 186.08 | 333.65 | 22.60 |
| Srinagar | 12.04 | 20.42 | 2.42 | 5.45 | 9.94 | 0.30 | 45.91 | 72.79 | 15.02 | 230.30 | 403.05 | 31.82 |
| Badgam | 48.05 | 78.77 | 12.76 | 7.65 | 14.21 | 0.12 | 22.45 | 32.19 | 11.17 | 205.34 | 359.60 | 28.12 |
| Baramula | 41.73 | 62.84 | 17.46 | 11.61 | 21.47 | 0.26 | 12.05 | 15.73 | 7.83 | 226.76 | 394.97 | 33.34 |
| Kupwara | 97.54 | 171.01 | 10.17 | 20.33 | 37.05 | 0.45 | 9.81 | 14.25 | 4.52 | 170.52 | 299.45 | 17.18 |
| Kargil | 91.86 | 52.34 | 143.98 | 3.69 | 2.00 | 5.92 | 5.95 | 0.50 | 13.15 | 306.78 | 483.05 | 74.29 |
| Leh | 63.89 | 70.35 | 55.07 | 25.12 | 25.64 | 24.42 | 6.31 | 3.18 | 10.58 | 358.91 | 535.97 | 117.20 |
| Doda | 22.88 | 38.88 | 3.91 | 9.06 | 16.04 | 0.78 | 1.91 | 2.49 | 1.22 | 256.45 | 430.00 | 50.62 |
| Udhampur | 10.96 | 16.62 | 4.58 | 1.68 | 3.06 | 0.15 | 0.73 | 0.52 | 0.93 | 278.67 | 479.06 | 52.69 |
| Kathua | 41.77 | 77.29 | 2.07 | 20.08 | 35.37 | 2.98 | 3.71 | 4.92 | 2.37 | 214.46 | 371.10 | 39.34 |
| Jammu | 14.76 | 26.88 | 1.10 | 5.65 | 10.13 | 0.59 | 1.65 | 2.27 | 0.94 | 251.95 | 437.12 | 43.10 |
| Rajauri | 48.76 | 87.91 | 1.12 | 5.12 | 9.32 | 0.42 | 1.07 | 0.92 | 1.26 | 252.70 | 417.67 | 51.95 |
| Punch | 40.79 | 77.15 | 0.15 | 11.71 | 21.93 | 0.30 | 3.39 | 3.61 | 3.13 | 197.87 | 330.39 | 49.76 |

Source: Census 1981

Table 4.9 Population and workers by Age and Sex, 1981 (lakhs)

| Area | Age Group | Population | | | Workers | | |
|---|---|---|---|---|---|---|---|
| | | Total | Male | Female | Total | Male | Female |
| Total | Total | 59.87 | 31.64 | 28.22 | 18.18 | 16.51 | 1.66 |
| | 0–14 | 24.54 | 12.58 | 11.95 | 1.09 | 0.85 | 0.23 |
| | 15–19 | 6.22 | 3.32 | 2.89 | 2.01 | 1.76 | 0.24 |
| | 20–24 | 5.01 | 2.65 | 2.35 | 2.40 | 2.15 | 0.24 |
| | 25–29 | 4.55 | 2.34 | 2.21 | 2.41 | 2.17 | 0.24 |
| | 30–34 | 3.74 | 1.94 | 1.79 | 2.06 | 1.87 | 0.19 |
| | 35–39 | 3.55 | 1.87 | 1.68 | 1.97 | 1.81 | 0.16 |
| | 40–49 | 5.45 | 2.96 | 2.48 | 3.05 | 2.85 | 0.20 |
| | 50–59 | 3.33 | 1.91 | 1.42 | 1.82 | 1.72 | 0.091 |
| | 60+ | 3.41 | 2.03 | 1.41 | 1.34 | 1.29 | 0.052 |
| Rural | Total | 47.26 | 24.92 | 22.34 | 14.54 | 13.17 | 1.36 |
| | 0–14 | 19.85 | 10.15 | 9.69 | 10.46 | 0.74 | 0.30 |
| | 15–19 | 4.71 | 2.53 | 2.17 | 1.67 | 1.46 | 0.20 |
| | 20–24 | 3.75 | 1.96 | 1.78 | 1.88 | 1.68 | 0.19 |
| | 25–29 | 3.49 | 1.78 | 1.70 | 1.86 | 1.67 | 0.18 |
| | 30–34 | 2.90 | 1.49 | 1.40 | 1.58 | 1.44 | 0.14 |
| | 35–39 | 2.76 | 1.45 | 1.31 | 1.53 | 1.40 | 0.12 |
| | 40–49 | 4.25 | 2.30 | 1.94 | 2.38 | 2.21 | 0.17 |
| | 50–59 | 2.65 | 1.52 | 1.13 | 1.48 | 1.40 | 0.079 |
| | 60+ | 2.87 | 1.70 | 1.17 | 1.17 | 1.12 | 0.047 |
| Urban | Total | 12.60 | 6.72 | 5.88 | 3.64 | 3.34 | 0.30 |
| | 0–14 | 4.69 | 2.42 | 2.26 | 0.14 | 0.11 | 0.027 |
| | 15–19 | 1.50 | 0.78 | 0.72 | 0.33 | 0.29 | 0.038 |
| | 20–24 | 1.25 | 0.68 | 0.57 | 0.51 | 0.46 | 0.050 |
| | 25–29 | 1.06 | 0.56 | 0.50 | 0.55 | 0.49 | 0.057 |
| | 30–34 | 0.84 | 0.45 | 0.38 | 0.47 | 0.43 | 0.042 |
| | 35–39 | 0.79 | 0.42 | 0.36 | 0.44 | 0.40 | 0.033 |
| | 40–49 | 1.19 | 0.66 | 0.53 | 0.66 | 0.63 | 0.033 |
| | 50–59 | 0.67 | 0.39 | 0.28 | 0.33 | 0.32 | 0.011 |
| | 60+ | 0.56 | 0.32 | 0.24 | 0.16 | 0.16 | 0.0052 |

Source: Census Deptt.

**Table 4.10**  District-wise total Gender Working force, 1981 (lakhs)

| District | Total Workers (Main + Marginal) | | | Other Workers | | |
|---|---|---|---|---|---|---|
| | Male | Female | Total | Male | Female | Total |
| Anantnag | 2.81 | 1.11 | 3.92 | 1.15 | 0.35 | 1.51 |
| Pulwama | 1.56 | 0.51 | 2.08 | 0.58 | 0.15 | 0.74 |
| Srinagar | 3.12 | 0.52 | 3.64 | 2.40 | 0.25 | 2.66 |
| Budgam | 1.62 | 0.66 | 2.28 | 0.60 | 0.13 | 0.74 |
| Baramula | 2.87 | 0.80 | 3.67 | 1.22 | 0.31 | 1.53 |
| Kupwara | 1.45 | 0.55 | 2.01 | 0.52 | 0.13 | 0.65 |
| Leh | 0.38 | 0.20 | 0.58 | 0.27 | 0.064 | 0.33 |
| Kargil | 0.28 | 0.23 | 0.51 | 0.17 | 0.067 | 0.24 |
| Jammu | 4.21 | 0.93 | 5.15 | 3.05 | 0.41 | 3.46 |
| Udhampur | 2.27 | 1.35 | 3.63 | 0.90 | 0.33 | 1.24 |
| Doda | 1.91 | 1.26 | 3.17 | 0.69 | 0.25 | 0.94 |
| Kathua | 1.44 | 0.57 | 2.02 | 0.68 | 0.15 | 0.84 |
| Rajouri | 1.30 | 0.84 | 2.15 | 0.43 | 0.16 | 0.60 |
| Poonch | 1.11 | 0.89 | 2.00 | 0.31 | 0.24 | 0.55 |
| J&K State | 26.41 | 10.47 | 36.88 | 13.04 | 3.06 | 16.11 |

*Source*: Census of India (1981), J&K, Registrar General of India.

workers is 307.60, this proportion varies considerably amongst districts, ranging between 455.84 in Kargil to 263.42 in Jammu. The districts in which the proportion of rural main workers is higher than the State average are Anantnag (319.35), Srinagr (322.37), Baramula (317.72), and Udhampur (318.76). Similarly against the state average of 169.65 the proportion of rural marginal workers amongst districts ranges from 252.31 in Udhampur to 71.39 in Leh (Ladakh). The lowest proportion of rural male marginal workers amongst districts is Badgam (22.93). Among females in the rural areas of the State, a proportion of 309.67 are marginal workers. The highest proportion of rural females in marginal workers is in Udhampur (447.38) and lowest in Leh (Ladakh) 120.75.

The proportion of rural non-workers which at the state level is 522.75 does not vary much among the districts. The highest proportion of rural non-workers is in Anantnag (563.93) and Jammu (563.42) and the lowest in the Udhampur (428.93). In addition to this Baramula (525.42), Doda (559.19), and Kathua (548.40) also have proportion of rural non-workers higher than the state average. In the case of rural males, a proportion of 427.33 are composed of non-workers. The highest proportion of male non-workers is in Jammu (455.38) and the lowest in Udhampur (367.34). Among the districts which have the proportion of rural male non-workers higher than the state average are Anantnag (436.23), Pulwama (431.11), Kupwara (430.66), Doda (441.20), Kathua (439.30), Rajauri (446.86), and Punch (432.28).

In the urban areas of state the proportion of main workers is 289.22. Among the district, the highest proportion of main workers is in Leh (Ladakh) 454.23 closely followed by Kargil (408.28) and the lowest in Punch (253.76). The districts which have proportion of urban main workers higher than the state average are Anantnag (295.11), Srinagar (293.70), Baramulla (292.15), Kupwara (298.20), Kargil (408.28), Leh (454.23), Doda (290.30), Udhampur (292.04), and Rajauri (307.65). Among 1000 urban males in the state, 497.54 are the main workers and among districts this proportion varies between 635.14 in Leh and 433.08 in Punch. The districts which have proportion of urban male main workers, higher than the state average are Anantnag (509.41), Pulwama (510.45), Srinagar (506.20), Kupwara (521.76), Kargil (537.89), Udhampur (499.26), and Rajouri (515.82). It is, however, interesting to note that the proportion of main work among the urban females is very low as compared with the corresponding proportion of urban males in this category. In the urban parts of the state only 51.11 per 1000 of the female population have been recorded as main workers and their proportion among the districts varies between 237.34 in Kargil and 32.32 in Kupwara.

The proportion of marginal workers in the urban areas of the State is 23.44 per thousand. The proportions, however, varies widely among the districts. It is as high as 188.69 in Kupwara and as low as 13.09 in Srinagar. The districts where the proportion of marginal workers is below 15 are Srinagar and Udhampur and those where this proportion is larger than the state average are Anantnag (32.14), Pulwama (101.02), Budgam (39.22), Baramula (32.14), Kupwara (188.69), Kargil (114.54), Leh (48.06), Doda (28.68), and Rajouri (43.20). In the case of urban males in the state a proportion of 6.58 are marginal workers. Among the districts the proportion of the urban male marginal workers varies between 46.36 in Kargil and 2.52 in Srinagar. The districts where this proportion is more than 15 are Pulwama, Kupwara, Kargil and Punch while Srinagar, Badgam, Baramula, Leh, Udhampur, Kathua, Jammu, Anantnag, Doda, and Rajouri have this proportion less than 15.

Among the districts the proportion of urban female marginal workers is more than the state average in Anantnag (56.82), Pulwama (192.72), Badgam (76.12), Baramula (59.93), Kupwara (359.09), Kargil (204.47), Leh (Ladakh) (107.98), Doda (47.24), and Rajouri (80.93). As compared to urban males, the incidence of marginal workers among urban females is markedly very high.

In the case of urban population of the state a proportion of 687.34 persons consist of non-workers. In majority of the districts of the state, the urban population is comprised, the highest proportion being in Punch (725.99) and the lowest in Kargil (477.18). The districts where the proportion of urban non-workers is more the state average are Srinagar (693.21), Udhampur (693.92), Jammu (706.17), and Kathua (703.05). In the case of urban females, a proportion of 906.17 are non-workers, the highest proportion of urban females non-workers among districts is in kathua (927.27) and the lowest in Kargil (558.19). In addition to Kathua, the proportion of urban females' non-workers is more than the state averages are Srinagar (925.21), Udhampur (919.90), Jammu (921.02), and Punch (924.99).

The data on the distribution of main workers by the broad industrial categories of cultivators, agricultural labourers, household industry and other workers reveal that nearly a proportion of 173 main workers in the state are cultivators. The next largest proportions are of other workers followed by household industry. Only a small proportion of 16.09 are engaged in household industry. This general trend is reflected in the case of distribution of male workers also. However, the largest proportion of females is comprised of cultivators followed by other workers. A small proportion of 1.29 of female main workers is agricultural labourers while 6.28 are in household industry.

In the rural areas the proportion of cultivators is slightly more than 212 followed by about 70 in other work. This is a sharp contrast with the distribution of workers in the urban areas where a proportion of 234 are other workers and only a small proportion of 6.80 to 24.97 are cultivators or agricultural labourers of in household industry. In the rural areas, the largest proportion of main workers among both the sexes in cultivation. In the urban areas both in the case of males and females, the largest proportion of main workers are other workers. It is, however, interesting to note that generally the participation of male main workers in household industry is higher than that of females. Also this proportion in urban areas is higher than the proportion of females in household industry in rural areas. It would be pertinent to note that by and large the workers in the household industry tend to concentrate in urban areas and this is particularly noticeable in Srinagar district which has a largest component of urban sector in its jurisdiction. Kargil has the highest proportion (336.47) of main workers in cultivation while in the case of Leh (Ladakh) the highest proportion (32.04) of the main workers is among agricultural labourers. In the household industry sector, the highest proportion is in Badgam (46.11), followed by Srinagar (43.97). Among other workers, the lowest proportion of main workers is in Kupwara (54.22) closely followed by Punch (56.25). Except Srinagar and Jammu, the proportion of main workers engaged as cultivators in other districts is higher than the state average (172.68). However, in the majority of the districts, the proportion of main workers engaged as agricultural labourers is higher than the state average (10.61). The proportion of main workers classified as other workers is, as mentioned, as high as (198.96) in Srinagar and as low as (54.22) in Kupwara.

Among male main workers, the highest proportion of cultivators is in Kupwara (389.98) while Srinagar is at its lowest with a proportion on only 85.81 of its main workers classified as cultivators. The proportion of male main workers classified as agricultural labourers in Kupwara (38.04) is highest followed by Leh (Ladakh) (32.86) and Kathua (29.66).

The proportion of male main workers in household industry varies from 69.44 in Srinagar to 1.12 in Kargil. Among the districts, the proportion of male main workers engaged in household industry is higher than the state (24.84) and in Srinagar (69.44), Badgam (67.52), and in Baramula (37.16). In case of male main workers classified as other workers it is 349.05 in Srinagar closely followed by Jammu (242.99) while the proportion is the least in Kupwara (97.29). The proportion of male other workers is higher than in the categories of agricultural labourers or household industry in all districts of state. The proportion of male main workers of all districts except Srinagar and Jammu is highest in cultivation as compared to corresponding proportions in other categories.

Among female main workers, cultivators constitute the highest proportion of 327.39 in Kargil against 37.51 in the State. The smallest proportion of female main workers engaged as cultivators is in Jammu (6.34) and Srinagar (9.48). The proportion of female main workers as agricultural labourers is the highest in Leh (Ladakh) (31.12) while it is the smallest in Pulwama (0.11). The proportion of such workers at the State level is 1.29. Among the female main workers, the highest proportion in household industry is in Badgam (21.76) while the lowest is in Jammu (1.12), the proportion for the state being 6.28. The proportion of female main workers in all districts in household industry is very much less than that in respect of the other categories.

In the rural areas, the highest proportion of main workers is of cultivators, the proportion ranging from 350.28 in Kargil to 153.00 in Jammu. The corresponding proportion for the state is 212.47. The highest proportion of main workers among agricultural labourers is in Leh and Kupwara. The proportion in household industry is comparatively smaller except in Badgam and Srinagar where a proportion of 50.00 and 35.97 of respective rural main workers are emerged in household industry. The lowest proportion is in Kargil (0.93).

The highest proportion of other workers has been recorded in Leh and the lowest proportion obtains in Punch. The highest proportion among rural male main workers working as cultivators is in Udhampur. The proportion of male main workers engaged as agricultural labourers in rural areas ranges from 38.07 in Kupwara district to 4.54 in Udhampur district as against the proportion of 20.74 at the state level.

Among female main workers in the rural areas, cultivators constitute the highest proportion in Kargil (337.05) as against 46.03 for the state. The other districts where the cultivators have the highest proportion than the state average are Leh (226.99), Doda (130.40), and Anantnag (63.87). The proportion of female agricultural labourers is, however, much smaller in comparison with the other economic categories, being only 1.47 for the state as a whole and ranging between 31.99 in Leh and 0.10 in Pulwama district. It is observed that generally the major proportion of female main workers in the rural areas is either cultivators or other workers. The proportion of rural female main workers engaged in household industry for the state is 5.59, the highest being in Badgam (23.48) and lowest in Kargil (0.66). The proportion of other workers among the female main workers in the rural areas of the state is 8.07, highest being in Leh (28.20) followed by Kathua (12.19) and lowest in Punch (3.04).

Main workers in urban areas are mostly composed of other workers. The proportion of cultivators in the urban areas, however, is also quite high in some districts like Kupwara (97.54), Kargil (91.86), and Pulwama (69.08). Likewise the proportion of main workers in urban areas engaged as agricultural labourers is more than the state average of 6.80 and in Pulwama (8.57), Badgam (7.65), Baramula (11.61), Kupwara (20.33), Leh (25.12), Doda (9.06), Kathua (2008), and in Punch (11.71). The proportion of urban main workers engaged in household industry swing between 45.91 in Srinagar and 0.73 in Udhampur, the state average being 24.97.

Among the urban male main workers, the highest proportion is accountable for other workers (406.86) followed by those engaged in cultivation (39.47), household industry (39.00) and agricultural labourers (12.21). In fact in all the districts other workers constitute the largest proportion among the male main workers in the urban areas. This proportion ranges between 535.97 in Leh (Ladakh) and 299.45 in Kupwara. Other workers also constitute the highest proportion (36.44) among urban female main workers in the state with the proportion in household industry (8.93) being the next highest followed by those in cultivation (5.13) and agricultural labourers (0.61). This is also true in case of urban male main workers in whose case the proportion of cultivators is greater than that in household industry, the least being in agricultural labour. As already discussed household industry constitutes the second highest proportion among urban female main workers (8.93) and among the districts this proportion varies between 15.02 in Srinagar to 0.93 in Udhampur. Unlike in the rural areas, the proportion of female main workers engaged in household industry is higher in urban areas. Against a proportion of 5.59 of the rural female main workers are engaged in household industry.

Similarly, in the case of urban female main workers, the proportion of main workers engaged as other workers is comparatively higher.

## Sector-Wise of Workforce at All India Level, 1981

According to the *census 1981*, the categories of workers were divided into cultivators, agriculture labours, manufacturing, Servicing, Repairs & HH industry, mining and quarrying, construction, trade and commerce, transport, storage and communication, and other service. As per census 1981, 63.88 per cent are engaged in agriculture. Manufacturing, servicing, and HH industries employed just 11.24 per cent of the total workforce. Later is followed by trade, commerce, transport, storage, and communication that account 8.73 per cent

However, the occupational structure of the state is like that of an under-developed economy just at national level where agriculture is the main stay of the people. It is because of the inadequate development of industries and services, that a major chunk of the labour force is engaged in agriculture which in turn leaves the agricultural sector overburdened. In the absence of well developed industrial base, the state suffers from large scale unemployment and under-employment. Such a gloomy picture of the state's economy calls for large scale change in occupational structure, which can be attained through the process of industrialization.

Table 4.11  Sector-wise Workforce as per census 1981, (Percentage)

| Sectors | J&K | All India |
|---|---|---|
| Agricultural Sector | 63.88 | 68.06 |
| Manufacturing, Servicing, Repairs & HH industry | 11.24 | 10.09 |
| Mining and Quarry | 0.18 | 0.50 |
| Construction | 2.83 | 1.50 |
| Trade, commerce, transport, storage & communication | 8.73 | 13.40 |
| Other Services | 13.14 | 7.10 |
| Total | 100.0 | 100 |

*Source*: Census of India/Pocket Book of Population Statistics (India), 1983.

# Labour Force Participation Rate Based on Activity Status, 1993–94

As per *NSS 50th R (1993–94)*, persons are classified into various activity categories on the basis of activities pursued by them during certain specified reference period. Three reference periods are used in NSS surveys, viz. (i) one year, (ii) one week, and (iii) each day of the reference week. Based on these three periods, three different measures of activity status are arrived at. It is clear from the table that the total rural working participation rate is 299/1000 and male accounts much more than female. With the same approach total urban working population is 231/1000. By the CWS Approach and CDS Approach, male working participation rate is much higher than female for the State in both rural and urban. The number of employed per 1000 persons during 1993–94 for J&K is given in Table 4.12.

**Table 4.12** Number of employed per 1000 persons for J&K, 1993–94

| Usual Principal Status Approach | | | | | |
|---|---|---|---|---|---|
| Rural | | | Urban | | |
| Male | Female | M+F | Male | Female | M+F |
| 500 | 95 | 299 | 491 | 81 | 231 |
| Current Weekly Status Approach | | | | | |
| Rural | | | Urban | | |
| Male | Female | M+F | Male | Female | M+F |
| 501 | 261 | 383 | 480 | 107 | 300 |
| Current Daily Status Approach | | | | | |
| Rural | | | Urban | | |
| Male | Female | M+F | Male | Female | M+F |
| 494 | 175 | 335 | 474 | 90 | 299 |

*Source*: NSS 50th Round, Revised Report No. 406.

Table 4.13  Trends of Workforce as per census 2001 (lakhs)

| Categories | Persons | age% | Males | age% | Females | age% |
|---|---|---|---|---|---|---|
| Main workers | 26.08 | 69.5 | 22.26 | 83.1 | 3.81 | 35.5 |
| Marginal workers | 11.45 | 30.5 | 4.52 | 16.9 | 6.92 | 64.5 |
| Cultivators | 15.91 | 42.4 | 10.04 | 37.5 | 5.86 | 54.7 |
| Agricultural Labourers | 2.46 | 6.6 | 1.90 | 7.1 | 0.56 | 5.2 |
| HH Industry workers | 2.34 | 6.2 | 1.26 | 4.7 | 1.08 | 10.1 |
| Other workers | 16.81 | 44.8 | 13.58 | 50.7 | 3.22 | 30.0 |
| Total workers | 37.53 | 37.01 | *26.79 | 71.38 | *10.73 | 28.62 |

*Source*: Compiled Census of India.

## Trends of Workforce for J&K, Census 2001

According to *census 2001*, total workers were classified into main workers, marginal workers, cultivators, agricultural labourers and Household industry workers and other workers. According to this source, the State J&K possess 37.53 lakh workforce which accounts 37 per cent workforce from the total population. Male contributes large proportion of 26.79 lakh against 10.73 lakh of women. Among categories of workers, main workers account maximum proportion of 26.06 lakhs (69.5 per cent) followed by marginal workers (30.5 per cent). The trends of workforce are reflected in Table 4.13.

## District-Wise Categories of Workers in J&K, Census 2001

J&K Government always tried to establish industrial units in the state. However, they failed largely due to the lack of political stability in the state. Thus, there was a very bleak chance of industries and investment in some districts that establish the variation among districts in industrial development and businesses. It furthermore succeeded in propelling the variation of workforce participation among different districts in J&K.

According to *Census 2001*, the work participation rate from total population of J&K was investigated to be 37.0 per cent and Punch having the highest rate at 54.0 per cent because large proportion is engaged in cultivation. Main workers stand at 69.5 per cent from total workers and Jammu having the highest at 82.2 per cent. Marginal workers from total workers stand at 30.5 per cent and Punch having highest at 57.0 per cent. Cultivators contribute high proportion of 42.4 per cent and district Udhampur is the leading one. Agricultural labourers shares 6.6 per cent and district Kupwara contributes highest of 19.8 per cent. In case of Household industry, district Badgam highest percentage (21.8 per cent) due to urbanization. The district-wise categories of workers according to census 2001 are shown in Table 4.14.

## Occupational Classification of Workforce, 2001

As per the census data of 2001, the category has gone down into four categories—cultivators, agriculture labours, House Hold industry workers, and other workers against eleven categories during 1981 census. Clearly from the table the share of rural and urban workers was 77.78 per cent and 22.22 per cent respectively in the State. The total Cultivators stood at 43.36 per cent of the total workers of the State, out of which 97.63 per cent (15.61X100/15.99) belonged to rural area and the remaining 2.37 per cent belonged to urban areas.

The total Agricultural Workforce was 6.72 per cent, rural (92.42 per cent), and 7.58 per cent for urban areas. The HH Industry stood at 6.22 per cent of the total workforce, 76 per cent belonged to rural areas and 23.93 per cent urban areas. Likewise, Other Workers stood at 43.675 per cent of total workers, 56.06 per cent belonged to rural areas and 43.94 belonged to urban areas. The above analysis is depicted in the table below with area and sex wise of workforce (2001) in terms of absolute size and percentage.

The sex-wise distribution of workforce is examined. The total number as regards to total male worker population for male cultivators was 51.5 per cent and 4.1 per cent from rural and urban areas respectively, while female stood at (60.4 per cent) rural and (8.2 per cent) urban. It is

**Table 4.14** District wise Categories of workers, 2001, Percent

| | Work participation Rate | Main workers | Marginal workers | Cultivators | Agricultural Labourers | HH Industry | Other Workers |
|---|---|---|---|---|---|---|---|
| J&K | 37.0 | 69.5 | 30.5 | 42.4 | 6.6 | 6.2 | 44.8 |
| Kupwara | 32.7 | 58.2 | 41.8 | 40.1 | 19.8 | 4.4 | 35.8 |
| Baramula | 31.8 | 72.9 | 27.1 | 33.3 | 11.6 | 12.1 | 42.9 |
| Srinagar | 32.0 | 81.8 | 14.2 | 7.6 | 4.5 | 13.4 | 74.5 |
| Badgam | 35.9 | 67.7 | 32.3 | 39.4 | 6.2 | 21.8 | 32.6 |
| Pulwama | 32.6 | 71.1 | 28.9 | 47.3 | 8.3 | 7.7 | 36.7 |
| Anantnag | 33.7 | 66.2 | 33.8 | 42.0 | 9.9 | 8.8 | 39.3 |
| Leh | 49.6 | 66.7 | 33.3 | 37.9 | 4.3 | 1.2 | 56.6 |
| Kargil | 46.6 | 68.9 | 31.1 | 46.3 | 1.1 | 1.5 | 51.0 |
| Doda | 46.0 | 61.0 | 39.0 | 64.1 | 4.2 | 1.5 | 30.2 |
| Udhampur | 49.3 | 67.0 | 33.0 | 68.2 | 1.9 | 0.9 | 35.1 |
| Punch | 54.0 | 43.0 | 57.0 | 65.8 | 3.8 | 2.2 | 28.2 |
| Rajauri | 45.2 | 54.3 | 45.7 | 67.5 | 1.6 | 1.4 | 29.5 |
| Jammu | 33.3 | 82.2 | 17.8 | 25.5 | 5.2 | 1.5 | 67.8 |
| Kathua | 37.3 | 78.8 | 21.2 | 50.6 | 5.5 | 1.5 | 42.5 |
| C.V | 19.42 | 1.53 | 0.33 | 3.69 | 75.24 | 106.09 | 3.19 |

*Source:* Compiled Census of India/India/ND/2005.

**Table 4.15** Category of Workers of 2001 Census, *lakhs*

| Categories | Area | Male | %age | Female | % | Total (M+F) | |
|---|---|---|---|---|---|---|---|
| Cultivators | R | 9.94 (51.50%) | 63.60 | 5.67 (60.40%) | 36.40 | 15.61 (54.40%) | 100 |
| | U | 0.29 (4.10%) | 76.70 | 0.088 (8.20%) | 23.30 | 0.378 (4.60%) | 100 |
| | U+R | 10.23 (38.70%) | 64.10 | 5.76 (55.01%) | 36.01 | 15.99 (43.36%) | 100 |
| Agricultural Labourers | R | 1.78 (3.90) | 77.90 | 0.50 (5.40) | 22.10 | 2.29 (8.00) | 100 |
| | U | 0.159 (2.20) | 84.40 | 0.029 (2.70) | 15.60 | 0.188 (2.30) | 100 |
| | U+R | 1.94 (7.40) | 78.40 | 0.53 (5.10) | 21.60 | 2.48 (6.72) | 100 |
| Workers in Household Industry | R | 0.86 (4.50) | 49.50 | 0.88 (4.50) | 50.50 | 1.74 (6.00) | 100 |
| | U | 0.32 (4.60) | 59.20 | 2.23 (2.10) | 40.80 | 0.55 (6.70) | 100 |
| | U+R | 1.13 (4.50) | 51.80 | 1.106 (10.50) | 48.20 | 2.29610 (6.22) | 100 |
| Other Workers | R | 6.69 (34.70) | 74.10 | 2.33 (24.80) | 25.90 | 9.031 (31.60) | 100 |
| | U | 6.34 (89.17) | 89.60 | 0.733 (68.3) | 10.40 | 7.079 (86.40) | 100 |
| | U+R | 13.043 (49.40) | 81.0 | 3.067 (29.40) | 19.0 | 16.110 (43.67) | 100 |
| Total | R | 19.29 (100) | 67.20 | 9.40 (100) | 32.80 | 28.69 (100) | 100 |
| | U | 7.121 (100) | 86.90 | 1.074 (100) | 13.10 | 8.195 (100) | 100 |
| | U+R | 26.41 (100) | 71 | 10.47 (100) | 29.0 | 36.88 (100) | 100 |

*Source*: Census of India for respective year Figures in Brackets represent the percentage of total population.

apparent from the table that in urban areas both male and female population is largely employed in the tertiary, that is, service sector.

## District-Wise Workforce by Sex, 2001

Broadly workforce is classified into three categories of main workers, marginal workers and non-workers. The census of India includes non-workers as the persons who did not work at all during the reference period. They constitute Students, household duties, pensioners, baggers, and persons having unidentified source of income.

While analysing the workforce categories at district level for the census 2001, variation is reflected among the districts. According to the *census 2001*, Jammu district accounts (4.20 lakh) highest proportion of workforce in the category of main workers followed by Srinagar. District Anantnag (1.35 lakhs) contributes the highest proportion in the category of marginal workers followed by Poonch (1.25 lakhs) and Doda. In the sub-categories of main workers, cultivators account highest proportions of 15.99 lakhs, and district Udhampur (2.29 lakhs) stands top (in primary activities-cultivators) among all districts in the sub-categories of main workers. It is followed by Doda which accounts 2.05 lakhs. According to census 2001, district Baramulla accounts highest proportion of agriculture labourers and district Srinagar in case of house hold industry.

## District-Wise Work Participation Rate for J&K, 2001

As per 2001 census, highest participation rate was found in Poonch district (54.1), followed by Leh (50.1) as compared to 1981, these districts rank 7th and 4th respectively. The lowest participating rate in 2001 census was found in Srinagar (30.8 per cent). Except Srinagar district the positions of all districts have undergone change some have improved their position and worsened. The other districts also improved like Doda from 11th to 4th Rajouri district rose from 9th to 5th, Kuthua from 10th to 7th, Jammu 13th to 10th, Anantnag 12th to 9th, and Leh 4th to 2nd.

**Table 4.16** Categories of Workforce by Sex, 2001 (lakhs)

| District | Main workers | | | Marginal workers | | | Non-workers | | |
|---|---|---|---|---|---|---|---|---|---|
| | Male | Fem. | Total | M | F | T | M | F | T |
| Anantnag | 2.32 | 0.24 | 2.57 | 0.48 | 0.86 | 1.35 | 3.27 | 4.50 | 7.77 |
| Pulwama | 1.32 | 0.13 | 1.48 | 0.24 | 0.37 | 0.61 | 1.77 | 2.62 | 4.40 |
| Srinagar | 2.84 | 0.26 | 3.11 | 0.28 | 0.25 | 0.53 | 3.20 | 4.98 | 8.18 |
| Budgam | 1.34 | 0.19 | 1.54 | 0.27 | 0.46 | 0.73 | 1.67 | 2.36 | 4.03 |
| Baramulla | 2.32 | 0.35 | 2.67 | 0.55 | 0.45 | 1.00 | 3.23 | 4.75 | 7.98 |
| Kupwara | 1.06 | 0.11 | 1.11 | 0.45 | 0.44 | 0.90 | 1.85 | 2.52 | 4.38 |
| Leh | 0.29 | 0.10 | 0.39 | 0.086 | 0.10 | 0.19 | 0.26 | 0.31 | 0.58 |
| Kargil | 0.21 | 0.12 | 0.34 | 0.085 | 0.10 | 0.17 | 0.32 | 0.31 | 0.63 |
| Jammu | 3.73 | 0.47 | 4.20 | 0.42 | 0.52 | 0.94 | 4.13 | 6.42 | 10.56 |
| Udhampur | 1.95 | 0.46 | 2.41 | 0.32 | 0.88 | 1.21 | 1.67 | 2.08 | 3.75 |
| Doda | 1.47 | 0.45 | 1.92 | 0.43 | 0.80 | 1.24 | 1.71 | 2.01 | 3.72 |
| Kathua | 1.23 | 0.34 | 1.58 | 0.20 | 0.23 | 0.43 | 1.41 | 2.00 | 3.42 |
| Rajouri | 1.03 | 0.11 | 1.14 | 0.27 | 0.72 | 1.00 | 1.22 | 1.41 | 2.63 |
| Poonch | 0.72 | 0.13 | 0.85 | 0.39 | 0.75 | 1.25 | 0.82 | 0.88 | 1.70 |
| State | 21.89 | 3.47 | 25.36 | 4.52 | 7.00 | 11.52 | 26.59 | 37.21 | 63.81 |

*Source* Compiled from Census of India.

**Table 4.17** Categories of Main Workers, 2001 (lakhs)

| | Cultivators | | | Agri. Labourers | | | Workers in HH Industry | | |
|---|---|---|---|---|---|---|---|---|---|
| | M | F | T | M | F | T | M | F | T |
| Anantnag | 1.21 | 0.46 | 1.67 | 0.30 | 0.093 | 0.39 | 0.13 | 0.19 | 0.33 |
| Pulwama | 0.77 | 0.22 | 0.99 | 0.14 | 0.037 | 0.18 | 0.064 | 0.095 | 0.15 |
| Srinagar | 0.25 | 0.047 | 0.29 | 0.14 | 0.024 | 0.16 | 0.32 | 0.19 | 0.51 |
| Budgam | 0.65 | 0.23 | 0.89 | 0.11 | 0.028 | 0.14 | 2.33 | 0.25 | 0.50 |
| Baramulla | 1.02 | 0.21 | 1.24 | 0.37 | 0.076 | 0.44 | 0.25 | 0.19 | 0.44 |
| Kupwara | 0.58 | 0.28 | 0.86 | 0.31 | 0.096 | 0.41 | 0.03 | 0.047 | 0.081 |
| Leh | 0.098 | 0.12 | 0.22 | 0.013 | 0.012 | 0.025 | 0.0023 | 0.005 | 0.0073 |
| Kargil | 0.10 | 0.15 | 0.25 | 0.0024 | 0.003 | 0.0053 | 0.0027 | 0.007 | 0.0097 |
| Jammu | 0.92 | 0.41 | 1.34 | 0.19 | 0.087 | 0.28 | 0.04 | 0.025 | 0.057 |
| Udhampur | 1.31 | 0.98 | 2.29 | 0.041 | 0.023 | 0.064 | 0.016 | 0.011 | 0.028 |
| Doda | 1.08 | 0.97 | 2.05 | 0.11 | 0.019 | 0.13 | 0.020 | 0.023 | 0.044 |
| Kathua | 0.64 | 0.39 | 1.04 | 0.098 | 0.015 | 0.11 | 0.016 | 0.010 | 0.026 |
| Rajouri | 0.82 | 0.65 | 1.48 | 0.027 | 0.005 | 0.032 | 0.016 | 0.011 | 0.028 |
| Poonch | 0.73 | 0.60 | 1.33 | 0.058 | 0.016 | 0.074 | 0.017 | 0.024 | 0.041 |
| State | 10.23 | 5.76 | 15.99 | 1.94 | 0.54 | 2.48 | 1.18 | 1.10 | 2.29 |

*Source*: Census (2001).

**Table 4.18**  District Wise Work Participation Rate for J&K State, 2001

| Districts above state level (36.6%) | | Below state level below (36.6%) | |
| --- | --- | --- | --- |
| Poonch | 54.1 | Budgam | 36.6 |
| Leh | 50.1 | Anantnag | 33.5 |
| Udampur | 49.2 | Pulwama | 32.1 |
| Doda | 46.0 | Kupwara | 31.5 |
| Rajouri | 44.9 | Baramullah | 31.5 |
| Kargil | 44.7 | Srinagar | 30.8 |
| Kathua | 37.2 | Jammu | 29.0 |

*Source*: District Census Handbook Kupwara (2001).
Coefficient of Variation = SD/Mean* 100.

## District-Wise Workers by Area, 2001

According to census 2001, district-wise workforce by area is examined and classified into three categories of main workers, marginal workers and non-workers. As the district level analysis is concerned for the workers it is examined Jammu district (4.34 lakhs) accounts highest proportion of main workers followed by Srinagar district. However, Baramulla (2.22 lakhs) is leading in case of rural areas and Srinagar (2.73) followed by Jammu in urban areas. In case of marginal workers, district Anantnag (1.33 lakh) followed by Doda playing leading role. In case of non-workers, district Jammu (10.60 lakh) followed by Srinagar possess highest proportion of non-workers in the state.

## District-Wise Workers in Agriculture and Non-Agriculture Sectors, 2001

Table below gives the information about the contribution of agriculture and non-agricultural sectors in total workers. It is examined Rajauri district accounts highest proportion of 70.48 per cent workforce and Srinagar accounts lowest proportion of 12.81 in terms of percentage in agriculture whereas in non-agriculture sector, Srinagar accounts 87.19

**Table 4.19** District wise Workers by Area, 2001 (lakhs)

| | Main Workers | | | Marginal Workers | | | Non-Workers | | |
|---|---|---|---|---|---|---|---|---|---|
| | R | U | T | R | U | T | R | U | T |
| Anantnag | 2.18 | 0.43 | 2.61 | 1.24 | 0.89 | 1.33 | 6.61 | 1.15 | 7.77 |
| Pulwama | 1.31 | 0.19 | 1.51 | 0.57 | 0.4 | 0.61 | 3.95 | 0.44 | 4.40 |
| Srinagar | 0.56 | 2.73 | 3.30 | 0.24 | 0.30 | 0.54 | 1.75 | 6.42 | 8.17 |
| Budgam | 1.33 | 0.19 | 1.52 | 0.68 | 0.04 | 0.73 | 3.56 | 0.47 | 4.03 |
| Baramulla | 2.22 | 0.48 | 2.70 | 0.90 | 0.09 | 1.00 | 6.60 | 1.38 | 7.98 |
| Kupwara | 1.16 | 0.07 | 1.23 | 0.87 | 0.16 | 0.88 | 4.21 | 0.16 | 4.37 |
| Leh | 0.25 | 0.12 | 0.38 | 0.18 | 0.13 | 0.19 | 0.44 | 0.14 | 0.59 |
| Kargil | 0.33 | 0.04 | 0.38 | 0.16 | 0.03 | 0.17 | 0.53 | 0.05 | 0.59 |
| Jammu | 2.18 | 2.14 | 4.34 | 0.78 | 0.15 | 0.93 | 5.89 | 4.70 | 10.60 |
| Udhampur | 2.01 | 0.43 | 2.45 | 1.18 | 0.028 | 1.21 | 3.06 | 0.70 | 3.76 |
| Doda | 1.78 | 0.15 | 1.94 | 1.22 | 0.012 | 1.23 | 3.42 | 0.31 | 3.73 |
| Kathua | 1.39 | 0.22 | 1.61 | 0.41 | 0.020 | 0.43 | 2.90 | 0.54 | 3.44 |
| Rajouri | 0.10 | 0.11 | 1.18 | 0.98 | 0.01 | 0.99 | 2.43 | 0.14 | 2.67 |
| Poonch | 0.78 | 0.07 | 0.86 | 1.14 | 0.003 | 1.14 | 1.56 | 0.15 | 1.71 |
| State | 18.62 | 7.46 | 26.08 | 10.62 | 0.83 | 11.45 | 47.02 | 16.87 | 63.89 |

*Source:* Census (2001).

per cent (highest) workers in non-agriculture sector and Rajauri accounts 29.52 per cent which is lowest of State.

## Workforce of State at National Level, 2001

The total workers are divided into two main categories of main workers and marginal workers. It is observed that J&K is insignificant in main workers and significant in marginal workers at national level. According to *2001 census*[121], the number of total workers of J&K State stood at 37.54 lakhs of which main workers constitute 26.09 lakhs (69.49 per cent) and marginal workers constitute 11.45 lakhs (30.51 per cent). Female workers constitute 28.61 per cent of total workforce and male constitutes 71.39 per cent. The population of the state increased from 101.44 lakhs to 125.49 lakhs from 2001 to 2011. The number of workers also registered an increase of 15.15 per cent during the same period.

**Table 4.20** Workers in Agriculture and Non-Agriculture sector in terms of percentage, 2001

| Districts | Agriculture | Non-Agriculture sector | Total |
|---|---|---|---|
| Kupwara | 63.31 | 36.69 | 100 |
| Baramulla | 46.07 | 53.93 | 100 |
| Srinagar | 12.81 | 87.19 | 100 |
| Badgam | 45.36 | 54.64 | 100 |
| Pulwama | 56.68 | 43.32 | 100 |
| Anantnag | 52.76 | 47.24 | 100 |
| Leh/Ladakh | 41.86 | 58.14 | 100 |
| Doda | 68.87 | 31.13 | 100 |
| Kargil | 50.79 | 49.21 | 100 |
| Udhampur | 64.92 | 35.08 | 100 |
| Punch | 70.10 | 29.90 | 100 |
| Rajauri | 70.48 | 29.52 | 100 |
| Jammu | 31.46 | 68.54 | 100 |
| Kathua | 57.10 | 42.90 | 100 |

*Source*: Census (2001).

**Table 4.21** Categories of workforce for J&K at National level, 2001, (lakhs)

| | | Total Workers | %age | Main Workers | %age | Marginal workers | %age |
|---|---|---|---|---|---|---|---|
| J & K | Persons | 37.54 | | 26.09 | 69.49 | 11.45 | 30.56 |
| | Males | 26.79 | 71.39 | 22.26 | 85.37 | 4.52 | 39.56 |
| | Females | 10.73 | 28.61 | 3.81 | 14.63 | 6.92 | 60.44 |
| All India | Persons | 4022.34 | | 3130.04 | 77.81 | 892.29 | 22.18 |
| | Males | 2750.14 | 68.37 | 2401.47 | 87.32 | 348.66 | 12.67 |
| | Females | 1272.20 | 31.62 | 728.57 | 57.26 | 543.63 | 42.73 |

*Source*: Directorate of Census Operations (J&K), 2001, Series II, Part XII-B.

## Comparison of NSS 55TH Round (1999–2000) and Census 2001

Although the 55th *round* of NSS held during 1999–2000 and the census 2001 are two different data sets, one based on sample while other is a complete enumeration, a comparison is worthwhile to see the conformity or divergence in the results of these two data sets. The NSS provides usual status definition of workforce categories like principal and subsidiary status and census provides the estimation of main and marginal workers.

Table below shows work participation rates according to NSS data and Census 2001. The total workers combine the principal and subsidiary workers of NSS and main and marginal workers of census. It may be seen from Table that work participation rates of both sources are very close to each other. The largest difference of 2 per cent is observed in respect with urban females. It has been generally alleged that census is under enumerating the female workforce in the State, but the census figures for rural women is very much close to that of the NSS. However, at the state level while male work participation rates are more or less close to census, this is not true for females. Particularly rural females show a marked level of divergence in the pattern of work participation, showing a very high level of dissimilarity.

When principal status workers of NSS are compared with main workers of census, we find that census gives us lower rates of participation. On the other hand, rates of subsidiary status workers of NSS are much lower than the marginal workers of census. When workers of NSS are compared with marginal workers of census, we find that census gives us higher rates of participation. The comparison of work participation rate for J&K, between NSS 55thR and census 2001 is reflected in Table 4.22.

## Activity–Wise Establishments and Employment, 2005

The *Economic Census*, conducted in 2005, indicates that there are 3.24 lakhs establishments in the State which are engaged in different economic activities. The total number of persons working in these establishments was recorded to be 7.52 lakhs, more or less equally distributed in rural and urban areas, that is, 51.53 per cent in urban areas and remaining 48.47 per cent in

**Table 4.22** Comparison of NSS 55th Round and Census 2001

**Work Participation Rate**

| NSS 55th Round (1999–2000) | | | | | | 2001 Census | | | | | |
|---|---|---|---|---|---|---|---|---|---|---|---|
| Rural | | | Urban | | | Rural | | | Urban | | |
| Persons | M | F | P | M | F | P | M | F | P | M | F |
| 44.2 | 54.8 | 32.7 | 28.1 | 47.8 | 6.2 | 37.9 | 49.2 | 25.8 | 32.7 | 51.8 | 9.50 |

**Work participation rate (Main), comparison of NSS 55th R and census 2001**

| NSS 55th Round | | | | | | Census 2001 | | | | | |
|---|---|---|---|---|---|---|---|---|---|---|---|
| Rural | | | Urban | | | Rural | | | Urban | | |
| Persons | Male | Fem | P | M | F | P | M | F | P | M | F |
| 30.0 | 53.3 | 4.6 | 26.8 | 47.3 | 4.1 | 23.8 | 38.7 | 7.7 | 29.5 | 48.6 | 6.10 |

**Work participation rate (Marginal), comparison of NSS 55thR & census 2001**

| NSS 55th Round | | | | | | Census 2001 | | | | | |
|---|---|---|---|---|---|---|---|---|---|---|---|
| Rural | | | Urban | | | Rural | | | Urban | | |
| Persons | M | F | P | M | F | P | M | F | P | M | F |
| 1.42 | 0.18 | 2.66 | 0.65 | 0.19 | 1.2 | 10.6 | 5.99 | 15.2 | 2.75 | 2.95 | 2.54 |

*Source:* NSS 55th Round and 2001 Census.

Table 4.23  Activitywise establishments and employment, 2005, thousands

| Major Activity group | Establishments | | Employment | |
| --- | --- | --- | --- | --- |
| Agriculture establishments | Size | %age | Size | %age |
| Farming of animals | 1.70 | 0.53 | 3.65 | 0.49 |
| Agriculture services | 0.58 | 0.18 | 2.81 | 0.37 |
| Fishing etc. | 0.29 | 0.09 | 0.37 | 0.05 |
| All Agricultural Activities | 2.58 | 0.80 | 60.84 | 0.91 |
| Non-Agricultural Establishments | | | | |
| Mining and Quarrying | 0.91 | 0.28 | 3.19 | 0.42 |
| Manufacturing | 67.32 | 20.72 | 154.19 | 20.52 |
| Elect. Gas and Water | 0.69 | 0.22 | 5.99 | 0.80 |
| Construction | 3.32 | 1.02 | 4.85 | 0.65 |
| Wholesale trade | 3.41 | 1.05 | 6.55 | 0.87 |
| Retail Trade | 153.27 | 47.17 | 203.16 | 27.03 |
| Restaurants and Hotels | 12.89 | 3.97 | 27.45 | 3.65 |
| Transport and Storage | 7.80 | 2.40 | 12.39 | 1.65 |
| Posts & Telecommunication | 6.43 | 1.98 | 10.83 | 1.44 |
| Financial Intermediation | 1.20 | 0.37 | 10.73 | 1.43 |
| Real estates, banking and services | 7.34 | 2.26 | 11.88 | 1.58 |
| Public adm. Defence social security | 7.54 | 2.32 | 99.92 | 13.30 |
| Education | 20.30 | 6.25 | 126.24 | 16.80 |
| Health and social work | 8.99 | 2.77 | 30.89 | 4.11 |
| Total Non-agricultural activities | 322.32 | 99.20 | 744.68 | 99.09 |
| All Establishments | 3.249 | 100.0 | 75.152 | 100.0 |

Source: 5th Economic Census (2005), MOSPI (Department of Statistics), CSO, New Delhi

rural areas. A careful analysis of the data indicates that activity known as 're-tail trade' with a share of 47.17 per cent occupies rank 1st in establishments followed by 'manufacturing' activity with 20.72 per cent share. On employment side it is again retail trade activity providing employment to 27.03 per cent workers out of 7.52 lakh persons closely followed by manufacturing activity wherein 20.52 per cent of total workers were working. The average annual growth rate in employment in the said establishments from 1998 to 2005 was 6.82 per cent. With this annual average growth rate in employment in such establishments, J&K topped all the States. The *5th Economic Census 2005* (MOSPI) indicates that there are establishments in the State which are engaged in different economic activities shown in Table 4.23.

## Trends of Workforce in J&K, 1999–2009

According to *economic survey 2009/10*, the categories of workers were divided into activities like agriculture, forestry, fishing, mining, manufacturing, electricity, gas and water supply, construction, transport storage and communication, financial intermediation, real estate, renting and business activities, public administration & defense, compulsory social security, and other services. It may be noticed that in 1999–2000, agriculture sector accounts 75.25 (45.22 lakh) per cent, and only 6 per cent by service sector of workforce The contribution of tertiary sector increased mildly. However, this data is doubtful as exact magnitude and reliable data is not possible. It is also different from other sources. It has been observed from other sources that contribution of workforce in agriculture is declining very fast and workforce is moving towards tertiary sector. The distribution of workforce from 1999 to 2009 is shown in Table 4.24.

## Labour Force Participation Rate Based on Activity Status, 2009–10

In NSS surveys, persons are classified into various activity categories on the basis of activities pursued by them during certain specified reference periods. Three reference periods are used in NSS surveys, viz. (i) one year, (ii) one week, and (iii) each day of the reference week. Based on these three periods, three different measures of activity status are arrived at. The activity status determined on the basis of the reference period of one year is known as the usual activity status (US) of a person and activity status determined on the basis of a reference period of one week is known as the current weekly status (CWS) of the person and the activity status determined on the basis of the engagement on each day during the reference week is known as the current daily status (CDS) of the person. The labour force participation rate of age 15–59 years is given in Table 4.25.

It is clear from the above table according to UP Status Approach that total rural working participation rate is 424 per 1000 and male (758/1000) are much more than female. With the same approach total urban working population accounts 472 per thousand and male contributes 764/1000 and female accounts small 167/1000. Similarly by the Current Weekly Status

**Table 4.24** Work Force of Jammu and Kashmir from 1999 to 2009, Lakhs

| Description | 1999–2000 | 2000–01 | 2001–02 | 2002–03 | 2003–04 | 2004–05 | 2005–06 | 2006–07 | 2007–08 | 2008–09 |
|---|---|---|---|---|---|---|---|---|---|---|
| Agriculture, Forestry | 45.23 | 46.37 | 47.52 | 48.00 | 48.75 | 49.49 | 50.23 | 50.96 | 51.68 | 52.41 |
| Fishing | 0.044 | 0.045 | 0.046 | 0.046 | 0.047 | 0.048 | 0.048 | 0.49 | 0.50 | 0.51 |
| Mining | 0.021 | 0.022 | 0.022 | 0.023 | 0.023 | 0.023 | 0.02 | 0.02 | 0.024 | 0.025 |
| Manufacturing | 3.31 | 3.39 | 3.48 | 3.51 | 3.57 | 3.62 | 3.68 | 3.73 | 3.78 | 3.84 |
| Electricity, Gas & Water supply | 0.081 | 0.084 | 0.086 | 0.086 | 0.088 | 0.89 | 0.91 | 0.92 | 0.93 | 0.94 |
| Construction | 1.59 | 1.63 | 1.67 | 1.69 | 1.72 | 1.74 | 1.77 | 1.80 | 1.82 | 1.85 |
| Wholesale & Retail sale Trade: Repair of Motor Vehicles and HH Goods | 2.90 | 2.97 | 3.05 | 3.08 | 3.13 | 3.17 | 3.22 | 3.27 | 3.31 | 3.36 |
| Hotels and Restaurant | 0.29 | 0.30 | 0.30 | 0.31 | 0.31 | 0.32 | 0.32 | 0.33 | 0.33 | 34.0 |
| Transport & Communications | 1.00 | 1.02 | 1.05 | 1.06 | 1.07 | 1.09 | 1.11 | 1.12 | 1.14 | 1.15 |
| Financial intermediation | 0.13 | 0.13 | 0.13 | 0.13 | 0.14 | 0.14 | 0.14 | 0.14 | 0.14 | 0.15 |
| Real est, & business activities | 0.23 | 0.24 | 0.24 | 0.25 | 0.25 | 0.25 | 0.26 | 0.26 | 0.27 | 0.27 |
| Public admt. & defense; compulsory social security | 2.24 | 2.29 | 2.35 | 2.37 | 2.41 | 2.45 | 2.49 | 2.52 | 2.56 | 2.59 |
| Other services | 2.97 | 3.04 | 3.12 | 3.15 | 3.20 | 3.25 | 3.29 | 3.34 | 3.39 | 3.44 |
| Total Work Force | 60.07 | 61.59 | 63.12 | 63.75 | 64.74 | 65.73 | 66.71 | 67.68 | 68.64 | 69.61 |
| Population | 97.95 | 100.42 | 102.91 | 103.95 | 105.56 | 107.17 | 108.77 | 110.35 | 111.92 | 113.50 |

*Source:* Directorate of Economics and Statistics, J&K State, 2011.

**Table 4.25** Labor Force Participation Rate (per 1000) for group 15–59, 2009–10

| Usual Principal Status Approach | | | | | |
|---|---|---|---|---|---|
| Rural | | | Urban | | |
| Male | Female | M+F | Male | Female | M+F |
| 758 | 93 | 424 | 764 | 167 | 472 |
| Current Weekly Status Approach | | | | | |
| Male | Female | M+F | Male | Female | M+F |
| 757 | 348 | 558 | 764 | 202 | 489 |
| Current Daily Status Approach | | | | | |
| Male | Female | M+F | Male | Female | M+F |
| 751 | 206 | 486 | 763 | 184 | 479 |

*Source*: NSS KI: (NSS 66th Round).

Approach and Current Daily Status Approach both in rural and urban areas male working participation rate is much higher than female for State of

## District-Wise Work Participation Rate for J&K State, 2011

Highest participation rate was found in Udampur district followed by Leh in 2011 and Poonch stands at 3rd rank. The lowest participating rate in *2011 census* is found in Kupwara. Except Kargil and Doda district the positions of all districts have undergone change. Some have improved their position and few districts have worsened their position than 2001 census.

## Occupational Classification of Working Force, 2011

According to *Census 2011* for J&K, Categories of workers were further divided into cultivators, agricultural labourers, workers in household industry and other workers. Among all these categories cultivators

**Table 4.26**  District Wise Work Participation Rate for J&K, 2011

| Districts above state level rate (38.8%) | | Below state level below | |
|---|---|---|---|
| Udampur | 55.1 | Srinagar | 36.6 |
| Leh | 49.5 | Pulwama | 34.5 |
| Poonch | 49.2 | Baramullah | 32.1 |
| Doda | 46.3 | Jammu | 31.5 |
| Budgam | 44.9 | Anatnag | 31.5 |
| Kargil | 44.7 | Rajouri | 30.8 |
| Kathua | 37.6 | Kupwara | 29.0 |
| J& K State | 39.5 | | |

*Source*: District Census Handbook Kupwara (2011).

**Table 4.27**  Occupational Classification of Working Force, 2011

| Categories | | Number (lakhs) | Percentage |
|---|---|---|---|
| Cultivators | Persons | 12.45 | 28.81 |
| | Males | 7.65 | 17.70 |
| | Females | 4.79 | 11.08 |
| Agricultural Labourers | Persons | 5.47 | 12.65 |
| | Males | 4.14 | 9.58 |
| | Females | 1.33 | 3.07 |
| Workers in Household Industry | Persons | 1.72 | 3.98 |
| | Males | 0.91 | 2.10 |
| | Females | 0.81 | 1.87 |
| Other Workers | Persons | 23.57 | 54.54 |
| | Males | 19.23 | 44.50 |
| | Females | 4.33 | 10.02 |

*Source*: Census of India, GoI.

maintains the dominance and female contributes high proportion as compared to males at state level.

According to Census 2011, cultivators calculated highest portion of 12.45 lakhs (28.81 per cent) among various categories. Even category of 'other workers' further sub-divided into various categories accounts highest proportion of 23.56 lakh (54.54 per cent).

## Working Force by Area and Sex, Census 2011

The data on workforce provided by the *2011 Census* reveals a distinct variation among districts in terms of area and gender. Workforce has been evaluated into rural and urban areas and by sex of male and female. The district-level analysis reflected that Jammu district accounts highest proportion of total workers followed by Srinagar district particularly in main working force category Jammu district accounts 4.10 lakhs followed by Srinagar district 3.30 lakhs. The district Jammu and district Srinagar maintain dominance since decades as both districts are the hub of various economic activities. The district-wise data of the above categories are analysed in Table 4.28.

## Working Population in Agriculture Sector, 2011

The ratio of working population in agriculture is decreasing day by day because of urbanization, modernization and diversification of occupation of the people. The percentage of people working in agriculture sector in the state has been deceased by 22.40 percentage points (63.88 (1981) to 41.48, 2011). The decrease in working population in agriculture is not uniform across the spatial units (districts) of the state. Six districts of the state have recorded much decline in the proportion of working population in agriculture than state average rate, while as in the other districts, the rate of decline of population engaged in agriculture is lower than the state average.

The state average is 46.95 per cent which indicates that 53.05 per cent population is engaged in activities other than agriculture. The working population with agriculture is not same throughout but exhibit regional variations which are visible across the districts of the state. The districts with more percentage of population engaged in agriculture are Doda (62.12 per cent), Ramban (61.5 per cent), Rajouri (61.45 per cent), and Kishtwar (59.64 per cent), etc. while as district Srinagar (5.15 per cent), Jammu (15.12 per cent), and Leh (34.42 per cent) have low percentage of people engaged in agriculture sector.

**Table 4.28** District wise Working force by area and sex, 2011 (lakhs)

| State/District | | Total Wkers | M | F | Main Wkers | M | F | Marg inal | M | F | Non-wrkers |
|---|---|---|---|---|---|---|---|---|---|---|---|
| J&K | T | 43.22 | 31.95 | 11.27 | 26.44 | 23.10 | 3.38 | 16.78 | 8.89 | 7.89 | 82.18 |
| | R | 31.13 | 22.12 | 9.01 | 16.69 | 145.31 | 2.16 | 14.43 | 7.58 | 6.84 | 59.94 |
| | U | 12.09 | 9.83 | 2.26 | 9.74 | 8.52 | 1.21 | 2.35 | 1.30 | 1.04 | 22.23 |
| Anantnag | T | 3.89 | 2.44 | 1.45 | 1.76 | 1.58 | 0.18 | 2.12 | 0.85 | 1.27 | 6.89 |
| | R | 2.95 | 1.75 | 1.19 | 1.19 | 1.06 | 0.12 | 1.76 | 0.69 | 1.07 | 4.99 |
| | U | 0.93 | 0.68 | 0.25 | 0.57 | 0.51 | 0.063 | 0.36 | 0.16 | 0.19 | 1.89 |
| Pulwama | T | 1.88 | 1.38 | 0.49 | 0.98 | 0.89 | 0.091 | 0.90 | 0.49 | 0.40 | 3.72 |
| | R | 1.57 | 1.13 | 0.43 | 0.77 | 0.69 | 0.074 | 0.80 | 0.43 | 0.36 | 3.22 |
| | U | 0.30 | 0.24 | 0.063 | 0.20 | 0.19 | 0.017 | 0.099 | 0.052 | 0.046 | 0.49 |
| Srinagar | T | 4.07 | 3.33 | 0.74 | 3.30 | 2.89 | 0.40 | 0.76 | 0.43 | 0.33 | 8.29 |
| | R | 0.05 | 0.04 | 0.02 | 0.03 | 0.03 | 0.002 | 0.03 | 0.02 | 0.02 | 0.12 |
| | U | 4.01 | 3.28 | 0.73 | 3.27 | 2.87 | 0.40 | 0.74 | 0.41 | 0.32 | 8.17 |
| Badgam | T | 2.14 | 1.62 | 0.52 | 1.32 | 1.16 | 0.15 | 0.82 | 0.46 | 0.37 | 5.39 |
| | R | 1.81 | 1.34 | 0.47 | 1.06 | 0.93 | 0.13 | 0.75 | 0.41 | 0.34 | 4.74 |
| | U | 0.33 | 0.28 | 1.06 | 0.25 | 0.23 | 0.023 | 0.074 | 0.047 | 0.027 | 0.65 |
| Baramul | T | 3.04 | 2.49 | 0.54 | 1.87 | 1.69 | 0.18 | 1.16 | 0.80 | 0.36 | 7.03 |
| | R | 2.38 | 1.91 | 0.46 | 1.32 | 1.19 | 0.15 | 1.05 | 0.72 | 0.33 | 5.87 |
| | U | 0.66 | 0.57 | 0.083 | 0.55 | 0.50 | 0.049 | 0.11 | 0.077 | 0.034 | 1.16 |

(continued)

**Table 4.28** Continued

| State/District | | Total Wkers | M | F | Main Wkers | M | F | Marginal | M | F | Non-wrkers |
|---|---|---|---|---|---|---|---|---|---|---|---|
| Kupwara | T | 2.29 | 1.90 | 0.38 | 1.23 | 1.11 | 0.12 | 1.05 | 0.79 | 0.26 | 6.41 |
| | R | 1.95 | 1.61 | 0.34 | 0.99 | 0.89 | 0.10 | 0.96 | 0.72 | 0.23 | 5.69 |
| | U | 0.33 | 0.28 | 0.041 | 0.24 | 0.22 | 0.020 | 0.088 | 0.067 | 0.021 | 0.71 |
| Kargil | T | 0.51 | 0.39 | 0.12 | 0.28 | 0.25 | 0.037 | 0.23 | 0.15 | 0.083 | 0.88 |
| | R | 0.44 | 0.34 | 0.10 | 0.23 | 0.19 | 0.030 | 0.22 | 0.14 | 0.077 | 0.80 |
| | U | 0.074 | 0.061 | 0.013 | 0.061 | 0.054 | 0.0073 | 0.013 | 0.0077 | 0.0054 | 0.089 |
| Leh | T | 0.75 | 0.53 | 0.22 | 0.57 | 0.45 | 0.13 | 0.18 | 0.085 | 0.094 | 0.58 |
| | R | 0.48 | 0.30 | 0.17 | 0.34 | 0.24 | 0.091 | 0.14 | 0.060 | 0.083 | 0.39 |
| | U | 0.26 | 0.22 | 0.044 | 0.23 | 0.19 | 0.032 | 0.036 | 0.025 | 0.012 | 0.18 |
| Doda | T | 1.51 | 1.01 | 0.50 | 0.79 | 0.68 | 0.11 | 0.73 | 0.33 | 0.39 | 2.58 |
| | R | 1.41 | 0.92 | 0.49 | 0.69 | 0.60 | 0.095 | 0.71 | 0.33 | 0.39 | 2.36 |
| | U | 0.10 | 0.086 | 0.016 | 0.096 | 0.082 | 0.014 | 0.006 | 0.004 | 0.0024 | 0.23 |
| Udham Pur | T | 2.43 | 1.63 | 0.79 | 1.52 | 1.27 | 0.25 | 0.91 | 0.36 | 0.55 | 3.11 |
| | R | 1.97 | 1.23 | 0.73 | 1.10 | 0.90 | 0.19 | 0.86 | 0.33 | 0.53 | 2.49 |
| | U | 0.46 | 0.40 | 0.062 | 0.42 | 0.37 | 0.046 | 0.043 | 0.027 | 0.017 | 0.61 |
| Kathua | T | 2.00 | 1.61 | 0.38 | 1.42 | 1.23 | 0.19 | 0.57 | 0.38 | 0.19 | 4.16 |
| | R | 1.72 | 1.37 | 0.34 | 1.18 | 1.02 | 0.15 | 0.54 | 0.35 | 0.18 | 3.54 |
| | U | 2.77 | 0.23 | 0.040 | 0.24 | 0.21 | 0.035 | 0.030 | 0.024 | 0.0057 | 0.61 |

| | | | | | | | | | | | |
|---|---|---|---|---|---|---|---|---|---|---|---|
| Jammu | T | 5.08 | 4.17 | 0.91 | 4.10 | 3.51 | 0.58 | 0.98 | 0.65 | 0.32 | 10.21 |
| | R | 2.36 | 1.95 | 0.41 | 1.70 | 1.50 | 0.20 | 0.65 | 0.45 | 0.20 | 5.28 |
| | U | 2.22 | 2.21 | 0.49 | 2.39 | 2.01 | 0.37 | 0.32 | 0.20 | 0.12 | 4.93 |
| Samba | T | 0.92 | 0.81 | 0.10 | 0.74 | 0.67 | 0.066 | 0.18 | 0.14 | 0.039 | 2.26 |
| | R | 0.74 | 0.66 | 0.087 | 0.57 | 0.52 | 0.051 | 0.17 | 0.13 | 0.036 | 1.90 |
| | U | 0.17 | 0.15 | 0.17 | 0.16 | 0.14 | 0.015 | 0.013 | 0.0098 | 0.0029 | 0.35 |
| Punch | T | 1.61 | 1.17 | 0.43 | 0.73 | 0.63 | 0.10 | 0.88 | 0.54 | 0.34 | 3.15 |
| | R | 1.47 | 1.06 | 0.41 | 0.61 | 0.52 | 0.085 | 0.85 | 0.53 | 0.32 | 2.91 |
| | U | 0.14 | 0.11 | 0.025 | 0.12 | 0.10 | 0.015 | 0.024 | 0.014 | 0.010 | 0.24 |
| Bandi Pora | T | 1.49 | 1.01 | 0.49 | 0.75 | 0.64 | 0.10 | 0.74 | 0.36 | 0.37 | 2.43 |
| | R | 1.24 | 0.83 | 0.41 | 0.59 | 0.51 | 0.084 | 0.64 | 0.32 | 0.32 | 2.02 |
| | U | 0.24 | 0.18 | 0.068 | 0.15 | 0.14 | 0.017 | 0.094 | 0.044 | 0.050 | 0.40 |
| Gander Bal | T | 1.00 | 0.73 | 0.27 | 0.52 | 0.46 | 0.061 | 0.47 | 0.26 | 0.21 | 1.96 |
| | R | 0.84 | 0.62 | 0.22 | 0.43 | 0.38 | 0.047 | 0.41 | 0.23 | 0.17 | 1.65 |
| | U | 1.63 | 1.11 | 0.052 | 0.098 | 0.083 | 0.014 | 0.065 | 0.027 | 0.037 | 0.30 |
| Shupiyan | T | 0.87 | 0.63 | 0.23 | 0.54 | 0.48 | 0.057 | 0.33 | 0.14 | 0.18 | 1.78 |
| | R | 0.80 | 0.58 | 0.22 | 0.49 | 0.43 | 0.052 | 0.31 | 0.14 | 0.17 | 1.68 |
| | U | 0.067 | 0.056 | 0.011 | 0.056 | 0.051 | 0.0049 | 0.011 | 0.0048 | 0.0064 | 0.096 |

(continued)

Table 4.28 Continued

| State/District | | Total Wkers | M | F | Main Wkers | M | F | Marg inal | M | F | Non-wrkers |
|---|---|---|---|---|---|---|---|---|---|---|---|
| Kulgam | T | 1.59 | 1.02 | 0.57 | 0.77 | 0.70 | 0.076 | 0.82 | 0.32 | 0.50 | 2.64 |
| | R | 1.26 | 0.81 | 0.45 | 0.61 | 0.54 | 0.062 | 0.65 | 0.26 | 0.39 | 2.16 |
| | U | 0.33 | 0.20 | 0.12 | 0.16 | 0.15 | 0.013 | 0.16 | 0.054 | 0.10 | 0.47 |
| Ramban | T | 0.87 | 0.68 | 0.18 | 0.52 | 0.46 | 0.055 | 0.35 | 0.21 | 0.13 | 1.96 |
| | R | 0.82 | 0.64 | 0.18 | 0.47 | 0.42 | 0.052 | 0.34 | 0.21 | 0.13 | 1.89 |
| | U | 0.043 | 0.039 | 0.004 | 0.040 | 0.037 | 0.0033 | 0.0028 | 0.0024 | 0.0005 | 0.074 |
| Kishtwar | T | 0.82 | 0.56 | 0.26 | 0.44 | 0.36 | 0.86 | 0.38 | 0.20 | 0.17 | 1.47 |
| | R | 0.78 | 0.52 | 0.25 | 0.40 | 0.32 | 0.079 | 0.37 | 0.20 | 0.17 | 1.37 |
| | U | 0.048 | 0.041 | 0.0073 | 0.044 | 0.37 | 0.0066 | 0.0041 | 0.0034 | 0.0007 | 0.099 |
| Reasi | T | 1.44 | 0.88 | 0.56 | 0.88 | 0.74 | 0.13 | 0.56 | 0.13 | 0.42 | 1.69 |
| | R | 1.33 | 0.80 | 0.53 | 0.79 | 0.67 | 0.12 | 0.54 | 0.13 | 0.41 | 1.53 |
| | U | 0.10 | 0.085 | 0.023 | 0.090 | 0.077 | 0.013 | 0.018 | 0.0078 | 0.010 | 0.16 |
| Rajouri | T | 2.90 | 1.84 | 1.06 | 1.30 | 1.10 | 0.20 | 1.60 | 0.74 | 0.85 | 3.51 |
| | R | 2.63 | 1.60 | 1.02 | 1.05 | 0.87 | 0.18 | 1.57 | 0.73 | 0.84 | 3.26 |
| | U | 0.27 | 0.24 | 0.033 | 0.24 | 0.22 | 0.021 | 0.026 | 0.014 | 0.011 | 0.25 |

*Sources:* PCA (2011).

**Pie Chart**

**District wise Agriculture working Population (2011)**

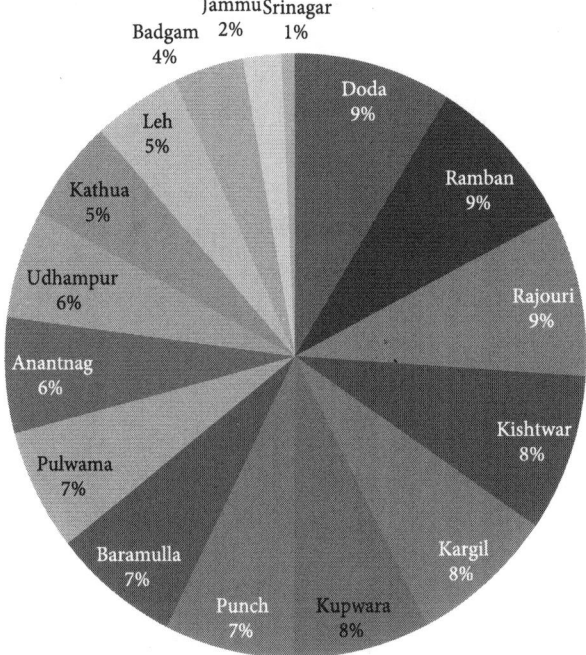

# Workforce Labour Force, Unemployment Data, 2011

As per Census 2011, the workforce participation rate for females is 19.11 per cent against 48.11 per cent for males. Rural sector has better female workforce participation rate of 20.8 per cent compared with 14.50 per cent in urban sector. Female participation in labour force has remained lower (20.4 per cent) than male participation (56.1 per cent) as women account for most of the unpaid work, and when women are employed in paid work; they are overrepresented in the informal sector and among the poor. It has been observed that LFPR is the lowest for urban females. The unemployment rate for women in rural area was 16.6 against 2.7 for men whereas it was 25.6 and 4.7 for women and men in urban areas during 2011.

**Table 4.29** Workforce, Labour Force, Unemployment Data, 2011

| | Rural | | | Urban | | | Rural+ Urban | | |
|---|---|---|---|---|---|---|---|---|---|
| | M | F | Person | M | F | Person | M | F | Person |
| Workforce Participation Rate, 2011 (Percent) | 46.3 | 20.8 | 34.2 | 52.68 | 14.5 | 35.23 | 48.11 | 19.11 | 34.47 |
| Labour force Participation Rate*, 2011 (Percent) | 55.9 | 26.3 | 41.9 | 56.3 | 14.5 | 36.2 | 56.1 | 20.4 | 39.05 |
| Labour force Participation Rate (per 1000) for persons aged 15 & above, 2011 | 727 | 199 | 477 | 179 | 709 | 454 | 723 | 194 | 471 |
| Unemployment Rate*, 2011 (Percent) | 2.7 | 16.6 | 3.9 | 4.7 | 25.6 | 7.8 | 3.07 | 20.56 | 5.85 |
| Unemployment Rate (per 1000) for persons aged 15 & above, 2011 | 70 | 153 | 86 | 45 | 166 | 68 | 64 | 156 | 82 |
| Worker Population Ratio (per 1000) for persons aged 15 & above, 2011 | 676 | 169 | 436 | 677 | 150 | 424 | 676 | 164 | 433 |

*Source* Census 2011 data, Office the Registrar General, India, NSSO, 68th Round; Employment and Unemployment Survey, Ministry of Labour & Employment, 2013–14.

## Comparison of Unemployment Rate at National Level

The *NSS Survey—68th Round* conducted during July 2011 to June 2012 throughout the country constitutes an important source of information on unemployment. The analysis of table reveals that the combined Unemployment Rate (R+U) under UPS and CWS is 4.9 per cent and 4.7 per cent, while as the indicator for CDS was 6.7 per cent. As against this the All India level indicator was lower than that of State level under all the three approaches as indicated in the below table. The unemployment rates revealed by 68th round of NSS for J&K State in comparison to all India figures is given in :Table 4.30.

The table further shows that at State level, the unemployment rates for females as per all the three approaches viz., UPS, CWS. and CDS were on the higher side when compared to corresponding figures for males. Further, there is a huge gap of female unemployment rate in comparison to national level as per all the three approaches. For example, as per UPS approach unemployment rate among female in J&K state is 20.2 per cent while at national level it is just 3.7 per cent means thereby that in J&K state as per the UPS unemployment rate among female is more than five times than at national level. Similarly as per CWS, and CDS unemployment

Table 4.30 Unemployment Rate for J&K State vis-à-vis All India, 2011

| Area | | J&K (% per 100 persons) | | | All India (%) | | |
|------|------|------|--------|---------|------|--------|---------|
| Area | | Male | Female | Persons | Male | Female | Persons |
| Rural | UPS | 2.7 | 16.6 | 3.9 | 2.1 | 2.9 | 2.3 |
| | CWS | 3.0 | 6.3 | 3.8 | 3.3 | 3.5 | 3.4 |
| | CDS | 5.0 | 11.8 | 6.1 | 5.5 | 6.2 | 5.7 |
| Urban | UPS | 4.7 | 25.6 | 7.8 | 3.2 | 6.6 | 3.8 |
| | CWS | 4.5 | 21.8 | 7.6 | 3.8 | 6.7 | 4.4 |
| | CDS | 5.3 | 24.2 | 8.4 | 4.9 | 8.0 | 5.5 |
| Combined | UPS | 3.2 | 20.2 | 4.9 | 2.4 | 3.7 | 2.7 |
| | CWS | 3.4 | 8.8 | 4.7 | 3.5 | 4.2 | 3.7 |
| | CDS | 5.0 | 14.7 | 6.7 | 5.3 | 6.6 | 5.6 |

*Source*: NSSO Report (July 2011–June 2012)

rate in the state among female is 8.8 per cent and 14.7 per cent while as at national level it is 4.2 per cent and 6.6 per cent, respectively. Thus, the results show that the problem of unemployment is more prevalent amongst females in the State.

## Unemployment Trend for J&K State

55th Round (1999–2012) to 68th Round (2011–2012)

The statistics of unemployment in J&K do not indicate any clear trend over the last years as is in shown in table. However it is quite clear that unemployment rate in the state is highest in urban areas than in rural areas. Within urban areas, the female unemployment rate has shown an increasing trend through all the three approaches. In rural areas female unemployment rate has increased from 4.4 per cent in 1999 to 16.6 per cent as per Usual statues which means that rural female unemployment has increased around four times in the last 13 years. Similar trend is evident from current weekly status as female unemployment has doubled from 3.3 per cent to 6.3 per cent from 1999 to 2012.

The table further shows that unemployment rate among male in urban areas has decreased in the last decade as per all the three approaches. Thus the analysis of the table makes it clear that in the state of J&K unemployment is mostly an urban phenomenon and that too in female population which needs a serious concern by government and policy makers.

## Unemployment in Northern States, 2011–12

As per the results of 68th Round of NSS (2011–12), the Unemployment situation of J&K in comparison to Northern States viz HP, Punjab, Haryana, Delhi, and at All India level is given in Table 4.32.

The analysis of table reveals that based on UP Status, J&K has the highest Unemployment rate of 4.9 per cent in comparison to its neighbouring States viz. Punjab (2.8 per cent), HP (2.0 per cent), Delhi (4.7 per cent), and Haryana (3.2 per cent). All India figures for Unemployment rate stood at 2.7 per cent only. The table shows that Unemployment rate

**Table 4.31** Unemployment rate trend, 1999–00/2011–12, Percent

| Years | Male | | | Female | | |
|---|---|---|---|---|---|---|
| | US | CWS | CDS | US | CWS | CDS |
| **Rural** | | | | | | |
| 55th (1999–2000) | 2.3 | 3.6 | 4.8 | 4.4 | 3.3 | 11.8 |
| 60th (2003–04) | 2.03 | 3.1 | 5.4 | 18.18 | 6.1 | 10.6 |
| 61th (2004–05) | 3.8 | 8.6 | 10.7 | 81.8 | 14.7 | 36.7 |
| 62th (2005–06) | 5.1 | 6.5 | 7.9 | 0.6 | 0.3 | 0.5 |
| 66th (2009–10) | 3.1 | 3.0 | 3.8 | 19.3 | 5.7 | 10.3 |
| 68th (2011–12) | 2.7 | 3.0 | 5.0 | 16.6 | 6.3 | 11.8 |
| **Urban** | | | | | | |
| 55th | 6.2 | 6.8 | 7.0 | 5.2 | 15.1 | 4.5 |
| 60th | 5.36 | 5.6 | 5.2 | 19.6 | 25.96 | 27.0 |
| 61th | 7.3 | 8.8 | 13.18 | 5.8 | 12.2 | 15.2 |
| 62th | 6.7 | 7.0 | 7.6 | 11.7 | 8.1 | 8.7 |
| 66th | 5.0 | 5.2 | 5.5 | 14.5 | 13.1 | 15.0 |
| 68th | 4.7 | 4.5 | 5.3 | 25.6 | 21.8 | 24.2 |

*Source*: Compiled from various Rounds of NSSO.

**Table 4.32** Unemployment in neighbouring States and at 'All India Level'

| States | Rural | | | Urban | | | Combined | | |
|---|---|---|---|---|---|---|---|---|---|
| | Male | Fem | Person | Male | Fem | Person | Male | Fem | Person |
| J&K | 2.7 | 16.6 | 3.9 | 4.7 | 25.6 | 7.8 | 3.2 | 20.2 | **4.9** |
| H.P | 1.8 | 1.8 | 1.8 | 2.1 | 11.0 | 4.2 | 3.2 | 20.2 | 4.9 |
| Punjab | 2.3 | 6.1 | 2.6 | 2.8 | 5.1 | 3.1 | 1.8 | 2.2 | 2.0 |
| Haryana | 2.6 | 4.2 | 2.5 | 4.0 | 5.6 | 4.2 | 2.5 | 5.6 | 2.8 |
| Delhi | 9.4 | 6.6 | 7.8 | 3.4 | 4.8 | 3.6 | 3.1 | 4.8 | 4.7 |
| All India | 2.1 | 2.9 | 2.3 | 1.2 | 6.6 | 3.8 | 2.4 | 3.7 | 2.7 |

*Source*: NSSO, 68th Report

for Males in J&K is 3.2 per cent only whereas that of females is 20.2 per cent which is far too high when compared to the unemployment of females in neighbouring States viz., Punjab (5.6 per cent), Haryana (4.8 per cent), Delhi (4.3 per cent), and HP (2.2 per cent).

Based on UPS there is a huge gap of unemployment amongst females in J&K (20.2 per cent) compared to the national aggregate (3.7 per cent). Further the unemployment is more prevalent in urban than in rural areas; unemployment rate in urban area of J&K based on 68th Round of NSS stood at 7.8 per cent against 3.9 per cent in rural area. The unemployment amongst urban male (4.7 per cent) is higher than that of rural males (2.7 per cent) in J&K. Rural female unemployment in J&K stood at 16.6 per cent which is far too high as compared to the neighbouring states viz., Punjab (6.1 per cent), HP (1.8 per cent), Haryana (4.2 per cent), and far too higher than the national average of 2.9 per cent only. It is quite clear based on the findings of 68thR, the rate of unemployment is more pronounced and visible in J&K compared to the national average.

Further increasing rates of literacy seem to exhibit a positive relationship with unemployment which is a serious area of concern for policy makers and development practitioners. The disproportionate growth of educated persons and employment opportunities have created a *chaotic* scenario where opportunities for employment are not substantial vis-à-vis educated workforce added. The literacy is growing at an annual average growth rate of 1.02 per cent, which results in addition to the educated youth year after year. This situation requires creation of ample opportunities in terms of employment avenues otherwise rise in literacy rate and number of literates will culminate into higher unemployment ratios.

## Workforce in Terms of Gender at National Level, 2011

According to 2011 census, the number of total workers in J&K stood at 43.23 lakhs of which the main workers account 26.44 lakhs (61.77 per cent) and the number of marginal workers constitutes 16.79 lakhs (38.83 per cent). Female workers account 26.09 per cent and male account 73.9 per cent from the total workforce The share of female in the Main workers is only 12.80 per cent against 47.02 per cent in marginal workers. It is analysed from the below table that male accounts higher proportion in both the main (61.80 per cent) and marginal workers (38.8 per cent). And the state is significant in main workers. However, contradictory to it, at All

**Table 4.33**  Categories of workforce for J&K at all India level (in Lakhs)

|  |  | Total workers | | Main workers | | Marginal workers | |
| --- | --- | --- | --- | --- | --- | --- | --- |
|  |  | Lakhs | age% | Lakh | age% | Lakh | age% |
| J & K (2011) | Total | 43.22 |  | 26.44 | 61.8 | 16.78 | 38.8 |
|  | Male | 31.95 | 73.9 | 23.05 | 87.2 | 8.89 | 52.9 |
|  | Female | 11.27 | (26.1 | 3.38 | 12.8 | 7.89 | 47.02 |
| All India | Total | 4817.43 |  | 2324.46 | 48.25 | 2492.96 | 51.74 |
|  | Male | 3318.65 | 68.89 | 1431.49 | 61.58 | 1587.16 | 63.66 |
|  | Female | 1498.77 | 31.11 | 892.97 | 38.41 | 905.80 | 36.34 |

*Source*: Directorate of Census Operations (J&K), Series II, Part XII-B.

India level, India is insignificant in main workers and significant in marginal workers. Male and female contributed the same position just at state level. At all India level, similarly the male accounts higher proportion of 3318.65 lakh and in terms of percentage, it accounts 68.89 points and further in categories of workers, the main workers accounts 1431.49 lakh that constitute 61.58 per cent and marginal workers levels 1587.16 lakh that accounts 63.66 per cent.

It is further important to mention here that marginal workers cover female workforce comparatively at national level. The total workers with categories of main workers and marginal workers in respect of gender for J&K at national level are reflected in Table 4.33.

## Workers in Respect of Area and Gender at National Level 2011

According to *2011 census*, the number of total cultivators in J&K stood at 12.4 lakhs of which the rural cultivators constitute 11.8 lakhs and the urban constitutes 64.9 thousand. Similarly total agricultural labour constitutes 5.47 lakhs, rural constitute 4.98 lakhs and urban constitute 49 thousand. Male accounts very high proportion of 61.52 and 75.68 per cent in both the categories of cultivators and agricultural labours for State and at national level the corresponding accounts 69.68 and 68.87 per cent. The classification of workers at national level is shown in Table 4.34.

**Table 4.34** Classification of Workers at National Level, 2011 (*lakhs*)

|  |  | Cultivators | Male | Female | Agri.Labour | Male | Female |
|---|---|---|---|---|---|---|---|
| J&K | T | 12.45 (1.04) | 7.65(61.5) | 4.79(38.4) | 5.47 (0.37) | 4.14 (75.6) | 1.33(24.3) |
|  | R | 11.80 (94.77) | 7.29 | 4.50 | 4.98 (91.04) | 3.76 | 1.22 |
|  | U | 0.64 (5.23) | 0.35 | 0.29 | 0.49 (8.95) | 0.38 | 0.11 |
| All India | T | 1186.92 | 827.06 (69.6) | 359.8(30.3) | 1491.62 | 1027.4(68.8) | 464.2 (31.2) |
|  | R | 1149.68 (96.8) | 798.39 | 351.29 | 1366.9 (91.3) | 965.30 | 401.29 |
|  | U | 37.24 (3.14) | 28.67 | 8.56 | 124.66 (8.6) | 62.10 | 62.93 |

*Source* Census of India, Registrar General of India.

## Job Seeker Youth Population in J&K, 2011

The District Employment and Counseling Centers of state maintain qualification-wise data on job seekers. Due to limited job opportunities, the number of job seeker youth has been increasing with every passing year. It is examined that *Matric up to Graduation* category accounts highest per cent of job seekers in 2011 followed by Graduates. The qualification-wise job seekers for 2011 are given in Table 4.35.

**Table 4.35** Job seekers registered with DECC, J&K, 2011

| Job seekers Categories | Percentage |
| --- | --- |
| Illiterate | 0.53 |
| below Matric | 12.8 |
| Matric &Above | 61.6 |
| Graduates | 14.3 |
| Post Graduates | 3.45 |
| Degree Engineers | 1.50 |
| Diploma Engineers | 3.22 |
| ITI Trained | 2.07 |
| Skilled (Other than ITI/Others) | 0.62 |
| Total | 86.6 |
| Grand Total | 100 |

*Source*: Directorate of Economics and Statistics, J&K State, 2011.

**Table 4.36** Working age group 15–59 of sex and residence, 2011, Percent

|  | Total | | | Rural | | | Urban | | | D.I |
| --- | --- | --- | --- | --- | --- | --- | --- | --- | --- | --- |
|  | T | M | F | T | M | F | T | M | F | |
| J&K | 65.9 | 65.1 | 66.8 | 64.9 | 64.0 | 65.8 | 70.0 | 69.2 | 70.8 | 0.057 |
| All India | 62.5 | 52.2 | 62.8 | 61.0 | 60.7 | 61.3 | 66.6 | 66.2 | 66.9 | 0.125 |

*Source*: Survey, SRS (2011).

## Working Age Group 15–59 in Terms of Sex and Residence at National Level, 2011

Table below provides working population in the age group 15–59 years at national level by sex and residence. The J&K State accounts 64.9 per cent in rural and 70.0 per cent in urban against 61.01 per cent and 66.6 per cent at national level. Thus it varies highly at national level and it is important mention here that J&K State accounts much better position in the rural areas. While the disparity index of state against All India is small in value. The table depicts the percentage of population in the age group 15–59 years by residence and sex.

## Trends by Type of Employment, 1999–2000 to 2011–12

During investigation into type of employment there has been a decline in self-employment and rise in casual wage employment. Only the service sector experienced a rise in self-employment. It means service sector employment is moving more towards self-employment and salaried wage employment. Table 4.37 depicts the trends of type of employment.

Table 4.37  Trends of type of employment, 1999–2000 to 2011–12, Percent

|  | 1999–2000 | 2011–12 |
| --- | --- | --- |
| Self-employment | 48.78 | 41.68 |
| Salaried employment | 36.12 | 29.44 |
| Casual wage employment | 15.10 | 28.88 |
|  | 100 | 100 |

*Source* Calculated from Employment and Unemployment Survey, NSSO, 1999–2000 and 2011–2012

## Distribution of Establishments & Employment, 2013

The percentage share of establishments and employment therein, by sector (rural/urban/combined) and by type of establishments (own account establishments/ establishment with at least one hired worker) have been presented in Table 4.38 respectively. According to *Sixth Economic Census* (6th EC), the percentage share of establishments and employment therein, there are total 0.86 per cent reported to be employed in the establishments and 0.83 per cent accounted in employment by the type of establishments.

## Distribution of Establishments and Employment, 2013

The type of establishments (own account establishments/establishment with at least one hired worker) have been analysed and category linked with at least one hired workers accounts higher percentage share establishments of 1.02 while without hired workers contributes higher per cent of 0.95 in employment by the type of establishment. The distribution of establishments and employment, 2013 is depicted in Table 4.39:

As per the 6th *Economic Censuses (2013)*, non-agricultural establishments grew at the rate of 0.13 per cent, while agricultural establishments grew at the rate of 1.07 per cent. As per the results of the Sixth Economic

Table 4.38  Distribution of establishments & employment, 2013 (Percent)

|  | Establishment | | | Employment | | |
|  | Rural | Urban | Combined | Rural | Urban | Combined |
|---|---|---|---|---|---|---|
| J&K State | 0.85 | 0.87 | 0.86 | 0.88 | 0.78 | 0.83 |
| All India | 100.0 | 100.0 | 100.0 | 100.0 | 100.0 | 100.0 |

*Source* Report of Sixth Economic Census, CSO, 2013

**Table 4.39** Distribution of establishments and employment by type of establishments, Percent

|  | Establishment | Employment |
| --- | --- | --- |
| Without Hired workers | 0.79 | 0.95 |
| With at least one Hired workers | 1.02 | 0.69 |
| Total | 0.86 | 0.83 |

*Source* Sixth Economic Census, MOSPI, 2013.

**Table 4.40** Area wise distribution of establishments and employment by type of establishments, 2013

|  | Broad Activity Groups | Agricultural Establishment | Non-Agricultural Establishment |
| --- | --- | --- | --- |
| Rural | Without Hired workers | 0.10 | 1.16 |
|  | With at least one Hired workers | 0.17 | 1.46 |
|  | Total | 0.11 | 1.24 |
| Urban | Without Hired workers | 0.29 | 0.93 |
|  | With at least one Hired workers | 0.41 | 0.85 |
|  | Total | 0.31 | 0.9 |
| Combined | Without Hired workers | 0.12 | 1.06 |
|  | With at least one Hired workers | 0.20 | 1.09 |
|  | Total | 0.13 | 1.07 |

*Sources*: Sixth Economic Census, Ministry of Statistics and Programme Implementation, CSO, www.mospi.giv.in.

Census, there were various establishments engaged in different economic activities. The distribution of total number of establishments and number of persons employed by broad activity groups, with break-up for each type of establishment (i.e. without hired worker and with at least one hired worker), is given in Table 4.40 by the percentage shares.

## Labour Force Participation Rate, 2016

Labour Force Participation Rate is the proportion of the working-age population, either by working or seeking for work. It provides an indication of relative size of the supply of labour available which can be engaged in the production of goods and services. As per *Economic Survey 2016–17*, the distribution of LFPR (per 1000) for persons of different age groups according to UPS and UPSS is given in Table 4.41.

Table 4.41 Labour Force Participation Rate at All India level, 2016.

| All India | | | | | | | | |
|---|---|---|---|---|---|---|---|---|
| **UPS** | 15–17 years | | | 18–29 years | | | 30 years & Above | | |
| | R | U | R+U | R | U | R+U | R | U | R+U |
| Male | 136 | 52 | 84 | 711 | 549 | 452 | 898 | 831 | 582 |
| Female | 56 | 17 | 167 | 232 | 163 | 550 | 310 | 176 | 477 |
| Person | 100 | 36 | 115 | 485 | 362 | 668 | 611 | 512 | 878 |
| **UPSS** | 15–17 years | | | 18–29 years | | | 30 years & Above | | |
| Male | 157 | 53 | 131 | 720 | 550 | 675 | 902 | 831 | 881 |
| Female | 77 | 19 | 62 | 281 | 167 | 250 | 365 | 180 | 311 |
| Person | 121 | 38 | 100 | 512 | 364 | 473 | 640 | 514 | 603 |
| **Jammu & Kashmir** | | | | | | | | | |
| **UPS** | 15–17 years | | | 18–29 years | | | 30 years & Above | | |
| Male | 17 | 11 | 16 | 459 | 381 | 444 | 863 | 803 | 867 |
| Female | 32 | | 25 | 144 | 149 | 145 | 77 | 119 | 89 |
| Person | 22 | 6 | 19 | 301 | 262 | 293 | 488 | 480 | 486 |
| **UPSS** | 15–17 years | | | 18–29 years | | | 30 years & Above | | |
| Male | 458 | | 407 | 186 | 87 | 169 | 2 | 3 | 2 |
| Female | 32 | | 25 | 144 | 149 | 145 | 80 | 119 | 91 |
| Person | 22 | 6 | 19 | 301 | 262 | 293 | 489 | 480 | 487 |

*Source*: Economic Survey (2016); UPS-Usual Principal Status Approach (UPS) & UPSS-Usual Principal Subsidiary Status Approach.

In case of age group 18–29 years, the state of Chhattisgarh had shown the highest 639 per 1000 LFPR followed by UT of Andaman & Nicobar Island with 605 per 1000 whereas the state of J&K has lowest, that is, 293 LFPR for this age group using both UPS and UPSS approaches. In J&K State, Female LFPR in the age group of 1829 years is 145 using both UPS and UPSS approaches where as at All India Level LFPR is 550 and 250 respectively for the same age group. At All India, persons having age 30 years & above, LFPR is 878 and 603 using UPS and UPSS approaches respectively. In J&K State, persons have age 30 years and above, LFPR stands at 486 per 1000 and 487 per 1000 using UPS and UPSS approaches respectively.

## Worker Population Ratio, 2016

Worker Population Ratio (WPR) signifies proportion of workers in the total population of specific age group. According to *JK Economic survey,* the person in the age group of 18–29 years had highest WP Ratio i.e. 607 per 1000 in the state of Chhattisgarh and the lowest in the state of J&K, that is, 221 per 1000 as observed during the survey period using UPS approach and 224 using UPSS approach. The distribution of WPR (per 1000) for persons of different age groups according to UPS and UPSS approach is given in Table 4.42.

In the J&K State, WPR of females in the age group of 18–29 years is 80 per thousand and 81 per 1000 using UPS and UPSS approaches respectively. For persons in the age group 30 years and above WPR at all India level is 573 per 1000 and 597 per 1000 respectively with UPS and UPSS approaches respectively. For J&K State, the corresponding figures stand at 480 and 483 per thousand respectively. For females in same age group for J&K State is 82 and 84 per 1000 using UPS and UPSS approaches respectively.

## Activity-Wise Distribution of Employed Persons, 2016

The employed persons are further classified based on the activity pursued by them during the reference period. Based on economic activities

Table 4.42  Worker Population ratio for J&K at National Level, 2016

| | All India | | | | | | | | |
|---|---|---|---|---|---|---|---|---|---|
| UPS | 15–17 years | | | 18–29 years | | | 30 years & Above | | |
| | R | U | R+U | R | U | R+U | R | U | R+U |
| Male | 111 | 40 | 93 | 631 | 486 | 593 | 890 | 826 | 871 |
| Female | 43 | 14 | 36 | 191 | 118 | 171 | 298 | 167 | 260 |
| Persons | 89 | 28 | 67 | 423 | 307 | 392 | 601 | 504 | 573 |
| UPSS | 15–17 years | | | 18–29 years | | | 30 years & Above | | |
| Male | 139 | 43 | 114 | 660 | 493 | 616 | 897 | 827 | 877 |
| Female | 67 | 16 | 54 | 247 | 124 | 213 | 358 | 172 | 304 |
| Persons | 106 | 31 | 87 | 465 | 314 | 424 | 635 | 507 | 597 |
| | Jammu & Kashmir | | | | | | | | |
| UPS | 15–17 years | | | 18–29 years | | | 30 years & Above | | |
| Male | 8 | 11 | 9 | 372 | 337 | 365 | 857 | 801 | 841 |
| Female | 9 | 8 | 7 | 73 | 107 | 80 | 70 | 114 | 82 |
| Persons | 9 | 6 | 8 | 222 | 220 | 221 | 481 | 476 | 480 |
| UPSS | 15–17 years | | | 18–29 years | | | 30 years & Above | | |
| Male | 9 | 11 | 9 | 374 | 348 | 369 | 862 | 801 | 845 |
| Female | 9 | 8 | 7 | 73 | 108 | 81 | 73 | 114 | 84 |
| Persons | 9 | 6 | 9 | 223 | 225 | 224 | 485 | 476 | 483 |

Source: Economic Survey (2016), J&K.

pursued by the employed persons in different reference periods, the persons aged 15–17 years, 18–29 years, and 30 years & above are broadly classified as Self Employed, Wage/Salaried Worker, Contract Workers, and Casual Labourers. At all India level, using UPS in the age group of 18–29 years highest number 390 per thousand persons are Self employed, 366 per thousand are casual workers, 190 per 1000 are salaried and only 54 per 1000 are contract workers. The distribution of employed persons in different activities by various age groups according to UPS and UPSS approaches is given in Table 4.43.

In J&K using the same approach 319 per 1000 persons are self-employed and salaried each and 286 per 1000 are casual workers and 76 per thousand are contract workers. Using UPSS approach, in India it has

**Table 4.43** Distribution of employed persons (per 1000) in different activities, 2016

| | All India | | | | | | | | |
|---|---|---|---|---|---|---|---|---|---|
| **UPS** | **15–17 years** | | | **18–29 years** | | | **30 years & Above** | | |
| | R | U | R+U | R | U | R+U | R | U | R+U |
| SE | 408 | 309 | 397 | 405 | 333 | 390 | 512 | 434 | 492 |
| WSE | 51 | 189 | 65 | 141 | 376 | 190 | 105 | 338 | 165 |
| CW | 36 | 77 | 40 | 46 | 84 | 54 | 24 | 49 | 30 |
| CSW | 506 | 426 | 497 | 408 | 207 | 366 | 359 | 179 | 313 |
| **UPSS** | **15–17 years** | | | **18–29 years** | | | **30 years & Above** | | |
| SE | 491 | 321 | 475 | 426 | 335 | 408 | 515 | 435 | 495 |
| WSE | 40 | 177 | 52 | 130 | 370 | 178 | 99 | 336 | 158 |
| CW | 29 | 78 | 33 | 44 | 85 | 52 | 23 | 49 | 30 |
| CSW | 441 | 425 | 439 | 400 | 209 | 362 | 363 | 180 | 317 |

| | Jammu & Kashmir | | | | | | | | |
|---|---|---|---|---|---|---|---|---|---|
| **UPS** | **15–17 years** | | | **18–29 years** | | | **30 years & Above** | | |
| SE | 435 | – | 376 | 305 | 379 | 319 | 466 | 423 | 454 |
| WSE | – | 322 | 44 | 283 | 464 | 319 | 239 | 472 | 302 |
| CW | – | 678 | 92 | 83 | 46 | 76 | 37 | 12 | 30 |
| CSW | 565 | – | 488 | 330 | 112 | 286 | 258 | 93 | 214 |
| **UPSS** | **15–17 years** | | | **18–29 years** | | | **30 years & Above** | | |
| SE | 409 | – | 357 | 304 | 394 | 322 | 462 | 423 | 451 |
| WSE | – | 322 | 42 | 281 | 452 | 315 | 237 | 472 | 300 |
| CW | – | 678 | 88 | 83 | 45 | 75 | 37 | 12 | 30 |
| CSW | 591 | – | 514 | 333 | 109 | 288 | 264 | 93 | 219 |

SE: Self Employed; WSE: Wage/Salaried Employed; CW: Contract Worker; CSW: Casual Worker.
*Source*: Economic Survey (2016).

been observed that in the age group of 18–29 year 408 per 1000 persons are self employed while 362 per 1000 are casual workers. Percentage of persons who are wage/ salaried and contract workers is 178 and 52 respectively. In J&K, using same approach for persons in the age group of 18–29 years, self-employed persons are 322, casual works are 288, wage/ salaried employed are 315, and contract works are 75 only. At national level, in the age group of 30 years and above self-employed, wage/salaried employed, Contract workers and casual workers using UPS approach are 492, 165, 30, and 313 per thousand respectively. Using UPSS approach values are 495, 158, 30, and 317 per 1000 respectively. Corresponding values for J&K State are 454, 302, 30, 214 per 1000 respectively using UPS approach and 451, 300, 30, and 219 per thousand respectively using UPSS approach respectively.

## Unemployment as Per Economic Survey, 2016

The persons in the age group of 18–29 years had R+U 132 per thousand of All India Level using UPS approach and 102 per thousand using UPSS approach. It is observed from the data that in J&K, in the age group 18–29 years R+U is highest among females, that is, 451 and 446 using UPS and UPSS approaches respectively. In J&K, R+U for males of age group 18–29 years is 178 and 169 using UPS and UPSS approaches respectively. In the age group of 30 years and above (R+U) at All India Level is 16 and 09 per thousand using UPS and UPSS approach against 13 and 08 per thousand for J&K State.

In the state of J&K, R+U is 246 per 1000 using UPS approach and 238 per 1000 using UPSS approach stands two fold at national level shown in Table 4.44.

## Labour Force, Workforce, & Unemployed (NSSO 61th/72thR)

The NSS provides data on two important parameters—labour force and workforce. Hence, labour force includes both employed and unemployed persons. The workforce is technical term used by NSS for the employed. During the analysis of labour force it increased from 4.01 million in 1999–2000 to 5.10 in 2014–15. While workforce increased from 3.94 million to 4.32 million during the same periods. In the fifteen year period, growth rate of labour force exceeded workforce. Notwithstanding this, the addition to the workforce has marginally fallen short of the additions to the labour force in successive periods

**Table 4.44** Unemployment Rate (per 1000) for persons of J&K, 2016

| | All India | | | | | | | | |
|---|---|---|---|---|---|---|---|---|---|
| **UPS** | **15–17 years** | | | **18–29 years** | | | **30 years & Above** | | |
| | R | U | R+U | R | U | R+U | R | U | R+U |
| M | 184 | 221 | 188 | 112 | 115 | 113 | 9 | 7 | 9 |
| F | 228 | 214 | 227 | 179 | 279 | 200 | 37 | 53 | 40 |
| P | 195 | 220 | 198 | 127 | 151 | 132 | 16 | 15 | 16 |
| **UPSS** | **15–17 years** | | | **18–29 years** | | | **30 years & Above** | | |
| M | 118 | 203 | 126 | 83 | 104 | 87 | 5 | 6 | 5 |
| F | 134 | 174 | 137 | 120 | 258 | 146 | 17 | 45 | 22 |
| P | 122 | 196 | 130 | 92 | 139 | 102 | 8 | 13 | 9 |
| | Jammu & Kashmir | | | | | | | | |
| **UPS** | **15–17 years** | | | **18–29 years** | | | **30 years & Above** | | |
| M | 508 | 396 | 452 | 191 | 114 | 178 | 8 | 3 | 6 |
| F | 712 | 713 | 712 | 496 | 280 | 451 | 95 | 49 | 79 |
| P | 613 | 541 | 577 | 264 | 162 | 246 | 14 | 8 | 13 |
| **UPSS** | **15–17 years** | | | **18–29 years** | | | **30 years & Above** | | |
| M | 458 | 356 | 407 | 186 | 87 | 169 | 2 | 3 | 2 |
| F | 712 | 713 | 712 | 491 | 272 | 446 | 87 | 49 | 73 |
| P | 588 | 522 | 555 | 259 | 140 | 238 | 8 | 8 | 8 |

*Source*: Economic Survey (2016).

of the NSS rounds leading to an increase in the absolute number of unemployed persons in the state. The trend of labour force, workforce at national level is below in Table 4.45.

The rapid increase in labour force creates pressure for creation of employment opportunities. If economic growth is jobless, the possibility of rapid growth of unemployment cannot be ruled out when labour force registers a high growth rate. During the period of 61st Round 2004–05 the percentage of the unemployed to the total labour force has also been increased. However, the *61st Round* 2.3 per cent is lower than the all India figure of 2.4 per cent. In *72th Round* of NSS data the trend was reversed subsequently J&K State stands at 1.85 against 0.78 at national level higher than national average.

**Table 4.45** Labor Force, Work Force and Unemployment (UPSS), Million

| | Jammu and Kashmir | | | All India | | |
|---|---|---|---|---|---|---|
| | 55<sup>th</sup>R (1999–2000) | 61<sup>th</sup>R (2004–5) | 72th R (2014–15) | 55<sup>th</sup>R (1999–2000) | 61<sup>th</sup>R (2004–5) | 72th R (2014–15) |
| Labor Force | 4.01 | 4.37 | 5.10 | 403.15 | 470.14 | 494.24 |
| Workforce | 3.94 | 4.27 | 4.32 | 394.17 | 458.99 | 481.74 |
| Unemployed | 0.07 | 0.1 | 0.08 | 8.98 | 11.15 | 3.8 |
| Unemployed/ Labor Force | 1.7% | 2.3% | 1.85 | 2.2% | 2.4% | 0.78 |

*Source*: Various Reports of NSS Data.

## Composition of Workers, 1983–2010

According to *NSSO data*, agriculture sector witnesses declining trend of workforce and service sector shows rapid and accelerated trend and the status for absorbing the workforce. In 1983 workforce in agricultural was 79.5 per cent and slumped finally to 61.05 per cent in 2009–10. The mining and quarrying accounts less contribution and slightly improved however never reached to 1 per cent. In case of construction, workforce absorbed significantly since 1983, 7.26 per cent in 1983, 6.0 per cent in 1993, 6.6 per cent in 1999, 7.10 and finally 6.19 per cent in 2009–10. The public administration, education, communication and other services performed tremendously and accounts 4.6 per cent in 1983 which accelerated to 10.60 per cent in 2010. However in overall service sectors growth rate is significantly increasing. The trends of workers in such activities are shown in Table 4.46.

## Trends of Workforce for J&K State, 1981–2011

During the three decades since 1981, the proportion of main workers always exceeded. Their proportion to total workers was 68.6 per cent against 31.4 per cent of marginal workers in 1981 and 69.5 and 30.5 per cent in 2001. Thereafter, main workers kept on declining steadily and stood at 61.17 per cent against 38.82 per cent in 2011. The analysis is depicted in the Table 4.47.

Table 4.46 Trends of Workers in various Categories, 1983–2010

| Occ. Cat. | Male | | | | | Female | | | | | Persons | | | | |
|---|---|---|---|---|---|---|---|---|---|---|---|---|---|---|---|
| | 1983 | 1993–94 | 1999–2000 | 2004–05 | 2009–10 | 83 | 93–94 | 99–00 | 04–05 | 09–10 | 83 | 93 | 99 | 04–05 | 09–10 |
| I | 71.7 | 61.3 | 66.9 | 53.8 | 43.7 | 96.0 | 95.6 | 93.4 | 86.6 | 78.4 | 79.5 | 76.0 | 74.4 | 64.0 | 61.05 |
| II | 0.28 | 0.10 | 0.00 | 0.40 | 0.64 | 0.05 | 0.10 | 0.0 | 0.0 | 0.02 | 0.20 | 0.10 | 0.0 | 0.30 | 0.33 |
| III | 5.51 | 5.71 | 4.40 | 9.90 | 11.12 | 2.07 | 0.90 | 3.90 | 9.70 | 7.14 | 4.40 | 3.60 | 4.20 | 9.80 | 9.13 |
| IV | 0.92 | 2.0 | 0.70 | 1.6 | 1.7 | 0.0 | 0.0 | 0.0 | 0.0 | 3.8 | 0.63 | 1.10 | 0.40 | 1.10 | 2.75 |
| V | 10.5 | 9.9 | 10.2 | 10.2 | 12.24 | 0.39 | 0.70 | 0.20 | 0.10 | 0.15 | 7.26 | 6.0 | 6.60 | 7.10 | 6.19 |
| VI | 2.7 | 4.3 | 5.4 | 7.1 | 6.4 | 0.4 | 0.2 | 0.4 | 0.3 | 0.2 | 1.9 | 2.5 | 3.6 | 5.0 | 3.3 |
| VII | 2.0 | 4.6 | 2.5 | 5.8 | 7.4 | 0.0 | 0.0 | 0.2 | 0.0 | 0.1 | 1.4 | 2.7 | 1.7 | 4.0 | 3.8 |
| VIII | 0.2 | 0.9 | 0.2 | 0.4 | 0.6 | 0.0 | 0.0 | 0.1 | 0.0 | 3.6 | 0.1 | 0.5 | 0.2 | 0.2 | 2.1 |
| IX | 6.4 | 11 | 9.7 | 10.01 | 14.81 | 1.1 | 2.5 | 1.8 | 3.3 | 6.4 | 4.6 | 7.5 | 6.9 | 8.5 | 10.60 |
| T | 100 | 100 | 100 | 100 | 100 | 100 | 100 | 100 | 100 | 100 | 100 | 100 | 100 | 100 | 100 |

*Source:* Various Issues of NSSO, 50th R, 55thR, 61st, and 66th NSSO Rounds.

Occupation Categories: I=Agriculture, etc.; II=Mining & Quarrying; III=Manufacturing; IV=Electricity, Water etc.; V=Construction; VI=Trade, Hotel and Restaurant; VII=Transport; VIII=Fin. Inter, bus. etc.; IX=Public Adm., Education communication; Service; etc.

Table 4.47  Analysis of Workforce from 1981 and 2011 (Lakhs)

| Year | Pop | Total Workers | Main Workers | Marginal Workers | Non-workers (*Lakhs*) |
|------|-----|---------------|--------------|------------------|------------------------|
| 1981 | 59.87 | 26.50 (44.3) | 18.18 (68.6) | 8.31 (31.4) | 33.37 |
| 2001 | 101.43 | 37.53 (37.0) | 26.08 (69.5) | 11.45 (30.5) | 63.89 |
| 2011 | 125.48 | 43.22 (34.44) | 26.44 (61.17) | 16.78 (38.82) | 82.26 |

*Source*: Compiled Census of India.

The rate of marginal workers during three decades from 1981 onwards was erratic. It declined to 30.5 per cent during 2001. Thus, the decrease in the main workers and increase in marginal workers was dramatic in 2011.

## Work Participation Rate (Area and Gender), 1981–2011

Crude work participation rate is analysed and categorized in main and marginal workers in respect of gender and residence for the reference periods of 1981, 2001, and 2011. It is important to note here that during 1991 no survey was done due to outbreak of violence in the State. The Crude work participation rate in respect of gender and geographical area (1981–2011) is depicted in Table 4.48.

The crude work participation rate of male reflects slight change, 55.81 per cent in 1981 and then proliferated 56.1 per cent in 2011. Female crude work participation decreased by high proportion from 31.31 to 20.4 per cent from 1981 to 2011 due to increase of girl enrolments in schools/institutions.

The crude work participation rate in rural was 47.73 per cent in 1981, which declined to 36.5 per cent in 2011. However, female participation decreased more than male. Female crude work participation decreased by 11.78 per cent (37.08–25.3) and male by only 4.37 per cent. The crude work participation rate in urban areas was 31.27 per cent in 1981, accelerated to 37.2 per cent in 2011.

The crude work participation rate of main workers was 30.37 per cent in 1981 and male accounts very high proportions of 52.20 per cent. In

Table 4.48  Crude Work Participation Rate for J&K, 1981–2011, (Percent)

| | 1981 | | | 2001 | | | 2011 | | |
|---|---|---|---|---|---|---|---|---|---|
| | T | M | F | T | M | F | T | M | F |
| Main+ Marginal | 44.26 | 55.81 | 31.31 | 36.63 | 49.83 | 21.96 | 38.85 | 56.1 | 20.4 |
| Rural (Main + Marginal) | 47.73 | 57.27 | 37.08 | 37.93 | 49.14 | 25.84 | 36.5 | 52.9 | 25.3 |
| Urban (Main +Marginal) | 31.27 | 50.41 | 9.39 | 32.71 | 51.80 | 9.50 | 37.2 | 56.3 | 14.5 |
| Main | 30.37 | 52.20 | 5.91 | 25.19 | 41.30 | 7.28 | 21.07 | 37.04 | 5.02 |
| Main (Rural) | 30.76 | 52.86 | 6.12 | 23.78 | 38.73 | 7.65 | 17.40 | 35.62 | 6.32 |
| Main (Urban) | 28.92 | 49.75 | 5.11 | 29.45 | 48.65 | 6.98 | 29.16 | 39.44 | 4.12 |
| Marginal | 13.89 | 3.61 | 25.40 | 11.44 | 8.53 | 14.68 | 13.37 | 14.18 | 12.26 |
| Marginal (Rural) | 16.96 | 4.41 | 30.97 | 14.15 | 10.41 | 18.19 | 15.08 | 18.14 | 16.44 |
| Marginal (Urban) | 2.34 | 0.66 | 4.27 | 3.26 | 3.15 | 3.40 | 10.58 | 8.34 | 7.66 |
| Non-agri Workers (Rural) | 18.39 | 25.81 | 5.61 | 38.90 | 41.29 | 33.98 | 53.42 | 57.72 | 45.24 |
| Non-agri.Workers (Urban) | 84.43 | 88.76 | 57.82 | 93.85 | 94.50 | 89.92 | 94.40 | 96.10 | 91.32 |

*Source:* Compiled Census of India.

2011, the same holds 21.07 per cent (main) and 37.04 per cent (male), the female accounts only 5 per cent

The crude work participation rate of main workers by residence (rural) was 30.76 per cent in 1981 and declined to 17.40 per cent in 2011. The crude work participation rate of main workers by residence (urban) was 28.92 per cent in 1981 and increased only 29.16 per cent. Male accounts very high proportions than female in during the same periods.

The crude work participation rate of marginal workers was 13.89 per cent and female accounts very high proportions of 25.40 per cent and male only 3.61 per cent in 1981. In 2001 work participation rate (Marginal) accounts 11.44 per cent and male rised to 8.53 per cent and female declined to 14.68 per cent The same accounts 13.57 per cent 14.18 per cent, and 12.26 per cent in 2011 means male incremented to 14.18 per cent and female decelerated further to 12.26 per cent. The crude work participation rate of marginal workers by rural was 16.96 per cent and female accounts very high proportions of 30.97 per cent and male accounts 4.41 per cent in 1981. In 2011 crude work participation rate (Marginal) by rural accounts 15.08 per cent and female accounts 16.44 per cent. The crude work participation rate of marginal workers by urban increased from 2.34 per cent to 10.58 per cent from 1981 to 2011. Male accounts only 0.66 per cent in 1981 and accelerated to 8.37 per cent in 2011.

The percentage of Non-agricultural Workers (Rural) to Total Rural Workers contributes 18.39 per cent in 1981 and 53.42 per cent in 2011. In both the periods male accounts higher proportions. However, the female increased tremendously from 5.61 in 1981 to 45.24 in 2011. The percentage of Non-agricultural Workers (urban) to Total Rural Workers contributes 84.43 per cent in 1981 and 94.40 per cent in 2011. In both the periods male accounts higher proportions.

## Growth Rate of Workers for J&K, 1983–2016

It comes out that as compared with 1983 to 1993–94, during the post-liberalization period 1993–94 to 2004–05, employment growth decelerated. In terms of sectoral employment, there is a marked deceleration in employment growth in agriculture. In the case of secondary sector, acceleration in their growth of employment took place and in the tertiary

**Table 4.49**  Growth Rate of UPSS Workers (R+U) for J&K State

|  | Agriculture | Secondary sector | Tertiary sector | All |
|---|---|---|---|---|
| 1983 to 1993–94 | 3.18 | 0.82 | 8.09 | 3.76 |
| 1993–94 to 2004–05 | –0.018 | 8.69 | 2.02 | 1.7 |
| 2004–05 to 2015–16 | 1.8 | 9.23 | 0.14 | 2.85 |

*Source*: Various Rounds, 61th & 73th NSS Round, Employment and Unemployment Survey.

sectors on the other hand, deceleration took place. But comparing the entire post-reform period 1993–94 to 2015–16 with the pre-reform period 1983 to 1993–94, it comes out that the employment growth rate decelerated for all major sectors except secondary sector. There is a visible acceleration in the growth rate of employment in the secondary sector. The Growth Rate of UPSS Workers (R+U) for State (1983/2015–16) is depicted in Table 4.49.

## Age Group of Workers in Terms of Percentage, 1981–2011

The age composition of total workers divides the whole age into three groups, that is, 0–14, 15–59, and 60+ and further classified workers into two main categories (Main & Marginal) in respect of gender and area wise.

It is examined among three groups, group 15–59 absorbs maximum proportion of workers, that is (84.79 per cent (M) & 81.92 per cent (F) in 1981 and 87.87 per cent & 86.58 per cent in 2001 and 88.24 per cent (M) and 87.44 per cent (F) in 2011. It is important to notice that female accounts higher proportion of child labour (014) than male in all the three periods. In case of (Main + Marginal) by Residence Rural, group 1559 possess maximum percentage 83.24 per cent male and 80.52 per cent female in 1981, 86.17 per cent male and 85.86 per cent female in 2001 and 85.64 per cent male and 84.44 per cent female in 2011. The age group of workers in terms of percentage (1981–2011) is delineated in Table 4.50.

**Table 4.50** Age Group of Workers in Percentage, J&K, 1981 to 2011

| | 1981 | | | | | | 2001 | | | | | | 2011 | | | | | |
|---|---|---|---|---|---|---|---|---|---|---|---|---|---|---|---|---|---|---|
| | Male | | | Female | | | Male | | | Female | | | Male | | | Female | | |
| | 0–14 | 15–59 | 60+ | 0–14 | 15–59 | 60+ | 0–14 | 15–59 | 60+ | 0–14 | 15–59 | 60+ | 0–14 | 15–59 | 60+ | 0–14 | 15–59 | 60+ |
| **Total Workers** | | | | | | | | | | | | | | | | | | |
| | 7.47 | 84.79 | 7.74 | 14.31 | 81.92 | 3.77 | 3.37 | 87.87 | 8.77 | 8.01 | 86.58 | 5.41 | 1.84 | 88.24 | 9.92 | 4.32 | 87.44 | 8.24 |
| **(Main + Marginal) by Residence (Rural)** | | | | | | | | | | | | | | | | | | |
| | 8.35 | 83.24 | 8.41 | 15.66 | 80.52 | 3.82 | 4.17 | 86.17 | 9.65 | 8.54 | 85.86 | 5.61 | 4.18 | 85.64 | 10.18 | 6.14 | 84.44 | 9.42 |
| **(Main + Marginal) by Residence (Urban)** | | | | | | | | | | | | | | | | | | |
| | 3.76 | 91.32 | 4.93 | 9.34 | 88.38 | 2.29 | 1.13 | 92.56 | 6.32 | 3.72 | 92.50 | 3.78 | 1.08 | 94.16 | 4.76 | 3.80 | 93.62 | 2.58 |
| **Main Workers** | | | | | | | | | | | | | | | | | | |
| | 5.20 | 86.97 | 7.83 | 13.88 | 82.94 | 3.18 | 1.53 | 89.56 | 8.92 | 5.36 | 89.20 | 5.43 | 1.90 | 90.60 | 7.5 | 6.68 | 88.24 | 5.08 |
| **Main Workers by Residence (Rural)** | | | | | | | | | | | | | | | | | | |
| | 5.64 | 85.79 | 8.57 | 20.71 | 76.04 | 3.25 | 1.79 | 88.13 | 10.1 | 5.92 | 88.11 | 5.97 | 2.44 | 88.26 | 9.3 | 4.96 | 86.76 | 8.28 |
| **Main Workers by Residence (Urban)** | | | | | | | | | | | | | | | | | | |
| | 3.50 | 91.60 | 4.89 | 9.19 | 89.05 | 1.76 | 0.91 | 92.90 | 6.19 | 3.23 | 93.39 | 3.38 | 0.70 | 93.92 | 5.38 | 2.22 | 94.42 | 3.36 |
| **Marginal Workers** | | | | | | | | | | | | | | | | | | |
| | 40.24 | 53.32 | 6.44 | 14.41 | 81.68 | 3.90 | 12.4 | 79.54 | 8.04 | 9.47 | 85.14 | 5.40 | 10.41 | 80.56 | 9.03 | 7.57 | 83.48 | 8.95 |
| **Marginal Workers by Residence (Rural)** | | | | | | | | | | | | | | | | | | |
| | 40.96 | 52.64 | 6.40 | 14.59 | 81.47 | 3.94 | 13.3 | 78.69 | 8.02 | 9.75 | 84.81 | 5.44 | 11.36 | 82.66 | 5.98 | 8.52 | 86.86 | 4.62 |
| **Marginal Workers by Residence (Urban)** | | | | | | | | | | | | | | | | | | |
| | 23.07 | 69.53 | 7.40 | 9.51 | 87.57 | 2.92 | 4.38 | 87.37 | 8.25 | 4.70 | 90.69 | 4.61 | 5.24 | 86.37 | 8.39 | 4.34 | 91.72 | 3.94 |

*Sources:* Census of India, Various Issues.

In case of (Main + Marginal) by Residence Urban, group 15–59 possess 91.32 per cent of male and 88.38 per cent of female in 1981, 92.56 per cent of male and 92.50 per cent of female in 2001 and 94.16 per cent male and 93.62 per cent in 2011 of workforce Group 1559 accounts maximum percentage of workforce in all the three periods even after sub-category of main and marginal workers. In case of age group (marginal workers), male propound hallmark in the child labour group (0–14) accounts 40.24 per cent of male in 1981 and particularly age group (0–14) of marginal workers by rural accounts 40.96 per cent of male.

## District-Wise Work Participation Rate for J&K, 1981–2011

Among all districts, the crude work participation was found to be highest in Kargil district (54.94 per cent) and lowest 34.90 per cent in Srinagar district during 1981. In 2001, Punch replaced Kargil and installed the top rank of having 53.97 per cent and Baramulla having lowest crude work participation rate of 31.76 per cent. In both periods of 1981 and 2001, Udhampur accounts highest per cent of male work participation rate. In case of female, Kargil accounts highest per cent in 1981 and punch contributes highest per cent in 2001. In 2011, Udhampur (51.96 per cent) replaced Punch and evaluated at top rank. The crude work participation rate at district level in terms of gender during the reference periods is depicted in Table 4.51.

## Distribution of Workers by Educational Status, 1981–2011

The increase in educational level of workforce has been much faster during 1981–2011 compared to earlier decades. It may be observed from table that the literacy level among male workers gone up dramatically since 1981. In 1981, the literacy level among male workers stood at 37.25 in 2001, 59.90 and 68.3 in 2011 in terms of percentage. Likely

Table 4.51 District wise Crude Work Participation Rate, 1981–2011, (Percent)

| Districts | 1981 | | | 2001 | | | 2011 | | |
|---|---|---|---|---|---|---|---|---|---|
| | Total | Male | Female | Total | Male | Female | Total | Male | Female |
| Kupwara | 48.86 | 56.93 | 39.46 | 32.67 | 45.34 | 18.69 | 30.45 | 44.34 | 18.56 |
| Baramulla | 45.44 | 56.66 | 32.56 | 31.76 | 46.83 | 15.06 | 32.93 | 48.80 | 17.06 |
| Srinagar | 34.90 | 52.62 | 14.60 | 31.99 | 50.14 | 10.68 | 41.96 | 57.24 | 26.68 |
| Badgam | 48.73 | 58.65 | 37.46 | 35.91 | 48.53 | 22.34 | 41.95 | 58.50 | 25.40 |
| Pulwama | 50.70 | 56.53 | 44.19 | 32.58 | 46.95 | 17.36 | 31.34 | 44.32 | 18.36 |
| Anantnag | 42.44 | 56.18 | 27.27 | 33.69 | 45.95 | 20.39 | 33.50 | 46.70 | 20.30 |
| Leh/Ladakh | 50.39 | 59.46 | 40.15 | 49.58 | 58.32 | 38.97 | 48.64 | 54.36 | 34.92 |
| Doda | 43.36 | 55.52 | 29.90 | 46.00 | 52.72 | 38.56 | 42.29 | 50.08 | 34.50 |
| Kargil | 54.94 | 59.53 | 49.57 | 46.64 | 50.08 | 42.53 | 43.22 | 46.10 | 40.35 |
| Udhampur | 54.58 | 62.04 | 46.35 | 49.28 | 57.83 | 39.35 | 51.67 | 58.80 | 44.54 |
| Punch | 46.56 | 56.04 | 35.86 | 53.97 | 57.68 | 49.93 | 43.65 | 49.60 | 37.70 |
| Rajauri | 44.98 | 55.18 | 33.73 | 45.15 | 52.15 | 37.19 | 36.73 | 42.26 | 31.20 |
| Jammu | 39.43 | 52.46 | 25.02 | 33.25 | 50.56 | 13.32 | 39.09 | 59.76 | 18.43 |
| Kathua | 43.40 | 55.34 | 30.37 | 37.34 | 50.64 | 22.58 | 31.80 | 38.28 | 25.32 |

*Sources*: Various Reports of Census of India (J&K).

the literacy level among female workforce, only one-tenth of the workforce was literate in 1981, which increased to one-third of the female workforce in 2001. The percentage of total male workers with educational level above matric was 5.05 per cent in 1981; it accelerated to 28.07 per cent in 2001 and 43.7 in 2011. The educational level of all workers during 1981–2001 is depicted in Table 4.52.

While trend in the educational level of workers is very increasing, but the educational level reveals that human resources need to be developed far more in coming decades, at least half the male workforce should be matriculate by 2020 and we strive to achieve one-third of the female workforce to be matriculate by that time. In the state of J&K literate male workers shows highest per cent during the reference period in both rural and urban areas. As expected, urban areas show higher educational level than the rural areas in both main and marginal categories.

**Table 4.52** Total workers of J&K at education level, 1981–2011 (Percent)

| | 1981 | | | | | | 2001 | | | | | | 2011 | | | | | |
|---|---|---|---|---|---|---|---|---|---|---|---|---|---|---|---|---|---|---|
| | Male | | | Female | | | Male | | | Female | | | Male | | | Female | | |
| | L | BM | AM | L | BM | AM | L | BM | AM | L | BM | AM | L | BM | AM | L | BM | AM |
| | 37.25 | 32.20 | 5.05 | 9.75 | 8.49 | 1.26 | 59.90 | 28.70 | 28.07 | 27.56 | 14.02 | 10.07 | 68.3 | 24.5 | 43.7 | 40.1 | 22.2 | 19.2 |
| Total Workers according to Education (Rural) | | | | | | | | | | | | | | | | | | |
| | 32.72 | 30.15 | 2.27 | 7.88 | 7.59 | 0.29 | 54.12 | 30.49 | 20.18 | 18.73 | 12.21 | 6.06 | 61.3 | 33.6 | 27.7 | 26.8 | 18.1 | 8.64 |
| Total Workers according to Education (Urban) | | | | | | | | | | | | | | | | | | |
| | 56.24 | 40.81 | 15.43 | 37.90 | 22.10 | 15.80 | 75.87 | 23.47 | 49.89 | 52.63 | 12.52 | 42.58 | 83.5 | 30.7 | 52.8 | 73.2 | 27.4 | 45.8 |
| Main workers according to Education | | | | | | | | | | | | | | | | | | |
| | 33.89 | 30.72 | 5.17 | 16.96 | 10.97 | 5.99 | 54.41 | 29.17 | 22.07 | 24.84 | 11.04 | 9.39 | 66.9 | 32.7 | 34.2 | 31.5 | 17.6 | 13.9 |
| Marginal workers according to Education | | | | | | | | | | | | | | | | | | |
| | 35.89 | 30.72 | 5.16 | 16.94 | 10.97 | 5.98 | 53.29 | 35.15 | 14.07 | 23.87 | 15.67 | 5.15 | 59.4 | 39.2 | 20.2 | 29.8 | 18.5 | 11.3 |

L means literacy level; BM means below matric; and AM means above matric.

*Source* Compiled Census of India.

## Comparison NSSO & Census Data: Non-Agricultural Workers

A striking observation which catches attention is the minor divergence between the two sources. Table 4.53 gives the information of non-agricultural workers in terms of percentage to total workers according to NSS 38th, 55th & 67th Round and Censuses of 1981 and 2001 and 2011. It is examined trend of the non-agricultural workers to total workers in urban areas is more than 80 per cent from the both sources during three reference periods. Even last two censuses of 2001 and 2011, urban workers exceeded more than 90 in terms of percentage.

## Trend of Workforce in Respect of Gender, 1981–2011

With population and number of educated increasing in the state, the avenues of employment generation have not increased proportionately. Workforce increases with the increase of population, however, the pace of workforce is very low than population. The analysis of workforce during 1981 period, the State accounts 26.50 lakh of workforce that stood 47.85 per cent from total population. Male accounts 17.66 lakh (66.64 per cent) and female accounts 8.83 lakh (33.35 per cent). During 2001, the total workforce accounts 29.51 lakh, stood 29.31 per cent from total population. Male accounts 26.41 lakh (71.60 per cent) and female accounts 10.47 lakh (28.39 per cent). In 2011, the same stood 43.22 lakh (34.44 per cent) with male 71.60 per cent and female 12.27 per cent.

During the three decade period 19812011, workers-population ratio is low due to rapid growth of population, low female participation, and under-enumeration and omission of unpaid family workers even when according to the accepted concept they are to be classified as workers.

That workforce increased 26.50 lakhs to 43.22 lakhs in consonance with population growth 59.87 to 125.48 lakhs from 1981 to 2011. It accounts that workforce increased at low pace. The male working population increased continuously and female working population decelerated due to increase of girls' enrolment in the schools. Furthermore, apparently in J&K, women do not undertake job due to social inhibitions.

**Table 4.53** Comparison Between NSSO & Census Data, (Percent)

| NSS 38th R | | | Census 1981 | | | NSS 55th R | | | Census 2001 | | | NSS 67th R | | | Census 2011 | | |
|---|---|---|---|---|---|---|---|---|---|---|---|---|---|---|---|---|---|
| T | R | U | T | R | U | T | R | U | T | R | U | T | R | U | T | R | U |
| 31.1 | 20.3 | 83.9 | 36.1 | 15.6 | 84.4 | 37.1 | 12.8 | 87.2 | 51.0 | 5.5 | 94.5 | 49.6 | 10.6 | 89.4 | 58.5 | 4.8 | 95.2 |

*Sources:* NSS Reports and Various Issues of Census.

## Trends of Workforce in Terms of Area, 1981–2011

J&K economy at the time of 1971 was overwhelmingly rural and agricultural in character. The cause is perceived due to migration when dynamic nature of workforce is examined area wise. It is found that rural workers decreased and urban workers increased. Migration is due to high job opportunity and high wages in urban areas. Since most industries are concentrated in and around urban areas. The only place of cities and towns undergoes industrialization and construction, with the result state's economy shift to cities. Migration took place by farmers for better jobs in urban areas. The area wise change in workforce and sectoral shift of labour force (primary to non-primary sector) is related with Simon Kuznets Hypothesis. The Kuznet's curve implies that as a nation undergoes industrialization, the centre of nation's economy will shift to cities. The area wise shift of workforce from rural and urban is shown in Table 4.55.

Table 4.54  Sex Wise Working Population of J & K, 1981–2011 (Lakhs)

| Year | Pop | Work force | %age | Male Workers | %age | Female Workers | %age |
|------|-----|-----------|------|--------------|------|----------------|------|
| 1981 | 59.87 | 26.50 | 47.85 | 17.66 | 66.64 | 8.83 | 33.35 |
| 2001 | 100.69 | 29.51 | 29.30 | 26.41 | 89.79 | 3.10 | 10.21 |
| 2011 | 125.48 | 43.22 | 34.44 | 30.95 | 71.61 | | 28.38 |

*Source*: Economic census, Govt. of India, various issues

Table 4.55  Area wise work force between rural & urban population, (lakhs)

| Year | Rural Pop. | Rural Workers | %age | Urban Pop | Urban Workers | %age | D.I |
|------|-----------|---------------|------|-----------|---------------|------|-----|
| 1971 | 37.58 | 11.46 | 30.5 | 8.58 | 2.27 | 26.47 | 0.086 |
| 1981 | 42.76 | 22.55 | 52.75 | 12.60 | 3.94 | 31.32 | 0.388 |
| 2001 | 75.64 | 28.69 | 37.93 | 25.05 | 8.19 | 31.71 | 0.119 |
| 2011 | 91.65 | 23.66 | 25.17 | 33.83 | 11.26 | 33.29 | 0.149 |

*Source*: Economic Census, Govt. of India, Various Issues.

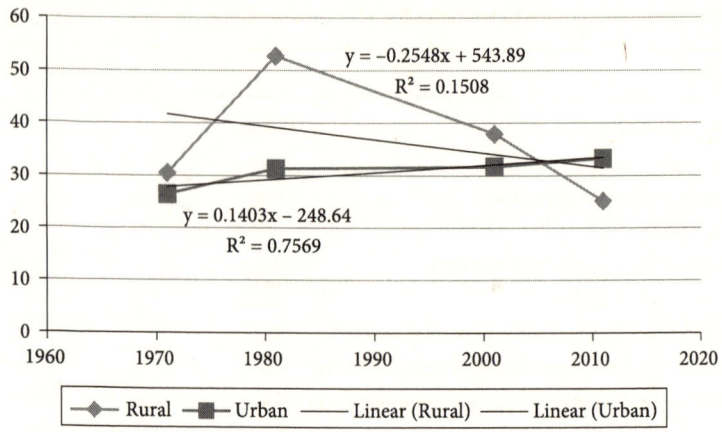

$$y = -0.2548x + 543.89$$
$$R^2 = 0.1508$$

$$y = 0.1403x - 248.64$$
$$R^2 = 0.7569$$

Efforts to examine urbanization, rate of workforce dwindled 30.5 per cent to 25.17 per cent in rural areas and whereas in urban areas increased from 26.47 to 33.29 in percentage terms during 1971 and 2011. Given all these perceptions, it is calculated that DI during 1981 is more than other decades.

## Categories of Workers, 1981–2011

We are witnessing a subtle but altering shift in the workforce pattern. As per reports of *Indicators of Regional Development (DES)*, the J&K State possess 43.23 lakh total numbers of workers which accounts 34.47 per cent from total population against 26.50 lakh and 44.26 per cent by 1981 census. It is pertinent to mention that cultivators have taken maximum proportion during 1981–2011.

## Trends of Labour Force into Three Major Economic Sectors, 1981–2011

The 1970 period was a period of near stagnation for J&K economy. At the time of 70s large people were engaged in agriculture which is judged and reflected by the unbalanced occupational structure with 71 per cent of

Table 4.56  Categories of workers for J&K, 1981–2011

| Years | | 1981 | 2001 | 2011 |
|---|---|---|---|---|
| Total population | Lakhs | 59.87 | 101.44 | 125.41 |
| Workforce | Lakhs | 26.50 | 37.54 | 43.23 |
| Workers per 100 of population | %age | 44.26 | 37.01 | 34.47 |
| Cultivators | Lakhs | 18.25 | 15.92 | 12.45 |
| Cultivators as %age of total workers | %age | 68.87 | 42.40 | 26.80 |
| Agricultural labourers | Lakhs | 0.77 | 2.46 | 5.48 |
| Agricultural labourers as %age of total workers | %age | 2.90 | 6.56 | 12.68 |
| Workers engaged in processing & manufacturing | Lakhs | 2.25 | 2.35 | 2.46 |
| Workers engaged in processing & manufacturing | %age | 8.49 | 6.25 | 7.38 |
| Other workers | Lakhs | 5.23 | 15.81 | 23.54 |
| Other workers as %age of Total workers | Lakhs | 19.74 | 44.79 | 54.52 |

*Source*: Survey conducted by the Directorate of Economics & Statistics (J&K); Census of India (J&K), Various Issues

working population or labour force occupied in agriculture or primary sector.

Among the three major sectors of economy—primary, secondary and tertiary sectors, there has been a decline, as expected, in the share of primary sector and increase in the share of tertiary in the total employment of labour force. Accordingly total labour force employed in primary sector was 71.55 per cent in 1971 which decreased to 41.48 per cent in 2011. It is due to advance of technology that absorbs less amount of labour force in agriculture fields. Secondary sector indicates a little erratic change and was around 10 per cent. The basic cause reflects lack of small scale and heavy manufacturing industries, poor road, and rail connectivity and lack of infrastructure has been a constant hurdle in the industrial development of the State. The structural transformation has been almost entirely from primary sector to tertiary sector, bypassing the secondary sector.

This phenomenon is at variance from the Kuznet's hypothesis, which has been supported by historical experience of many newly industrialized countries. There is a terrific rise in the percentage of the labour force employed in **service sector**. In 1971 the total labour force employed in

**Table 4.57** Trends of Labour force into Economic sectors, 1971–2011 (%age)

| Sectors | 1971 | 1981 | 2001 | 2011 |
|---|---|---|---|---|
| Primary | 71.55 | 63.88 | 50.10 | 41.48 |
| Secondary | 8.94 | 12.07 | 6.21 | 8.41 |
| Tertiary | 18.10 | 24.05 | 43.71 | 51.11 |
| | 100 | 100 | 100 | 100 |

*Source*: Economic census, Govt. of India, Various Issues. District Handbook, Department of Planning, 2011.

*Note*: In 1991, no census was held in J&K due to outbreak of violence.

**Table 4.58** Workforce Shift from Primary to Non-Primary Sector (%age)

| Year (Decadal) | 1981 | 1991 | 2001 | 2011 |
|---|---|---|---|---|
| Workforce in primary sector (%age) | 63.88 | 57.96 | 50.10 | 41.48 |
| Workforce in non-primary sector (%age) | 36.12 | 42.04 | 49.90 | 58.52 |
| Total | 100 | 100 | 100 | 100 |

*Sources* (1) Census of India (Various Issues), Govt. of India, (2) Digest of Statistics; J&K.

tertiary sector was 18.10 per cent which rises to 51.11 per cent in 2011 by tourism sector, communication, and transport. The trends of labour force into three economic sectors during the period, 1971–2011 in terms of percentage are shown in Table 4.57.

## Workforce Trend in Two Main Sectors, 1981–2011

The employment percentage share of primary sector has decreased continuously during the entire reference time period. It has decreased from 63.88 per cent in 1981 to 41.48 per cent in 2011 while as in non-primary sector percentage share has increased from 36.12 per cent in 1981 to 58.52 per cent in 2011. Therefore, 22.40 percentage points' of employment shifted from primary sector to non-primary.

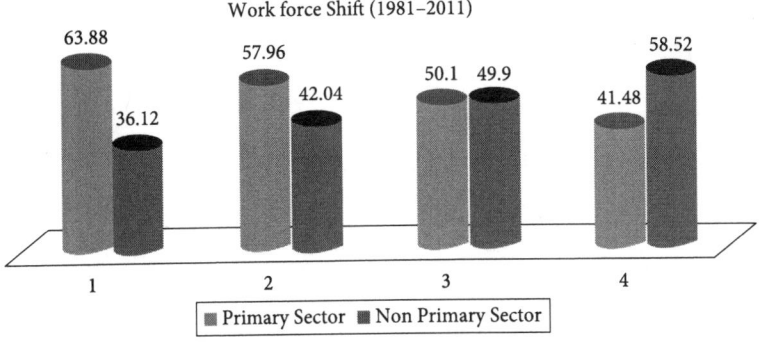

Work force Shift (1981–2011)

## Share of Child Labour (5–14) in Workforce in J&K State, 1981–2011

The child labour in Kashmir is a cause of concern for the government. Like other States, the State of J&K is also beset with the problem of child labour in view of its unique geographic features and other peculiarities. According to census 1981, the State of J&K had nearly 1 per cent of child workers. Its share increased steadily up to 2011. One important cause for increase in child labour in Kashmir is the prevailing strife in the valley. The ongoing armed struggle in the valley with political background has snatched patronage of many children making them orphans and increasing the number of widows with resultant increase in the number of households with female headship. The loss of breadwinners is bound to compel the children of such families to adopt menial occupations for subsistence and survival of families *(Reports of NCPCR)*. The share of Child Labour in workforce in the state, 1981–2011 is shown in :Table 4.59.

Table 4.59  Share of Child Labour (5-14) in work force in Kashmir, 1981–2011

| Year | 1981 | 2001 | 2011 |
|---|---|---|---|
| Percentage of Child Labour | 0.85 | 5.7 | 7.6 |

*Source\*:Census of India/NCPCR/Rehabilitation of Child Labourers in India' (1991).

## Sectoral Output-Labour Ratio, 1993–94
## to 2014–15

At the onset of effects of new policy regime, in 1993–94, the share of primary, secondary and tertiary sector in the State economy (NSDP) was 37.52, 17.59, and 44.89 per cent respectively. It was a period when the tertiary sector had started taking off. The share of a sector when related to PCY of the state shows that level of per capita income of a state and the primary sector share are inversely correlated. That is higher per capita income means the lower share of primary sector and vice-versa. On the other hand, there is a positive correlation between PCY level and the share of secondary and the tertiary sector.

In the year 2004–05, all states including J&K joined the tertiary sector led growth bandwagon except the states of Chhattisgarh, Jharkhand, HP, and Punjab. The output/labour ratio gives the output produced per unit of labour. It gives efficiency of labour for a particular sector.

In 2000–01, the output/labour ratio in primary, secondary and tertiary sector was 0.97, 0.55, and 1.28 respectively. That is to say, at the time of take off stage of tertiary sector, the efficiency of labour was the highest in tertiary sector as compared to the other two sectors. Two important facts emerged. First, invariably, the state with higher output/labour ratio in tertiary sector has a higher PCY and second, during the new policy regime, the output/labour ratio has improved in almost all the states including J&K State. The state with higher labour efficiency is leading towards tertiarization process. This is a lesson for the state trailing for revolution that if higher growth level of income and higher PCI is to be achieved, the key to success lies in the development of human resources. The tertiarization of a region is a function of intellectual capital endowments.

Table 4.60 Sectoral output/Labour ratios in relation to PCY for J&K

| Years | Primary | Secondary | Tertiary |
|-------|---------|-----------|----------|
| 1993–94 | 0.83 | 1.27 | 1.09 |
| 2000–01 | 0.97 | 0.55 | 1.28 |
| 2004–05 | 0.94 | 0.41 | 1.57 |
| 2014–15 | 0.99 | 0.52 | 2.08 |

Calculated

**Table 4.61** Output share by Primary & Non-Primary Sector (%age)

| Year (Decadal) | 1981 | 2001 | 2011 |
|---|---|---|---|
| Output of Primary sector (%age) | 47.40 | 32.59 | 21.98 |
| Out-put of non-primary sector (%age) | 52.61 | 67.41 | 78.02 |
| | 100 | 100 | 100 |

*Source*: Census of India; Digest of Statistics, Directorate of Economics and Statistics (Govt. of J&K).

**Table 4.62** Workforce and Output of Primary Sector, 1981–2011

| Year (Decadal) | 1981 | 1991 | 2001 | 2011 |
|---|---|---|---|---|
| Workforce in Tertiary sector (in %) | 21.87 | 32.53 | 43.67 | 54.53 |
| Out-put of Tertiary sector (in %) | 39.7 | 44.72 | 47.19 | 52.26 |

*Sources*: Census of India & Digest of Statistics; Govt. of J&K, Various Issues.

The analysis of structural change is indicative of the fact that transformation of State economy from primary to tertiary sector has bypassed the secondary sector altogether. The employment and output share in the tertiary sector has grown at a synchronous pace however; the output share has outnumbered the corresponding employment share which is matter of concern from the policy point of view.

The share of primary sector in output has decreased by 25.42 per cent in contrast of workforce increased by 22.40 percentage points from 1981 to 2011. However, when fall of output is more than fall of employment in primary sector then the work supports Chenery's pattern of structural change.

It becomes clear that there is the presence of asymmetry between the output and employment share in shifting from primary to the non-primary sector. Same statement as noted by T. S. Papola at national level, *A sharper decline in the contribution of agriculture in GDP than in its share in employment implies a decline in its relative productivity and increase in income differentials between agriculture and the non-agriculture sectors.* An opposite trend is seen in services, where the increase in GDP share has been faster than in employment.

It is clear that the employment and the output share in the tertiary sector move in the same direction, at different speed leads to a high degree of employment and output equality in the state economy which is a viable change so for the 'Standard Structural Change Theory' is concerned as it leads to income and productivity.

However, during the three decade period 1981 to 2011, the employment elasticity of the tertiary sector dwindled 0.62 to 0.13 (Digest, 2011, DES). Therefore, the tertiary sector justified as fragile to become the absorber of last resort of the workforce in the state economy. The matter of concern for the state economy is that whether the tertiary sector sustains or not as it has by-passed the secondary sector of the state economy which is not feasible shift so for the 'Standard Structural Change Theory' is concerned. So, policy makers have to frame the policies for the state economy that the secondary sector may get encouraged so that we complete the first stage of the Structural Change Theory.

J&K economy has shown high levels of growth and PCY in recent years accompanied by an unprecedented shift of labour from agriculture to non-agriculture during the last decades. The reallocation of labour from traditional to modern segments in an economy having large surplus labour was conceived in the Lewisian framework as the process by way of which both accumulation of capital and exhaustion of surplus labour takes place.

Historical evidence from advanced countries as well as those of growing economies since 1960 suggests a negative association between growth in GDP per capita and the share of the labour force in the primary sector. The casual relationship between the process of accumulation of capital that drives growth and that of structural change was captured in Arthur Lewis's seminal work on underdeveloped economies. Lewis (1954) brought to the fore the central concern of developing countries having resource constraints such as low levels of investment and savings and at the same time reserves of surplus labour and highlighted how to generate capital accumulation from the surplus labour that these developing economies. The answer to this question relied in appreciating the fact that economies having large volume of surplus labour in primary sector have the option to increase accumulation of capital in the modern sector at a more or less unchanged real wage so long as labour is not a scarce factor. Hence development is conceived as processes that progressively utilize available labour in a productive way and gradually reduces the share of decreasing returns activities in the economy, be it in agriculture or in non-agriculture.

In this context, we discuss the present scenario of J&K economy which shows high levels of growth and PCY by an unprecedented shift of population from agriculture to non-agriculture since 1981. Now, how does the structural change in employment in Kashmir since 1980s approximate Lewisian transformation? There is no doubt about the fact that the rapid growth in non-agricultural employment over the decades in J&K appear to be the kind of structural transformation *Lewis* conceived. Not only is there a market shift in employment from agriculture to industry and services, but it has almost happened keeping real wages in the modern sector more or less unchanged. Nevertheless, the Lewisian transformation does not imply only accumulation of surplus in the modern sector facing a fixed real wage scenario subsequently there should be gradual process of the exhaustion of the surplus labour.

At this moment leaving aside the dynamic issues related to technology and investment of accumulated surplus the simpler version would say that with a given technology, accumulation of surplus shall continue to increase as more and more labour are drawn out from traditional sector presuming that this transfer is engaging disguised unemployed population to productive employment, that is, where labour produces more than they receive.

In this context shift in employment from agriculture to industry is justified on the ground that it essentially reallocates labour from diminishing returns activities to activities with increasing returns. And increasing returns scenario implies higher growth and higher labour productivity accompanied by no limit to employment at the subsistence wage level. The incentives for migration from traditional sectors, according to *Lewis*, could be a reasonable real wage gap, the inter-sectoral 'hill' between wages in two sectors. Although the shift employment from agriculture to non-agriculture with employment in the informal sector being the larger share cannot be explained by wage differentials alone. Informal employment in non-agriculture may grow because of many reasons depending on productivity and incomes in the agriculture as well as relative income sharing opportunities in agriculture and non-agriculture. If the growth in agriculture slows down and the sector fails to produce additional employment opportunities, according to *Harris-Todaro model*, a small increase in the formal sector employment may result in large rural-urban migration. And in the extreme case, when the formal sector employment happens to be contracting then also in all possibilities it could be accompanied by a relative large informal sector because those retrenched from formal sectors would find jobs in the informal sector.

It would be quite reasonable to conclude that the expansion of non-agricultural employment is a result of the push factor, that is, a result of declining incomes in agriculture and second, informal sector appears to be the last resort for those thrown out of formal sector jobs. In either of these cases, there is no reason to believe that this process relocates labour from low productivity income sharing segment to the high-productivity income generating opportunities.

## Area-Wise Workers by Broad Industry Division, 1993–2012

Percentage distribution of workers in the principal status by broad industry division depicts that in the year 1993–94, statistics are indicative of the fact that in rural area, the dominant occupation is the primary sector. Structural change in employment pattern shows that in rural areas, the employment share of primary sector that was 64.1 per cent in 1993–94 has come down to 40.01 per cent in the year 2011–12. Employment share of secondary sector has improved to 25.24 per cent in 2011–12 as compared to 16.1 per cent in the year 1993–94.

Tertiary sector employment share improved from 19.5 per cent to 34.75 per cent during the same period. In urban area the share of primary is almost negligible in the year 2011–12. But the secondary sector employment has improved from 18.1 per cent in 1993–94 to 25.0 per cent in the year 2011–12. Share of tertiary sector that is still above the national mark of 60 per cent has slightly gone down. So, the Table 4.63 shows that tertiary sector is the major employer in urban areas and it is picking up in the rural areas.

Another dimension of employment structure is the sex-wise distribution of labour force across the sectors, over a period of time (table). In the year 2011–12, share of services sector employment 70.0 per cent for the

Table 4.63  Area wise workers by Broad Industry Division (Percent)

|  | Sector | Rural Male | Rural Female | Total Rural | Urban Male | Urban Female | Total Urban |
|---|---|---|---|---|---|---|---|
| 1993–94 | Primary | 59.9 | 86.7 | 64.1 | 6.9 | 15.1 | 8.0 |
|  | Secondary | 18.2 | 4.9 | 16.1 | 19.7 | 4.9 | 18.1 |
|  | Tertiary | 21.8 | 7.8 | 19.5 | 73.8 | 78.0 | 73.8 |
| 1999–2000 | Primary | 66.1 | 74.8 | 66.7 | 11.6 | 0.1 | 10.7 |
|  | Secondary | 15.7 | 10.4 | 15.3 | 22.2 | 27.7 | 22.5 |
|  | Tertiary | 14.4 | 14.9 | 17.9 | 66.4 | 72.3 | 66.6 |
| 2007–08 | Primary | 50.0 | 48.4 | 49.9 | 6.8 | 5.3 | 6.6 |
|  | Secondary | 22.3 | 26.0 | 22.7 | 24.3 | 31.9 | 25.3 |
|  | Tertiary | 27.6 | 25.6 | 27.5 | 68.8 | 62.8 | 68.1 |
| 2011–12 | Primary | 45.0 | 46.21 | 45.11 | 5.2 | 4.5 | 5.4 |
|  | Secondary | 25.03 | 28.0 | 24.74 | 24.6 | 28.9 | 24.5 |
|  | Tertiary | 29.97 | 25.7 | 30.15 | 70.0 | 66.6 | 70.1 |

*Source*: NSSO, Various Rounds.

male and 66.6 per cent for the female in urban areas. In secondary sector, the employment share of female has been 28.9 per cent against the mark of 24.6 per cent for male. So the urban area is characterized by higher share of female workforce in secondary sector and slightly lower share in service sector. In rural area, the employment share, in secondary, of female is higher than the male. Temporal change in employment structure shows that the female share in primary sector in rural areas has drastically gone down and has moved to secondary and tertiary sector. In urban areas, the female workforce relieved by primary sector has gone to basically the secondary sector. In the structural change, the female has been gainer in moving to secondary and tertiary sector in the last two decades.

## Growth Rate of Labour Force for J&K State, 2007–12/2012–17

According to *NCEUS Report (2011)*, growth rate in labour force between 2007/2012 was 1.59 million which increased to 1.76 million during

**Table 4.64**  Growth Rate in Labour Force, 2007–12/2012–17 (in million)

| Labour Force, 2007 to 2012 | | | Labour Force, 2012 to 2017 |
|---|---|---|---|
| Rural | Male | 1.52 | 1.77 |
| | Female | 0.97 | 1.43 |
| | Total | 1.26 | 1.66 |
| Urban | Male | 2.95 | 2.24 |
| | Female | 2.25 | 1.03 |
| | Total | 2.84 | 1.92 |
| Total | Male | 1.88 | 1.86 |
| | Female | 0.93 | 1.39 |
| | Total | 1.59 | 1.76 |

*Source*: Report from National Commission for Enterprise in the Unorganized Sector.

**Table 4.65**  Labour Force for 2012 and 2017 (in millions)

| Labour Force for 2012 | | | Labour Force Projections for 2017 |
|---|---|---|---|
| Rural | Male | 2.61 | 2.85 |
| | Female | 1.36 | 1.46 |
| | Total | 3.96 | 4.30 |
| Urban | Male | 1.11 | 1.24 |
| | Female | 0.19 | 0.20 |
| | Total | 1.30 | 1.43 |
| Total | Male | 3.72 | 4.08 |
| | Female | 1.54 | 1.65 |
| | Total | 5.26 | 5.74 |

*Source* National Commission for Enterprise in the Unorganized Sector.

2012/2017. The cause of increase in rural areas was due to Employment Schemes like NREGA and NRHM. The growth rate in labour force during the reference period declined in the urban areas and however, female dwindled steeply.

## Labour Force Age Group-Wise (UPSS), 2007, 2012, & 2017

The size of economically active population is determined by the age structure. Growth of population in the working age group (15–59) is at present around 2.4 per cent, substantially higher than growth of overall population. Since labour force participation is not uniform across age groups, the size of labour force is influenced by age structure.

The question is whether the deceleration in the labour force growth would continue into the future. It could be so if it has been caused by a structural change in the economy. Some decline in labour force growth could be due to a slower growth in working age population. The decline in participation rates observed needs to be carefully examined in terms of trends in different segments of the population and by different age groups and in a longer-term perspective. It is seen that decline in participation rates across age groups, in most of the cases, either fit into a longer term trend or changes are not very significant.

The decline in the LFPR in the younger age group reflects longer term trend of shift in activity status of this group towards education. This trend is likely to continue in future. In this background, the future projections of labour force in relation to working age population have to be considered. The participation rates for younger age groups have dropped much more than other age groups. In the 10–14 years age group, decline will be to near zero in the next 5–8 years as elementary education becomes compulsory.

## Sectoral Employment Shares for J&K State, 1983–2015

With economic development, agriculture is expected to decline in importance in terms of its share in employment and output. Proportion of primary sector in total employment has declined from 79.5 per cent in 1983 to 35.30 per cent in 2014–15. However the proportion of tertiary sector in employment increased tremendously from 8.1 to 38.46 per cent between 1983 and 2014–15. The share in secondary sector rose nearly twofold of 12.14–22.64. The sectoral share of employment for State from 1983 to 2014–15 in terms of percentage is shown in :Table 4.67.

**Table 4.66** Age-Sex MCWS Labour Force of J&K in 2007 (in million)

| Group | Rural | | | Urban | | | Rural + Urban | | |
|-------|-------|--------|-------|------|------|------|------|------|------|
|       | Male  | Female | Total | M    | F    | T    | M    | F    | T    |
| 0–4   | 0.00  | 0.00   | 0.00  | 0.00 | 0.00 | 0.00 | 0.00 | 0.00 | 0.00 |
| 5–9   | 0.00  | 0.00   | 0.00  | 0.00 | 0.00 | 0.00 | 0.00 | 0.00 | 0.00 |
| 11–14 | 0.01  | 0.01   | 0.03  | 0.00 | 0.02 | 0.02 | 0.01 | 0.03 | 0.04 |
| 15–19 | 0.23  | 0.10   | 0.33  | 0.01 | 0.01 | 0.03 | 0.25 | 0.12 | 0.36 |
| 20–24 | 0.36  | 0.14   | 0.50  | 0.12 | 0.02 | 0.14 | 0.48 | 0.17 | 0.65 |
| 25–29 | 0.33  | 0.11   | 0.44  | 0.15 | 0.03 | 0.17 | 0.47 | 0.14 | 0.61 |
| 30–34 | 0.27  | 0.10   | 0.37  | 0.14 | 0.02 | 0.16 | 0.42 | 0.11 | 0.53 |
| 35–39 | 0.25  | 0.09   | 0.34  | 0.13 | 0.02 | 0.15 | 0.38 | 0.11 | 0.49 |
| 40–44 | 0.22  | 0.07   | 0.30  | 0.12 | 0.01 | 0.13 | 0.34 | 0.09 | 0.43 |
| 45–49 | 0.19  | 0.05   | 0.25  | 0.10 | 0.01 | 0.11 | 0.29 | 0.07 | 0.36 |
| 50–54 | 0.15  | 0.04   | 0.19  | 0.08 | 0.01 | 0.08 | 0.23 | 0.04 | 0.28 |
| 55–59 | 0.11  | 0.03   | 0.15  | 0.05 | 0.00 | 0.05 | 0.16 | 0.04 | 0.20 |
| 60+   | 0.23  | 0.04   | 0.27  | 0.05 | 0.00 | 0.06 | 0.28 | 0.04 | 0.33 |
| Total | 2.36  | 0.08   | 3.16  | 0.95 | 0.16 | 1.11 | 3.31 | 0.95 | 4.26 |

Age-Sex MCWS Labour Force of Jammu & Kashmir in 2012 (in million)

| Group | Rural | | | Urban | | | Rural + Urban | | |
|-------|-------|--------|-------|------|------|-------|------|------|-------|
|       | Male  | Female | Total | M    | F    | Total | M    | F    | Total |
| 0–4   | 0.00  | 0.00   | 0.00  | 0.00 | 0.00 | 0.00  | 0.00 | 0.00 | 0.00  |
| 5—9   | 0.00  | 0.00   | 0.00  | 0.00 | 0.00 | 0.00  | 0.00 | 0.00 | 0.00  |
| 11–14 | 0.00  | 0.00   | 0.00  | 0.00 | 0.01 | 0.01  | 0.00 | 0.01 | 0.01  |
| 15–19 | 0.18  | 0.10   | 0.27  | 0.00 | 0.01 | 0.03  | 0.18 | 0.11 | 0.29  |
| 20–24 | 0.38  | 0.17   | 0.55  | 0.13 | 0.03 | 0.16  | 0.51 | 0.19 | 0.71  |
| 25–29 | 0.39  | 0.13   | 0.52  | 0.17 | 0.03 | 0.20  | 0.56 | 0.16 | 0.72  |
| 30–34 | 0.31  | 0.10   | 0.42  | 0.16 | 0.02 | 0.18  | 0.47 | 0.12 | 0.60  |
| 35–39 | 0.26  | 0.09   | 0.35  | 0.15 | 0.02 | 0.17  | 0.41 | 0.11 | 0.51  |
| 40–44 | 0.23  | 0.07   | 0.30  | 0.14 | 0.01 | 0.15  | 0.37 | 0.08 | 0.45  |
| 45–49 | 0.21  | 0.06   | 0.27  | 0.12 | 0.02 | 0.13  | 0.33 | 0.07 | 0.40  |
| 50-54 | 0.17  | 0.04   | 0.22  | 0.10 | 0.01 | 0.10  | 0.27 | 0.05 | 0.32  |
| 55–59 | 0.13  | 0.04   | 0.17  | 0.07 | 0.00 | 0.07  | 0.20 | 0.04 | 0.25  |
| 60+   | 0.27  | 0.04   | 0.31  | 0.07 | 0.00 | 0.07  | 0.34 | 0.05 | 0.38  |
| Total | 2.54  | 0.84   | 3.38  | 1.10 | 0.16 | 1.16  | 3.64 | 1.00 | 4.63  |

**Table 4.66** Continued

Projected Age-Sex MCWS Labour Force of J&K State in 2017 (in million)

| Group | Rural | | | Urban | | | Rural + Urban | | |
|---|---|---|---|---|---|---|---|---|---|
| | Male | Female | Total | M | F | Total | M | F | Total |
| 0–4 | 0.00 | 0.00 | 0.00 | 0.00 | 0.00 | 0.00 | 0.00 | 0.00 | 0.00 |
| 5–9 | 0.00 | 0.00 | 0.00 | 0.00 | 0.00 | 0.00 | 0.00 | 0.00 | 0.00 |
| 11–14 | 0.00 | 0.00 | 0.00 | 0.00 | 0.01 | 0.01 | 0.00 | 0.01 | 0.01 |
| 15–19 | 0.16 | 0.08 | 0.25 | 0.00 | 0.01 | 0.01 | 0.16 | 0.10 | 0.26 |
| 20–24 | 0.36 | 0.16 | 0.52 | 0.13 | 0.02 | 0.15 | 0.49 | 0.18 | 0.67 |
| 25–29 | 0.45 | 0.15 | 0.59 | 0.18 | 0.03 | 0.21 | 0.63 | 0.17 | 0.80 |
| 30–34 | 0.38 | 0.13 | 0.51 | 0.18 | 0.02 | 0.20 | 0.56 | 0.15 | 0.71 |
| 35–39 | 0.29 | 0.10 | 0.40 | 0.17 | 0.02 | 0.19 | 0.46 | 0.12 | 0.59 |
| 40–44 | 0.25 | 0.07 | 0.32 | 0.15 | 0.01 | 0.17 | 0.40 | 0.09 | 0.49 |
| 45–49 | 0.22 | 0.06 | 0.28 | 0.13 | 0.02 | 0.15 | 0.35 | 0.08 | 0.43 |
| 50–54 | 0.19 | 0.05 | 0.24 | 0.11 | 0.01 | 0.12 | 0.31 | 0.06 | 0.37 |
| 55–59 | 0.16 | 0.05 | 0.21 | 0.08 | 0.01 | 0.09 | 0.24 | 0.06 | 0.29 |
| 60+ | 0.32 | 0.05 | 0.37 | 0.09 | 0.00 | 0.09 | 0.41 | 0.06 | 0.47 |
| Total | 2.78 | 0.91 | 3.69 | 1.23 | 0.17 | 1.40 | 4.01 | 1.08 | 5,08 |

*Source*: The Challenges of Employment in India, Volume II, NCEUS; MCWS (Modified Current Weekly Status) Approach in Labour Force Measurement.

**Table 4.67**  Sectoral Share of employment (UPSS) for J&K (Percent)

| Sector | 1983 | 1993–94 | 2004–05 | 2014–15 |
|---|---|---|---|---|
| **Primary Sector** | 79.5 | 76.59 | 64.84 | 38.30 |
| Mining & Quarrying | 0.20 | 0.10 | 0.30 | 0.26 |
| Manufacturing | 4.68 | 4.01 | 10.06 | 10.78 |
| Construction | 7.26 | 6.0 | 7.10 | 11.60 |
| **Secondary Sector** | 12.14 | 10.11 | 17.46 | 22.64 |
| Trade & Hostelling etc. | 1.9 | 2.5 | 5.0 | 9.38 |
| Transport & Communication etc. | 1.4 | 2.7 | 4.0 | 11.48 |
| Finance, Insu., Real est. & business Services | 0.4 | 0.6 | 0.2 | 8.03 |
| Community, social & personal services | 4.6 | 7.5 | 8.5 | 9.57 |
| **Tertiary Sector** | 8.1 | 13.3 | 17.7 | 38.46 |
| All Non Agricultural | 20.24 | 24.0 | 43.70 | 61.7 |
| Total | 100 | 100 | 100 | 100 |

*Source*: Estimates based on various rounds of NSSO data, Rounds of 38thR, 50thR, 6thR & 72nd of NSS.

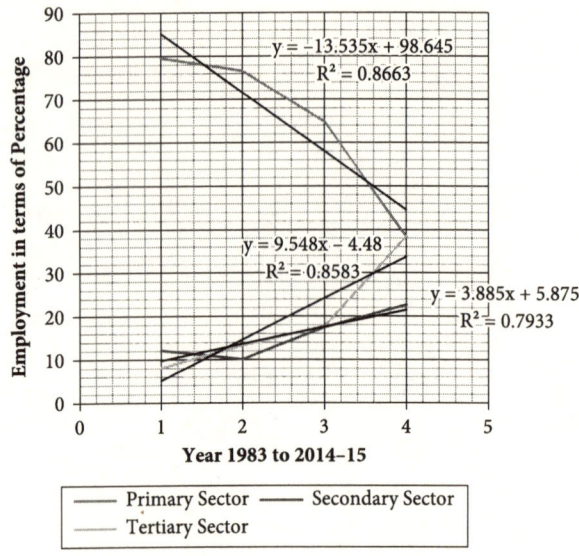

y = −13.535x + 98.645
R² = 0.8663

y = 9.548x − 4.48
R² = 0.8583

y = 3.885x + 5.875
R² = 0.7933

Year 1983 to 2014–15

——— Primary Sector  ——— Secondary Sector
——— Tertiary Sector

The decline in employment share of agriculture has been mostly compensated by an increase in the share of secondary sector in the pre-reform period but since the economic reforms the tertiary sector has been the main gainer of employment. Within the secondary sector, construction (7.26 per cent to 11.60 per cent) followed by manufacturing (4.40 per cent to 10.50 per cent) has sharply increased its share in employment. In the tertiary sector, transport and Communication (1.4 per cent to 11.48 per cent) experienced a fast increase in its share in employment. Financial services (0.4–8.03) also registered a fast increase in its employment. Community, social and personal services which used to the largest activity in the tertiary sector, is now the small in terms of employment. In every decade, the share of tertiary sector in employment growth increases by 9.54 per cent and primary sector declined by 13.58 points.

The linkages between agriculture and other sectors of the economy have been extensively investigated in the study work. In the early analysis, agriculture assumed to play the role of providing labour and raw material for the development of industry and services. It held that surplus labour forces available in the agriculture sector could be transferred for rapid industrialization as well for tertiary sector growth. In the subsequent analysis, the intersectoral linkages, both from the demand and supply sides gained prominence.

# 5

# Issues of Unemployment and Underemployment

Unemployment is a curse for any nation. No nation can develop unless its labour force is engaged in gainful employment. In fact, the whole national income is the sum total of wages, rent, profit, and interest, which is simply share of different factor payments. So, when these factors are employed then national income increases and economic growth takes place. Unemployment means a situation when able and willing are not getting jobs as per their own capabilities.

Occupation is one of the important determinants of one's social status, while as unemployment is a state that reflects the failure of the youth to achieve certain socially expected and accepted goals. However, it is verily the society that provides the required means for its individuals to achieve the expected goals. Proper education, family background, personal interest, available facilities, socio-political standing, etc. are some of the factors responsible for one's success in the society and vice-versa related to their unemployment (Ahmad, 2016).

The state of J&K has shown high economic growth but has not been able to meet the aspirations of the youth who are looking for opportunities for education and employment. Frequent disturbances have created an atmosphere of uncertainty, impacting employment creation which has alienated the youth.

The current unrest environment surfaced since 90s makes it difficult to attract large scale private investment into the state, especially in the industrial sector. The alternative is to focus on the agriculture and services sectors that have the potential to generate jobs quickly. However, agriculture sector responds quickly, that is, in a short run to the investments and productivity.

In order to understand the situation of J&K, it is important to understand the rapid demographic transition bearing historically unprecedented numbers of young people. These demographic changes potentially witnessed

*Jammu & Kashmir*. Bilal Ahmad Khan, Oxford University Press. © Oxford University Press 2022.
DOI: 10.1093/oso/9780192849656.003.0005

rapid rate of population against workforce. The population increased at exceeding rate, cause the abysmal problem of unemployment rate. The workforce registered an increase of 14.4 per cent against undesirous 23 per cent of population between 2001 and 2011 period (Digest, 2011–12, DES).

Young people are a major human resource for development, key agents for social change, and driving force for economic development and technological innovation. However, the same resource is a daunting and major challenge. The youth challenge is considered as the most critical for the economic development of conflict zone of Kashmir. The critical aspects of the challenge are mostly related to labour market entry where young people encounter difficulties in finding and maintaining a decent job. Failure to integrate youth into the labour market has appalling consequences for the development.

Education level is increasing at an alarming rate. However, the problem youth face is that they cannot earn their livelihood after completing their degrees. They remain jobless most of the time. The problem of educated unemployment constitutes a serious and menacing problem. The educated unemployed are more dangerous than uneducated person. Even the grievance if long continued the situation is explosive and constant threat to the security and stability of the State. The unemployed person belong to the category are '*not dumb*' drive cattle, but intelligent people and will not accept an uneven viable position lying down. If educated people remain idle, then state of affairs deserves strong condemnation. It involves wastage of human resources (Bhatt & Anwar, 2013).

The problem of educated unemployment in the context of J&K State involves a more social waste than a private loss. The government has been fully subsidizing the education at all the stages of education ladder. However due to non-utilization and under-utilization, the educated manpower produced from the existing system decreases the social return (Nisar, 2007).

J&K is one of those developing state which continue to have the problem of unemployment and underemployment despite continuous policy emphasis and programmes to eliminate the problem. What is important at this moment is to look in to the reasons for the ever-increasing unemployment in the state and recognize our strength and potential. The State faces this problem despite its strong human and natural resources due to ferocities and lackadaisical policies, pursued by the subsequent governments which converted state economy into fragile economy and make the state of J&K into conditions of what is known as *dependency syndrome*. Thus ferocities and imprudent policies have eroded our strengths (Haq, 2015).

Underdevelopment and unemployment in J&K state is the manifestation of *mismatch* between physical and human resources technically known as structural unemployment. In simple words this type of unemployment exists when a large segment of working-age population does not possess the appropriate skills and knowledge. The State owes many resources in connection with employment generation however, suffer shortage of skilled labour. This acute shortage of manpower has encouraged migration of casual workers from other states of India. As per report from 2001 census, there are nearly 1.65 lakhs in-migrants and 2.24 lakh out-migrant workers in J&K State. It means 2.24 lakh are spread throughout India for job which accounts lack of job avenues in the state. Thus, the state is rendering huge unemployment problem because result huge out-migrants take place for the search of job. Consequently, the impact seems extremely ambivalent. On the one hand, there are no job opportunities in the state and on the other hand, hopes are strained due to lack of skilled labour.

But the important points that our youth are not entering into the ventures, is a matter of their psychological makeup, imprudent policies, and missing enlightened institutions which can be broken only by big push in education. It is the job of the academics in the higher educational institutions not only to create and disseminate the knowledge, but also to find the ways and means of its application through innovations. Education institutions are less significant and lot resentment among parents, students and industry due to lack of innovation and entrepreneurship in the universities. There must be link between university and industry. Whatever is produced from the university should be required in the industry. This brings us a very important corollary that human resource through education system and physical resources are moving in diverse directions with the result the input–output relation in a production function, as taught in the text books, does not hold for J&K (GK, 28 April 2015).

Even there is no perfect source of the magnitude of educated unemployment in the state of J&K. That is why efforts government always remain unavailing to achieve the target. Alhough, the government fails to make effective steps to make registration compulsory in employment exchanges. The records in the employment exchanges cannot be taken as an accurate estimate of the magnitude of unemployment. The number of applications on the register of exchange stood at 130.47 thousand in 1992 against 66.74 thousand in 1984. It accelerated to 111.07 thousands in 2016 (JK Economic Survey, 2016–17). The decrease in registration level

**Table 5.1**  Trend values of unemployment in J&K State, thousands

| Year | Unemployment Trend | Log | Growth Rate |
|------|--------------------|-----|-------------|
| 1984 | 66.74 | *4.200804* | 8.74098 |
| 1992 | 130.47 | *4.871143* | 3.151475 |
| 2000 | 167.23 | *5.11937* | −5.52531 |
| 2008 | 106.13 | *4.664665* | 0.570319 |
| 2016 | 111.07 | *4.710161* | – |

*Sources*: Various issues, JK Economic survey (DES)

is possible due to the fact that all unemployed do not get registered themselves. Table 5.1 depicts trend values of unemployment based on various
J&K Annual Economic Surveys.

## Chart

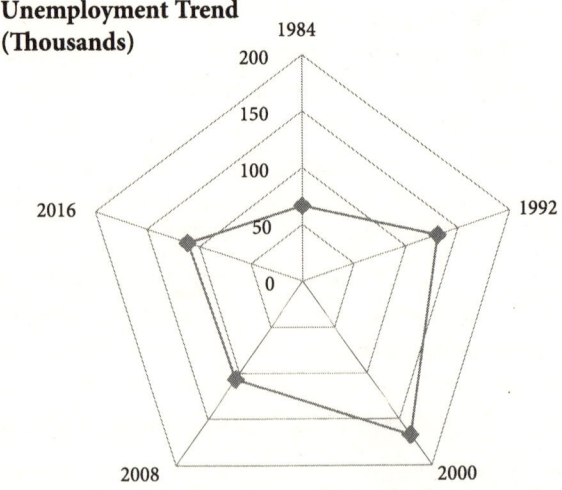

Log = ln(trend value)
Growth Rate = (exp ((next year trend−present year trend)/gap) −1)*100

It is elucidated that education level and unemployed rate ranching
at same direction. The analysis between the levels of education and the

rate of unemployment is that young people with some education do not want to engage in low-productivity, low-income work, and in informal sectors. They tend to seek non-manual work, preferably in the organized sector. They have a very good reason for doing this, since the service sector actually offers the best quality jobs. The very fact is that their families have some capacity to support them. Thus unemployment is a luxury in the J&K state, which at least some of them can offer, since aspirations; ability to afford unemployment and level of education all move together, the outcome is a positive relationship between levels of education and the rate of educated unemployed (GK, Ali, 2007).

General education does not equip the educated with particular technical skills. The educated, therefore, may not necessarily find employment even when the organized sector generates employment at a rapid pace. Moreover, wage differentials corresponding to differentials in the level of education are really market determined, excessive level of education leads to their unemployment, rather than narrowing of wage differentials between educated and illiterate.

Thus, a positive relationship between the rate of unemployment and the level of educational could be established. It is observed that rate of unemployment is best indicator of labour market mismatches, generated by spread of general education.

## Qualification Wise Unemployed Job Seekers, 1981–2011

The Table 5.2 gives a clear picture regarding qualification-wise number of unemployed persons in terms of percentage registered in different employment exchanges of the State. The unemployment at different levels of general education registered shows matriculate unemployed is higher than graduates and post-graduates. In 1981, the illiterate and matriculate up to Graduation accounted 26.15 and 23.92 per cent followed by below matric category (14.21 per cent) respectively. The matriculates show an increasing trend during 1981 to 2016. The matriculation up to graduation rose to 58.11 per cent from 23.92. While the illiterate category shows steep decline. The qualification-wise unemployed person from 19812016 periods is depicted in Table 5.2.

**Table 5.2** Qualification–wise Unemployed persons Register, 1981–2016, per cent

| Category | 1981 | 1991 | 2001 | 2011 | 2016 |
|---|---|---|---|---|---|
| Illiterate | 26.55 | 19.93 | 12.74 | 6.12 | 0.19 |
| Below Matric | 14.21 | 16.34 | 18.62 | 5.15 | 7.72 |
| Matric & Above | 23.92 | 38.10 | 36.77 | 41.46 | 58.11 |
| Graduate | 11.42 | 9.94 | 13.05 | 14.13 | 19.74 |
| Post-Graduate | 3.22 | 2.10 | 4.94 | 3.45 | 6.28 |
| Degree Engineers | 0.49 | 0.63 | 2.85 | 6.01 | 1.87 |
| Diploma Engineer | 0.51 | 0.62 | 2.78 | 12.89 | 2.77 |
| ITI Trained | 3.12 | 2.38 | 2.76 | 8.29 | 2.38 |
| Skilled (other than ITI) | 15.74 | 9.94 | 5.48 | 2.48 | 0.58 |
| Total | 100 | 100 | 100 | 100 | 100 |

*Sources*: JK Economic Survey, various issues, Govt. of J&K

**Chart (Colum)**

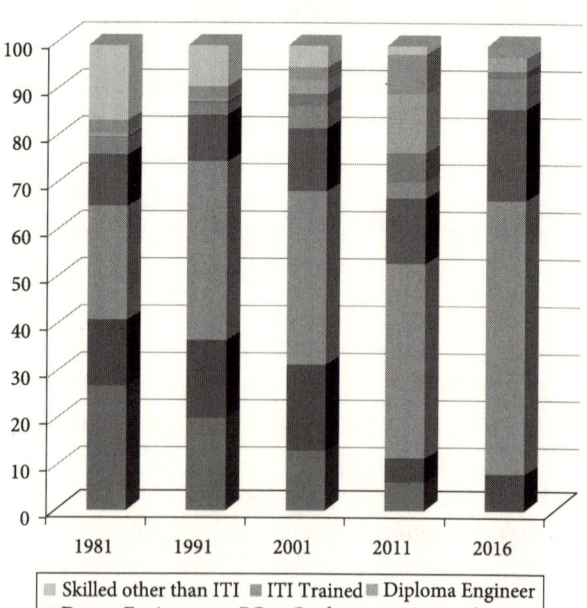

The graduate unemployed shows regular increasing trends since 1991. These observations prove that incidence of unemployment is comparatively more pronounced among matriculation and above (undergraduates).

Thus, the employment exchange data indicates the large magnitude of job seekers as the number of such persons has been swelling very fast. It is important to mention here that the figures given in the table do not give us exact magnitude of the unemployment in the State. It has two main defects. First, all the unemployed persons do not get themselves registered with the employment exchanges. Second, some of the registered may not be actually unemployed but only in search of better jobs.

The present problem of the degree holders and technical persons is that they are involuntarily unemployed, in which most unemployed are graduates and post-graduates. The growth of job for graduate and technical degree holders was lower than the growth rate in their number. Market rigidities and structural limitations prevent wage rates from declining to levels, where all graduates may be employed. The private rate of returns to graduate education is greater than private rate of return to matriculation. The cost of higher education is low which encourages the people to take higher education. Matriculates have to wait for some years for getting the job and in the waiting period higher education is the best way to utilize time (Bhatt & Anwar, 2013).

Among the middle-income families *demonstration effect* operates, which makes parents to send their sons for higher education. The expansion of education has also led to devaluation of education. A decade ago a clerical job required matriculation, now the same job requires post-graduation.

The J&K being a developing state, the level of unemployment and under-employment trend is being high. The industries like tourism, handicrafts, and handlooms are measured in terms of their potential to create large employment opportunities shows low performance as the same industries are very intensive with violence. Being labour intensive in character, these industries are capable of absorbing more labour per unit of output as well as investment. Prior to the turbulent phase, their position privileged in the international markets. The glorious cultural tradition possessed by the artisans and tourists gave name and fame for their craft works and beautiful destinations throughout the world.

The historical perspectives reviewed in various literatures, highlight the progress of these industries flourished referred for invention of job opportunities. Till 1989, have been the major economic activities of the state. However, all sectors were hard hit following the outbreak of militancy during 90s. The economic stability as well as employment opportunities of its people disrupted to a large extent.

The study has also demonstrated that the socio-cultural significance of tourism, measured in terms of employment is very large. However, the impacts of tourism are extremely ambivalent. On the one hand, tourism plays an important and certainly positive role in the economic development, cultural exchange and further promotes international relations of state. On the other hand, many hopes that were placed on tourism as an engine of economic development have been disappointed and strained due to violence in state. So, tourism needs pertinent care on sound efficacies.

The State lost 29 million tourists from 1989–2002 leading to revenue loss of $ 3.6 billion due to out-break of insurgency (Khan, 2015). Tourism is the leading industry employment potential and state revenue. The revenue generation is expected to increase manifold provided the situation remains normal and tourists influx increases in a desired manner.

The state is revived to some extent depends upon the normalcy produced in the state. It is found that trends of employment in the three main sectors have proliferated by consensus intervention of various parties involved over some frequent years, to facilitate cooperation in an anarchic world. The self-interest parties in the state seek to establish cooperation through mutual agreement under certain conditions is also instrumental to some extent. Regimes are tailored to suit the specific interest of the state. The year-wise employment trend level of three main sectors (Tourism, Handicrafts, and Handlooms) is delineated in Table 5.3 from 1987–88 to 2016–17.

The recorded size of above industries reflected high fluctuated erratic trend. However, it is important to analyse that size decelerated steeply in all the industries during the peak turbulent period of 1995–96. The main cause was the Azadi Movement, which led to chaos, militancy, and insecurity.

In 2016, Kashmir had suffered a 55 per cent decline since 1978. The situation is going from bad to worse. We have just only 15–20 per cent occupancy in hotels and advance bookings even on the peak season

**Table 5.3** The Employment level of Three main Industries, *(lakhs)*

| Year | Employment in Tourism | Log | Growth Rate | Handicrafts | Log | Growth Rate | Handlooms | Log | Gr. Rate |
|------|----------------------|------|-------------|-------------|------|-------------|-----------|------|----------|
| 1987–88 | 12.86 | 2.55 | –33.24 | 1.79 | 0.58 | –4.46 | 0.056 | –2.88 | –5.38 |
| 1995–96 | 0.76 | 0.27 | 22.47 | 1.30 | 0.26 | 6.10 | 0.038 | –3.27 | 18.08 |
| 2009–10 | 10.60 | 2.36 | –11.42 | 2.81 | 1.03 | –3.96 | 0.331 | –1.10 | –8.79 |
| 2016–17 | 5.12 | 1.63 | – | 2.20 | 0.78 | – | 0.198 | –1.66 | – |

*Source:* Census from Handlooms in India, Ministry of Textile, GoI/ Digest of Statistics (DES)
Report of Tourism Department, Govt. of J&K, various issues

**Table 5.4** Employment trend at All India level, *Location Quotients,* lakhs

| Year | Employment In Tourism | | LQ | Employment In Handicraft | | LQ | Employment In Handloom | | LQ | Total Employment | |
|---|---|---|---|---|---|---|---|---|---|---|---|
| | J&K | India | | J&K | India | | J&K | India | | J&K | India |
| 1980 | 09.75 | 396.11 | 1.54 | 1.44 | 8.69 | 10.4 | 0.061 | 26.31 | 0.14 | 39.50 | 2420.13 |
| 1985 | 12.86 | 404.24 | 2.15 | 1.75 | 8.70 | 13.5 | 0.053 | 23.77 | 0.15 | 40.78 | 2766.19 |
| 1990 | 0.92 | 452.56 | 0.12 | 2.25 | 10.01 | 14.7 | 0.047 | 25.19 | 0.12 | 46.05 | 3060.54 |
| 1995 | 0.76 | 423.42 | 0.18 | 1.30 | 14.02 | 9.5 | 0.038 | 31.97 | 0.12 | 35.64 | 3689.91 |
| 2000 | 3.44 | 483.13 | 0.57 | 3.29 | 19.67 | 13.6 | 0.037 | 47.51 | 0.63 | 49.51 | 4022.34 |
| 2005 | 12.64 | 424.39 | 2.31 | 3.48 | 22.84 | 8.3 | 0.035 | 45.73 | 0.59 | 56.86 | 4398.21 |
| 2010 | 10.60 | 339.31 | 2.38 | 2.80 | 29.94 | 7.12 | 0.331 | 43.31 | 0.58 | 63.22 | 4817.38 |
| 2015 | 16.74 | 373.15 | 3.81 | 3.57 | 37.76 | 6.7 | 0.152 | 41.88 | 0.25 | 69.88 | 4991.78 |
| | | | 1.63 | | | 10.4 | | | 0.32 | | |

*Source* Government of J&K, Economic Survey (Various Issues), Srinagar, Directorate of Economics and Statistics; Census from Handlooms in India, Ministry of Textile, GoI; Census of India (Various Issues), NSSO (Various Years).

Location Quotients: A tool for comparing regional industry composition

State's Industry Employment

LQ = State's Total Employment

Country's Industry Employment

Country's Total Employment

If LQ >1, then area has proportionally more workers employed in a specific industry than the larger comparison area.

If LQ >1.25, then area industry has potential to be classified as exporter

If LQ<1, then may indicate opportunity to develop businesses in the local area

only, down from 70–80 per cent a year ago. Hoteliers and travel agents are now forced to look for another business. It is worth mentioning that Government could give much importance on maintenance of civic law and order and internal security.

The calculated value of Location quotients for tourism and handicraft exceeds much more than 1.25 values at various points of time (Table 5.4). However, periods of 1990, 1995, and 2000 exhibit less than 1 value doesn't imply the low employment potential of industries but the adverse impact of the terrorism in the same years as per *J&K in Indian Economy* source is concerned.

The State has proportionally more workers employed in a specific industry than the larger comparison area. For instance, the average relative concentration of handicraft employment of state compare to all India is 10.4 times higher.

The decline of these industries began towards the beginning 90s and become more accentuated by the middle of the 1996 due to the highest horrific events recorded in the turbulent phase that convoked with convoluted susceptibility on potential industries. The militancy and militarization (occupied productive and tourist spots land area) compelled to encouraged import of handicraft and handloom made goods which led to decay of these industries. Ultimately, converted state economy into fragile economy and make the state of J&K into conditions of what is known as 'dependency syndrome'. Subsequently, the wrecked economy eroded by the main sectors ruined lakhs of job avenues in the state. Although lot of damage has been done so far, yet there seems to be some ray of hope and situation can be reversed when industries are put in gear through prudent policies and by peaceful environment. This situation was not remedied by any alternative growth of new forms of industries (Yasmen, 2013).

It is clear that turbulent sustenance resulted erratic changes in the key sectors of economy. With political instability and unrest circumstances, sectors declined in importance in terms of its share in employment as well as in growth.

Unemployment is a social issue of serious concern. The survey carried out by NSSO provides estimates on various characteristics pertaining to employment and unemployment at the National as well as State level. Unemployment rate as per Usual Principal Status (UPS) in J&K has come down from 5.3 per cent to 4.9 per cent during the period July 2009 to June 2012, that is (66th & 68th Round of NSS respectively) which is still higher than the unemployment rate of 2.7 per cent at all India level.

The labour market did not function perfectly and could give rise to various problems. The new institutional arrangements that resulted, unemployment insurance and minimum wages prominent among them and further altered the operation of the market. The obvious way of doing so is by comparing labour markets over time. Research has revolved around *three* topics: changing structure of labour markets, incidence and effects of unemployment, and the policy response.

## Changing Structure of Labour Markets

Unfortunately the J&K state has also been troubled by acts of terrorism by the neighbouring country of Pakistan. The ongoing conflict since 1989 has not only deteriorated the social, but the economic setup as well. The state affected by conflicts had undermined development efforts, affected the living conditions of vulnerable groups and created mass unemployment.

Thus unrest circumstances have retarded economic growth and development of a state to a large extent. The economic sectors get encouraged whenever the normalcy is produced in the state. This phase of development is supporting the *Amartya Sen's Economic Theory* by way of positive relationship between economic development and peace (Bilal, 2013).

The abrupt fleeing of the non-local workers (hailing from Bihar and UP) form the major chunk of workforce in Kashmir for construction and other development activities, brought crisis in the labour market in Kashmir. As per reports (labour bureau, 2015), J&K constitute 55 per cent non-local workers. However, non-local workers had reduced the work space for locals to large extent and caused unemployment in the State. People prefer migrant labour over Kashmiri ones as migrant labourers are technically sound and work on time and charge less. Even following the vicious cycles of killings and continual shutdowns hesitated them to stay in the valley.

While decomposed the labour force in various sectors, reflects the changing structure of labour market and sector responsible more for generating employment. A declining share of labour force in agriculture and allied sectors anticipated sustained rise in real PCY and favourable to economic development. However, the slow pace of decline is a cause for concern and policy action. During the earlier phase of 80s, labour market clearly reflects the backwardness of economy as majority of the people were engaged with agricultural activities and primary sector stood the main occupation of the people, though there was gradual decrease hitherto. According to census 1981 and census 2011, the total percentage of labour force employed in primary sector dwindled by 22.4 per cent points. Secondary sector indicates a little erratic change and stood around 10 per cent during three decades as lack of small scale and heavy manufacturing industries, rail connectivity, and lack of infrastructure has been a constant hurdle in the industrial development of the State. There is a terrific and continuous rise in the percentage of labour force employed in service sector since 1981. In 1981 the total labour force employed in tertiary sector was 12.89 per cent which rises to 31.35 per cent and 54.53 per cent in 2001 and 2011 census, respectively. The main cause was by development of tourism sector, communication, and transport (District Handbook, 2011). *Kuznet and Colin Clark* prefer to call them service industries. Generally productivity in tertiary sector is very high. Hence, transfer of population primary industries to secondary and eventually to tertiary activities is considered a reliable index of economic progress.

This gives fillip to the process of urbanization by way of migration of workforce that took place rapidly from rural to urban areas due to high job opportunity and wages in urban areas and most industries are concentrated in and around urban areas. According to Annual JK Economic Survey (DES), 2013–14, deceleration of workforce from 30.5 to 25.17 per cent in rural areas and accelerated 26.47 per cent to 33.29 in urban areas between 1981 and 2011 supported the *Simon Kuznets Analysis* that implies as a nation undergoes industrialization as the centre of nation's economy will shift to cities. As internal migration by farmers looking for better jobs in urban areas, causes significant rural–urban inequality gap. Rural population decreases and urban population increases. Inequality is expected to decrease when a certain level of average income is reached and processes of industrialization such as democratization and rise of welfare state allow for trickle down of benefits from rapid growth and increase of per capita income.

## Incidence and Effects of Unemployment

Insofar as the unemployment is unevenly distributed, its burden fall disproportionately on manual and unskilled workers for whom job attachment is low and frequent unemployment spells. However, unavoidable circumstances are one of the principal cause in which firms shed workers, skilled, and unskilled, were equally vulnerable to job loss (Jk Digest, 2011–12).

Despite high unemployment, government after government has failed to create ample number of jobs to suffice the aspirations of job seekers.

State has a weak private and industrial scenario that makes getting job a hectic task and this ads frustration and agony to unemployed youth. Currently, the public sector of the state is in quite unhealthy shape with weak performance. Ironically, the PSUs of the J&K state have properties worth billions of rupees at prime locations but unable to harness their rich potential fully in J&K so as to provide employment opportunities to youth.

Unemployment is the root of a number of social and economic problems because when a person is unemployed or even underemployed, he or she is unable in managing bread and butter for himself and his family. Rising rate of unemployment is one of the main reasons for late marriages and violence. Poverty is the immediate consequence of unemployment because when a person is unemployed, he earns nothing and becomes poor. According to JK Economic Survey 2016, the total percentage of population living below poverty line is 10.35 per cent for the year 2011–12 *(Tendulkar Methodology)*. Thus, unemployment is directly linked with poverty i.e. unemployed one faces a lot of different problems. In response to this, he/she indulges in various illegal activities which are against what Emile Durkheim called the *collective consciousness*. Unemployment causes income inequalities, with a very few cornering a very large chunk of total income and very large number getting a very small proportion. Again consequences of unemployment make resources under-utilized.

Ground realities and surveys suggest that the menace of unemployment among the educated youth in J&K has touched new heights with lakhs of candidates applying for a few thousand posts advertised by recruitment agencies. Critics maintain that successive governments have failed to tackle the alarming problem of unemployment while youth continues to be dilemma (Anwar & Bhat, 2013). Actually education system is very defective and is not job oriented, it is degree oriented. It is defective on the ground that is more general than the vocational. The first and foremost concern of today's youth in Kashmir is quality education. Youth demands better education, skill-based education. Thus, the people who have general education are unable to do any work. They are not able to find the ways of self-employment. It leads to unemployment as well as underemployment. Thus, it acts as an obstacle on the way to get job.

According to *NSSO 64th Round*, the unemployment of J&K is increasing at an alarming rate and ranked first (6 lakh jobless) in North

India. In 2011, report a US-based development agency 'Mercy Corps' found that 48 per cent Kashmiri youth are unemployed. The main causes of unemployment were, less opportunities than other states, underdeveloped or no industrial sector, inefficient Govt., shutdowns, severe winters, and bad connectivity and declining of Art and crafts. According to JK Economic Survey 2016–17, the state government itself admitted that the unemployment is the biggest challenge faced by the government with 58.79 thousand unemployed youth registered from Kashmir division compared to 45.78 thousand youth registered in Jammu division.

Most of the rural people are engaged directly as well as indirectly in agricultural operation. However, agriculture in the state is basically a seasonal affair. It provides employment only in a particular season of the year. Thus, agriculture has limited scope for job creation. The answer to unemployment problem lies only in the growth of micro, small, and medium enterprises (MSME) sector having huge employment generation potential and depends if promoted properly by creating a congenial and conducive climate. However, the environment for the industries is lugubrious due to ferocity in J&K. As a result of which the job seekers suffer a serious loss (GK, 28 March 2018).

The State government does not want the industries to be established in the state. It just pays lip service. The only incentives come from the central government. The state politicians know if industry is developed, people will try their hands in the industries, and the craze for government jobs will decrease. That will reduce the clout and influence of those politicians, who try to influence the people with the government jobs only. They have to protect their fiefdom.

J&K is facing the brunt of turmoil resulting in negligible investments with business marred by uncertainties. The industries have come only in the Jammu region due to peace, work culture, and better connectivity. Even the small industries are not up to the mark. As the central government has launched the 'Udaan' scheme, however, that may take much time to show the results. The highest unemployment is by the reason that outsiders can't buy any land and hence they do not open industries under Article 370. Besides, there is no mineral wealth which can be exploited by the local industrialists.

The J&K is an isolated one as the youth are not aware and interested in different available jobs (like Junior Statistical Officers) at national level.

The J&K is facing a severe dearth as the posts are lying vacant and aspirants of J&K State have been given special relaxation. The state government takes least pains in motivating educated youth for appearing in the various examinations conducted at national level (Kashmir Reader, 21 September, 2017).

During the planning period unemployment in absolute terms has increased. The main objective of our economic policies, right from the First FYP has been the provision of gainful employment opportunities. However, every plan ends up with a greater backlog of unemployed people. That is, at the end of each FYP period, this state has more unemployed than at the beginning. This has happened because during the planning period trend rate of growth was considerably lower than the targeted growth (*Brighter Kashmir*, 29 January 2018).

The employment opportunities are not keeping pace with the population growth. Education system prepares youths for *white-collared jobs*. Highly educated are waiting for the job in the situation of uncertainty and who also belong to extremely poor sections of the society. Young populations across the world are generally seen as drivers of socio-economic growth, but in Kashmir, the youth bulge is a problem and lack of avenues to engage youth in meaningful ways drives youth towards destructive activities. Unemployed youths are betrayed by the anti-social elements and for destabilizing economy by using them as tools for creating mayhem (*State Times*, 13 December 2017).

In context of uncertain and industrially backwardness both the state and central Government are working on to develop entrepreneurship as a resource to cope up with the problem of unemployment. The uncertain and conflict situation further dampens the risk appetite of the youth for entrepreneurship and self-employment. Nothing is being done so that the huge job market that lies in between government sector and self-employment can be tapped. There is not a single effort to fill the gap between the labour shortage and unemployment (Haq, 2015).

J&K economy, by and large, continues to be in a state of underdevelopment. The volume of economic activities which could provide increasing avenues of employment, determined largely by agriculture and non-agricultural sector remain low. This unfortunate situation of slow growth characterized the state economy even after turbulent period. After the attainment of independence, there was a favourable atmosphere for rapid industrialization but performance remained far short of the plan-targets after militancy. It is obvious that the unemployment situation is grim indeed. However, it is necessary to find out the causes responsible for the wide spread unemployment.

## PROBLEMS/CHALLENGES

1   Less productive investment, that is, no manufacturing sector exists, Industrial graveyard (*Business Today*, 5 November 2017). Kashmir is the highest militarized zone in the world, consequently, production adversely hit. This kind of military presence per square foot is highest in the world. There is no part of the world which has this kind of concentration of military presence. This is the maximum concentration zone in the world.

2   No internal resource mobilization (huge amount is spending on internal security (15th Finance Commission, Finance Department J&K).

3   Not able to invite FDI as militancy and violence deterrent investors, (J&K PHD Chamber of Commerce and Industry, 2011).

4   Inadequate attention paid by State government to industrial development (Economic Features of J&K, IJEDR, 2013).

5   Irregular power supply and State receives only 15 per cent of generated power as royalty from major power projects run on J&K rivers (Economic Survey, 2016).

6   Lack of investment in private and public sector consequently no long run employment policy (Butt & Pandow, 2012).

7   Poor tourism avenues due to out-break of violence (GK, October 2017).[228]

8   Poor women work quality (poor access to credit and inadequate skill training, etc. (District Level HH Survey, J&K, 2008).

9   Lack of multinational companies thus, low job opportunities (Daily Excelsior, 27 October 2018).

10  Increase of In-migrant workers leads unemployment to local workers (GK, 4 July 2017).

11  Rough terrain and ferocity hurdled to industrial development (J&K Economic Survey, 2011–2012).

12  Unskilled youth available as militancy eroded and due to lack of skill development training programme (Expert Report for J&K, 2011).

13  Diversion of resources from productive to unproductive sectors (CAG, Govt. of J&K, 2011).

14  Shortage of capital and entrepreneurial abilities (GK, 28 March 2018).

15  Theoretical education unable to keep pace with the changing market demands (J&K Higher Education Plan, 2011–12).

16  Rapid population growth has, thus, created hurdles in the way of fast growth of economy and job opportunities (Census, 2011).

17  Bad Governance failed to fulfil the targets of plans and every plan ends up with backlog (J&K Development Report, 2011).

18  Slow capital formation also inhabited the growth potential activities.

## PROBLEMS/CHALLENGES

| 19 | High incidence of child labour (NCPCR, 2012). |
| 20 | Inequalities and disparities existed across regions and social groups cause underemployment and poverty (Inequalities in J&K, EPW, 18 February 2018). |
| 21 | Sub-division of ancestral land results uneconomical size of land holdings (Land Commission Report, 1968, J&K Govt.). |
| 22 | Lack of connectivity between consumption market and producing centres (Development Report of Planning Commission, 2011). |
| 23 | High corruption and creation jobs for political interests (GK, 26 September 2013). |
| 25 | Current account deficit and fiscal deficit (Economic Survey, 2017). |
| 26 | Lack of awareness of different jobs available at centre level (The Raising Kashmir, 02 August18). |
| 27 | Mismatch between physical and human resources (GK, 28 April 2015). |
| 28 | Lackadaisical and imprudent policies pursued by subsequent governments. |
| 29 | Negative growth in agriculture viz. −1.44 & −5.06 in 2013 & 2015 at constant (2004–05) prices is a cause of concern to policy makers (Survey, 2016–17). |
| 30 | Underemployment due to Inadequate availability of production. People not get employment for the whole year due to shortage of electricity, coal and raw materials (J&K Industrial Policy, 2004). |

Keeping the above points in view, there are many more obstacles of the unemployed, facing acute pressure in every field for getting job. Thus, the real challenge in front of policy makers is to create enough jobs in the market for educated workforce. As per NSSO Survey, youth unemployment among illiterate is less as compared to educated youth. Even the illiterate youth is willing to do all sorts of work whereas educated ones look for jobs in their respective fields.

Even no effort has been made to know the exact or approximate number of the jobless youth in the state (J&K Budget Analysis, 2017–18). While government proposes 'Aadhaar-seeded registration with the Employment Department' be made necessary, in order to get the actual numbers of unemployed people. However, the fact is that only those people register themselves at Employment Exchanges, who want to opt for some self-employment scheme. Thus data will not be exact or at the best it will provide much-inflated figures. That is a real obstruction for a target-oriented policy formation to cope with unemployment.

It is time for policy makers to think and try to eradicate the unemployment of J&K and overhaul the system for urgent action. The problem of unemployment in the state of J&K is one of the most serious challenges to the Government, Policy Makers, and the Society as a whole. The government till now does not show any serious means to tackle it.

As the 'policy response' in context of this section is concerned (elaborated in Chapter 6), the central and state government adopted a variety of measures in response to the emergence of high rate of unemployment. The response was conditioned by the contemporary perceptions of the nature of the unemployment. Prior to turbulent phase, the unemployed were referred as vagrants or vagabonds, however, terrorists or stone-palters now. The unemployment had been seen as a problem of State rather than the individual. The effects of unemployment on the behaviour of the unemployed and specifically on their incentive to seek work have been a subject of great controversy over last three decades (Naqshbandi, 2011).

The J&K State has been in isolation from other states in complementary policies by the central government in light of contemporary issues. So, in order to provide gainful employment on sustainable basis and tackle the disturbed condition, Union and State government made many schemes in order to engage J&K Youth. A study describes the highly politicized nature of unemployment and the difficulty of facing its effects as the long-term unemployed resort to illegal activities.

The central government must display greater involvement and consider the needs and wants of the Kashmiri people to make the people feel recognized. This can be achieved by sending greater assistance to people in the valley ending corruption, injustice and inefficiency. Investment on infrastructure will improve the life of the people and would lead to less resentment against India (Subhash, 2002).

The fragility of the economy and the weak governance in Kashmir played a significant role in creating the conditions for conflict. What is needed, therefore, is the reconstruction of enabling conditions for functioning peacetime economy.

## Trend of Migrant Workers in J&K

Migration from Kashmir to various parts of the India was very old. The J&K had been emigrating to promote trade, political and religious links with several states and countries from centuries. The trends and implications of migration from Kashmir varied from time to time. However, since 1989 a mysterious and malicious atmosphere spread that obliterated the whole system and forced migration took place. The situation of gloomy and infringement made Hindus and Pundits intractable and insure in the state.

The violence distorted and halted the entire developmental sectors particularly human sector. The uncertain and conflict situation kept the educational sector in crappy with the changing market demands. Consequently shortage for trained and skilled labour emerged in the Kashmir Valley. The vacuum created by the scarcity of skilled workers makes room for migrant labourers. The acute shortage of manpower, in the farm and construction sector over the recent decades has encouraged migration of casual workers from other states. Conversely, lack of job avenues due to absence of industries accentuated huge out-migration to the local job seekers.

As per report from *2001 census,* 1.65 lakhs in-migrants and 2.24 lakh out-migrant workers took place in J&K State. It is important to mention that there is a dire need of new job avenues as 2.24 lakh spread throughout India for job. State rendered huge unemployment and is counted among the top job seeker state (6.31 lakh, *Digest, 2011*) in the country due to the absence of desirable industrial growth and limited scope for absorption in the private sector. Due to limited job opportunities available for job seeker youth, the number of job seeker youth has been increasing with every passing year and huge out-migrants takes place for the search of job. Table 5.5 reflects the in-migrant and out-migrant trend for the state.

**Table 5.5**  In-migrants and Out-migrants for Jammu and Kashmir State

| In-migrants (2001) | Out-migrants (2001) | In-migrants (Percent) | Out-migrants (Percent) | D.I | Migration Rate (per 100) 1991–2001 | Migration Rate (per 100) 2001–11 |
|---|---|---|---|---|---|---|
| 165084 | 224236 | 42.40 | 57.59 | 0.17 | 0.4 | 0.37 |

*Source* Census of India (2001), Migration Data, Table D-1, NSSO 67th R & Col. Estimated from Census 2011 by LTSR; Economic Survey of India 2017, Organization for Economic Co-operation and Development

David *Sopher's* Disparity Index measures the relative disparity 0.17 between in-migrants and out-migrants during the reference period of 2001. Thus, deficiency of manual labourers is a major problem faced by the state. Farmers, contractors, businessmen, and other categories of employers complete their operations in time by migrant workers due to scarcity of native manual workers.

The present education facilities in the state do not have the capacity to provide diversified employment for the new generation in the state itself. So the newly educated workforce in state has become highly mobile willing to earn a living in any part of the world today. They usually seek out *white-collar jobs* in profession such as banking, engineering, or management, leaving the state scarce of conventional/traditional labour. At the same time high wages, rapid urbanization, and shortage of skilled workers make Kashmir attractive destinations for migrant labourers. The vacuum created by the scarcity of local skilled labour makes room for them. Employers also prefer workers from other states as they demand wages much lower than that of their native counterparts. Thus emergence of migrant labourers in to the labour market of State was a relief to the manual labour deficit market and they supply cheaper labour force in the labour market.

Migrant workers help to the economic development of the state by providing the required labour force and hold important position in the economy of the state. Thus the role of migration cannot be underestimated. It is a mechanism through which the short-term supply and demand for labour in a labour market is counterbalanced and helps in manpower planning. Moreover, migrants are agents of changes. They can make changes in the wage rates, employment patterns, living and working conditions, trade union attitudes and policies, government policies, and so on. They contribute much to the economic and social development of destination even if they may be looked down by the natives. Many native labourers find it difficult to work in native places even the migrant workers undertake various activities at lower wage rates irrespective of nature or status of the work. They are ready to undertake dangerous, hazardous, hard, difficult, and filthy occupations, which are rejected by native's workers (Wasim, 2008).

Migrant workers have been instrumental in keeping alive the economy of J&K State. They carry out sowing and harvesting of crops, including paddy, work in brick kilns, construction work, and pack fruit to be exported to other states. The rapid flow of migrant workers in state has an effective role in the developmental sphere on one hand and putting a huge pressure on the basic amenities on the other, which may become a future threat for the long-term economy of the state. Another problem is that authorities in the state are unaware of the actual number of migrant workers. The local labours remained unemployed and migrant workers accepted low wage employment. They are simply taking away capital and are contributing to their own states' economies (Ali, 2007).

Displacement creates a peculiar vulnerability and impoverishment. It is argued that turbulent period had serious long implications and that displacement is not just an aberration in the life of citizen. What should be a matter of great concern is that with lacuna in the system incidents of violence such as what happened in Kashmir since 1989 continue to occur. The topography of cramped spaces with narrow streets, shared mountain walls and additional living spaces constructed into already cramped spaces can make rioting easy, policing difficult, and afford anonymity to trouble makers. Displacement is not just a humanitarian issue of providing for the needs of those affected by violence, but the issue of denial of fundamental rights of citizens and therefore an issue with political ramification. More alarming is the fact that even the justice system so far has allowed the state government to elude responsibility. During the mid-period of violence, mobs of more than lakh people roamed the streets with impunity committing crimes such as arson, theft, murder, rapes, and burning and stabbings against members of minority community. People migrated and displaced have been forced to move out of valley (Mehta & Jaswal, 2004).

The share and rate of in-migrants and out-migrants since 1981 is examined at national level. Prosperity of the region prior to 1980 acted as pull factor for a significant number of people from poorer regions not only from near but also from the far. J&K continued to enjoy a lead among Indian states in terms of beautiful resources. It is evaluated that during 1981, the share of in-migrants in terms of percentage at national level is 1.05 per cent against out-migrants 0.44. Then the trend figure of in-migrants has been declined. It indicates that during 1981, the place of Kashmir was more attractive for the out-side people. The rate and share in in-migrants and out-migrants depicted in Table 5.6.

**Table 5.6** Rate and Share of In-migration and Out-migration

| Year | Total In-migrants from other states (lakh) | Total out-migrants to other states (lakh) | Total population (lakh) | Rate of in-migration | Rate of out-migration | Share of total In-migration in percentage (All India level) | Share of total Out-migration in percentage (All India level) |
|------|------|------|------|------|------|------|------|
| 1981 | 0.47 | 0.27 | 59.87 | 0.78 | 0.45 | 1.05 | 0.44 |
| 2001 | 0.86 | 1.22 | 100.69 | 0.86 | 1.21 | 0.52 | 0.74 |
| 2011 | 0.91 | 1.37 | 125.48 | 0.72 | 1.09 | 0.47 | 0.87 |

*Sources:* Compiled from census of India.

**Table 5.7** Percentage distribution of reasons for migration during 1991–2011

| Year | Sex | Work/ Employment | Business | Education | Family moved | Marriage | Natural Calamities | Others |
|------|------|------|------|------|------|------|------|------|
| 1991 | Male | 29.6 | 3.7 | 9.8 | 32.3 | 0.7 | 0.4 | 23.5 |
|      | Female | 5.9 | 1.2 | 4.6 | 51.5 | 24.6 | 0.2 | 12.0 |
|      | Total | 18.3 | 2.4 | 7.2 | 41.9 | 12.6 | 0.3 | 18.75 |
| 2001 | Male | 42.7 | 1.6 | 9.5 | 26.3 | 0.8 | 4.4 | 14.7 |
|      | Female | 12.5 | 0.9 | 14.9 | 34.2 | 21.5 | 4.1 | 11.9 |
|      | Total | 27.6 | 1.2 | 12.2 | 30.25 | 11.15 | 4.2 | 13.3 |
| 2011 | Male | 46.4 | 4.6 | 8.8 | 29.1 | 1.0 | 4.7 | 5.4 |
|      | Female | 22.5 | 2.7 | 9.5 | 27.6 | 20.2 | 4.3 | 13.2 |
|      | Total | 34.45 | 3.65 | 9.15 | 28.35 | 10.6 | 4.5 | 9.3 |

*Source*: Census of India.

## Reasons for Migration

Table 5.7 shows, the reasons for migration and reason for migration in case of males and females vary significantly. Whereas work or employment was the most important reason for migration among males and marriage was the most important reason cited by the female migrants. The other important reasons of migration are moved with household and moved after birth. Migration primarily occurs due to disparities in regional development. The lack of employment opportunities in one region and better employment prospects and infrastructure facilities in the other region motivate people to migrate developed region. The poor regions have stagnated rural economy, which lags behind in the process of development. Underdevelopment, unavailability of resources, poverty and low wages in rural areas push the people to migrate developed areas. It is important to know what has happened to the migration pattern during the last three decades. It was examined that the inception of militancy brings change in the pattern of migration in state of J&K. Hence, it was felt that there is a need to analyse the recent census data on migration which might throw some light on the pattern of migration in the context of development. The present study is a humble attempt in that direction.

Percentage distribution of reasons for migration during 1991–2011.

# 6

# Prospects of Employment Generation in Jammu & Kashmir

There is mounting evidence to prove that lack of investment and an indifference to the needs of youth incur a high cost in terms of lost development opportunities, unemployment, and mental disruption. There is no doubt that the youth have been at the centre of socio-economic and socio-political changes. It is believed that demographic situation provides our young with an extraordinary opportunity to compete in whatever sphere they choose. We have an opportunity to turn our very large and very young people into a productive asset. That could contribute significantly to the economic growth and employment generation. Both the government and society must join hands for this nation-building task and concentrate on protecting the emotional and physical health of the youth, their skill-based education, and provision of recreational facilities, employment, and above all incorporation of self-confidence, motivation and courage to move forward (Dar, 2016).

The youth of Kashmir, confronting a problem like unemployment has always been in the forefront of movements and political changes. It is unfortunate that the youth, despite their contributions to national developments, find themselves trapped in a culture marked by violence and frustration. This is the best time for state to invest in youth and reactivate and relocate their energies if there is any need for economic growth and social development.

The most serious problem our youth is facing at present is unemployment. This monstrosity is eating up our youth slowly and gradually. The youth in state don't have jobs due to lack of healthy entertainment, health resources and awareness. The frustration emanate from unemployment resulted multitude of other problems. This is the right time to look into the problems of youth and give them viable solutions. We need proper

*Jammu & Kashmir.* Bilal Ahmad Khan, Oxford University Press. © Oxford University Press 2022.
DOI: 10.1093/oso/9780192849656.003.0006

education counselling system if we require a maximum output from our youth. We should create and disseminate the knowledge by ways and means of its application through innovations.

Employment generation is the key channel through which economic growth translates into prosperity for the population. In a growing economy, employment growth with rising productivity is the most effective mechanism available to the poor to participate in the growth process and raise their standard of living. High economic growth, therefore, unless accompanied by quality employment opportunities will raise inequalities. Thus, gainful employment generation is the bedrock of attaining growth with equity and alleviates poverty.

Emphasis is laid for enhancing employment opportunities to achieve the long-cherished objectives of inclusive growth. Focused attention is given to the necessary infrastructure regarded as the engine of economic growth. It is the physical infrastructure that strengthens the economy, boosts investment, attracts prospective entrepreneurs, and reduces the unemployment incidence through numerous positive forward and backward linkage effects of primary, secondary, and tertiary sectors of the economy.

The state has shown high economic growth but has not been able to meet the aspirations of the population especially the youth. The 'Expert Group, 2011' (constituted by PM for J&K, 2010) was set up in the context of enhancing the employment opportunities in J&K and to formulate a jobs plan involving both the public and private sectors, especially for the youth on employment over two primary issues of one identifying and enhancing employment opportunities in the various sectors and second skill development for improving employability of youth.

What is important at this moment to decipher is to look in to the reasons for the ever-increasing unemployment in the state. The number is increasing and continues to inflate year after year. Since neither the requirements in different government offices nor the resources of the state would do and would permit to create as many jobs, as the number of jobless, therefore, the unemployment of educated jobless youth continues to attain dangerous proportions. Besides, J&K State lacks private sector initiative of industry which is often an important driver for skill acquisition. Thus creating a large number of jobs will require a two-pronged strategy.

The first would be to identify sectors with large employment generation potential and suggest interventions to kick start the growth process and the second, a human resource development initiative focused on improving skill sets through improving access to education and focused placement-oriented training.

To increase the access of the youth to educational opportunities and optimize their full academic potential and turn to productive activities, the Expert Group recommended four initiatives—(I) a Special Scholarship Scheme for J&K (SSS J&K), (II) faculty development programmes(III) initiative by Delhi Public School, and (IV) special initiatives by Indira Gandhi National Open University (IGNOU) for J&K. If the capacity of the educational institutions in J&K is to be built up, it is essential to enhance the faculty skill set (Expert Group, 2011).

The state of J&K, facing serious challenges of development despite its strong human and natural resources, merits attention of the academia and policy makers, to adopt a realistic development model in conformity with its own attributes. The job of higher educational institutions is not only to create and disseminate the knowledge, but also to find the ways and means of its application through innovations. However, transition to knowledge society is a very complex task requiring radical changes to be made on all the fronts simultaneously and effectively (Greater Kashmir, 28 April 2015).

Researcher attempted to convey that underdevelopment and unemployment in J&K, in essence, is the manifestation of *mismatch* between physical and human resources technically known as structural unemployment. In simple words, this type of unemployment exists when a large segment of working age population does not possess the appropriate skills and knowledge necessary to engage itself in exploiting its given resource endowments.

In such a situation the state must make a radical shift in its policies especially in the education sector to remove this impediment so as to give birth to specialized workforce capable to manage all the potential sectors on modern lines and according to the socio-economic requirements of the society. This must ultimately give rise to a vibrant private sector capable to shift the employment burden away from the government.

The government must in turn give way to the private sector to emerge because it is not the business of the government to do the business. The private sector is not the one comprising a few industrialists and business tycoons, but the one consisting of our own youth. To inculcate such a capability among the youth means that our youth must be sufficiently equipped with entrepreneurial abilities necessary to vibrate all the potential sectors (sleeping giants) of our economy.

It is clear in unequivocal terms that our curricula ought to be designed to accommodate such a strategy. There is no single university of India does fall among the first two hundred universities of the world in terms of provision of quality education, and that we need to provide education according to the needs and requirements of the societies.

The J&K economy bestowed with a rich base of resource endowments by all means is not only capable to survive as an independent economic entity, but fulfils all those conditions required to provide a base for sustainable development. Ironically face a situation of massive unemployment, especially educated unemployment, even though in presence and availability of abundance of resources of which our state furnishes a classic example. However, due to lackadaisical policies, pursued by the subsequent governments and the political strife during the last almost four decades, all the strengths of our economy have ultimately been converted into its weaknesses making the state of J&K to look like a state as if it cannot survive on its own producing the conditions of what is known as 'dependency syndrome'.

However, it may be pointed out that nature has bestowed every country or region with certain peculiar features characterized in its strengths and weaknesses which through properly crafted policies can bring the dividends by exploiting the strengths and eliminating the weaknesses. But unfortunately in case of the J&K economy, the lackadaisical policies and their implementation fasten with internal strife on account of guerrillas have actually eroded the strengths and enlarged the weaknesses. Although lot of damage has been done so far, yet there seems to be some ray of hope. Situation can be reversed provided prudent policies are put in gear through enlightened institutions, which, of course, seems to be the priority of the present dispensation.

The point researcher always raise, is that it is high time to come out of the generally accepted dogma that growth and development in an underdeveloped region are subservient to big push by a few industrial giants that will percolate the benefits down the society in accordance with the *'trickle-down' theory* based on Adam Smith's 'Invisible hand' principle. Often argument in economics is made on the lines that output (growth) is a function of inputs like men (human resources) and material (physical resources), but in case of J&K State this has failed to realize owing to some unexplained phenomenon. It is clear that for the growth to respond, presence of men, and material is only a necessary condition but not a sufficient condition.

The sufficient condition states that for the growth to respond the quality of inputs (men and material) must match or, in other words, the inputs used in the production process must be complementary to each other. This brings to a very important corollary that in J&K State, the human resource development through prevailing education system and physical resources or societal requirements are moving in diverse directions with the result the input–output relation in a production function, as taught in the text books, does not hold. Thus, until this mismatch between human skills and the geographic resource endowments are addressed unemployment and under development is bound to emerge. Now, once the malady is diagnosed applying the solutions should become easier. The remedy to this problem apparently seems to lie in revamping our education sector by crafting appropriate policies giving due consideration to the type of curriculum most suitable to produce graduates and post-graduates with the appropriate skills to harness our resource potential in line with our socio-economic requirements.

But the moot question that why youth are not willing to enter these ventures, is a matter of their psychological makeup, imprudent policies and missing enlightened institutions creating a vicious circle which can be broken only by big push in education and must convert into virtuous circle of prosperity only in the long run. While so doing an attempt should be made to prepare an entrepreneurial class of young educated youth that will strengthen the supply side of the economy by automatically creating the employment opportunities with their own skills and efforts amidst difficult situations.

However, such entrepreneur class cannot be produced through short term technical courses, as currently the thrust seems to be, but by involving them from the very beginning of their basic education. Any short-term attempt may produce a semi-entrepreneur technical class with undesirable demand side effects on the job markets making it difficult for the governments to supply the jobs.

To establish the broad contours of the problem it is important to estimate the employment–unemployment trend at national level for which the NSSO is an important source. As per various rounds of *NSSO*, the labour force in J&K increased from 4.01 million in 1999–2000 to 4.37 million in 2004–05 and 5.10 million in 2014–15 correspondingly workforce increased from 3.94, 4.27, and further 4.32 million. Notwithstanding this, the addition to the workforce has marginally fallen short of the additions to the labour force in successive periods of the NSS rounds leading to an increase in the absolute number of unemployed persons in the state. The trends of labour force, workforce, and unemployment (UPSS) of J&K state at All India level are given below in Table 6.1.

The rapid increase in labour force creates pressure for creation of employment opportunities. If economic growth is jobless, the possibility of rapid growth of unemployment cannot be ruled out when labour force registers a high growth rate. During the period of 61st Round 2004–05 the percentage of the unemployed to the total labour force has also been increased. However, the 61st Round 2.23 per cent is lower than the all India figure of 2.4 per cent. In *72nd Round* of NSS data the trend was reversed. Subsequently in 72nd Round J&K State stands at 1.85 against 0.78 at national level higher than national average.

It will be interesting to decompose the workforce and find out the potential sectors responsible for employment generation. As expected the share of the primary sector in employment has been consistently declining dropping from 55.6 per cent in 1999–2000 to 44.89 per cent in 2009–10. The share of secondary and tertiary sector increased, however the 67th *round* of NSSO however provides some corroborated evidence of higher job creation by the services sector as compared to industry. However, the slow pace of economic growth in agriculture is a cause for concern and policy action.

As NSSO collects data on the activity status of the workforce gives useful insights for gauging the quality of employment generated. Usually economic development involves transition from self-employed to RWS

**Table 6.1** Labour Force, Work Force and Unemployment (UPSS) Million

| | Jammu and Kashmir | | | | | All India | | | | | Disparity Index (J&K Vs India) | |
| --- | --- | --- | --- | --- | --- | --- | --- | --- | --- | --- | --- | --- |
| | 55thR | 61thR | Gr. Rate | 72th R | Gr. Rate | 55thR (1999–2000) | 61thR (2004–5) | Gr. Rate | 72th R (2014–15) | Gr. Rate | D.I (55th R) | D.I (72th R) |
| Labour Force | 4.01 | 4.37 | 2.17 | 5.10 | 1.73 | 403.15 | 470.14 | 4.07 | 494.24 | 0.55 | 0.28 | 0.50 |
| Workforce | 3.94 | 4.27 | 2.03 | 4.32 | 0.13 | 394.17 | 458.99 | 3.87 | 481.74 | 0.53 | 0.29 | 0.61 |
| Unemployed | 0.07 | 0.12 | 9.32 | 0.08 | -2.44 | 8.98 | 11.15 | 5.56 | 3.80 | -11.27 | 0.24 | 0.63 |
| Unemployed/ Labour force | 1.7 % | 2.23 % | – | 1.85 % | – | 2.2% | 2.4 % | – | 0.78% | – | – | – |

*Sources:* 55th NSSO Round (1999–2000), 61thRound (2004–2005), 72th R (2014–2015).

**Table 6.2** Trends of Workforce in terms of size and percentage

|  | Workforce (lakhs) | | | | | | | | Shares in Percentage | | |
| --- | --- | --- | --- | --- | --- | --- | --- | --- | --- | --- | --- |
|  | 55th (1999–2000) | Log | 61st (2004–05) | Log | Gr. Rate | 67th (2009–10) | Log | Gr. Rate | 55th | 61st | 67th |
| Primary | 16.34 | 2.795 | 22.57 | 3.116 | 8.36 | 26.22 | 3.266 | 3.82 | 55.6 | 53.9 | 44.89 |
| Secondary | 4.79 | 1.566 | 9.62 | 2.263 | 19.04 | 13.66 | 2.614 | 9.16 | 16.3 | 23.6 | 24.39 |
| Tertiary | 8.29 | 2.115 | 10.46 | 2.347 | 5.98 | 18.52 | 2.804 | 12.10 | 28.1 | 25.5 | 31.71 |

Source: Report of the Expert Group on Employment in J&K, 2011, NSSO (Various Issues).

(Regular Wage and Salaried) status. NSS data on the RWS workers is considered a good approximation of organized sector employment. In J&K, the Regular Wages & Salaried (RWS) workers increased in absolute numbers by 3.69 lakhs in the period 1999–2000 to 2009–10 but the share fell by 1.53 per cent. The workers in the self-employed (SE) category increased by 19.43 lakh between the 55th and 67th Rounds and the share increased by 4.65 per cent, thus shows positive relationship. A possible explanation is that a number of employment intensive sectors in like horticulture, tourism and handicrafts have still not scaled up and are run by small household enterprises often characterized by proprietor—owners. The absolute number of workers in the casual labour (CL) category increased marginally but their share in the total jobs declined in the last reference period.

However, the *DECC data* shows a much higher figure of unemployed at 4.48 lakhs in November 2009 and 5.89 lakhs in March 2010. The variations in the two sets of data could be due to conceptual and methodological differences. It may thus be useful to view the NSS number of unemployed as the baseline number for strategizing on the number of jobs that need to be created and the DECC numbers regarding 'job seekers', as the aspirational ceiling number.

As per statistics available with the Directorate General of Employment & Training (Report, 2017) about 1.50 lakhs unemployed youth have registered themselves with the different Employment Exchanges in the state for immediate attention. In order to reduce the unemployment the

**Table 6.3** Workforce distribution by activity status and shares

| | Workforce (lakhs) | | | Activitywise (Percent) | | |
|---|---|---|---|---|---|---|
| | Self-Employed | Regular Wages & Salaried | Casual Labour | SE | RWS | CL |
| 55th | 20.21 | 5.43 | 3.79 | 68.7 | 18.4 | 12.9 |
| 61st | 31.27 | 7.08 | 4.29 | 73.30 | 16.6 | 10.1 |
| 67th | 39.64 | 9.12 | 5.28 | 73.35 | 16.87 | 9.77 |

*Source*: NSSO (Various Reports).

following points must be considered to frame the policies to eradicate the plague of unemployment.

I. Promotion of labour intensive generation activities, for example, horticulture, regeneration of degraded forests, watershed development, etc.

II. The non-farm activities in the rural areas should be given preference. There is lot of service activities required in the remote and rural areas in the field of education, health, and in respect of information technology.

III. The major employment generation sectors like tourism and handicrafts are required to be encouraged and new tourist spots should be explored.

The State of J&K has certain inherent strengths that can be utilized to improve the income of its people and to provide gainful employment opportunities on sustainable basis, which are like strong base of traditional skills not found elsewhere; untapped natural resource; a natural environment which has been very profitably utilized by other countries for high income-environment friendly tourism industry (DES, 2011–12).

In order to sustain growth and employment in its economy, the State Government

Should articulate an Employment Policy focus on:

- Improving productivity and income of traditional skill-based industries,
- Shifting agricultural workforce to high value-added;
- Transforming service industry, by setting up a world-class infrastructure;

Creating a vibrant self-employed-professional workforce,
The policy would need to incorporate the following objectives:

- To exploit full growth potential of sectors and sub-sectors.
- Setting up new enterprises in manufacturing services sector.
- To assist self-employed workers to upgrade themselves through provision of credit, marketing, technological, and training facilities.

- To improve prospects of long-term growth by creating physical infrastructure such as transport and communication services.
- Improve efficiency of utilization of resources.

## Sectoral Initiatives towards Employment Generation

The economy of J&K has suffered from disturbed conditions prevailing from almost three decades. It would, therefore, be necessary to put the economy back on the rails to enable the average person to get employment opportunities. This would require giving fillip to the economic activities that have traditionally been the mainstay of the State's economy and continue to hold significant potential for growth and employment. Such activities include agriculture (including horticulture), handicrafts and handlooms, tourism, etc. It would be equally necessary to ensure diversification of the State economy, especially expanding the industrial base by promoting private capital inflows into the State through various incentives and concessions (Digest, 2016).

The government is taking all possible steps and making all possible efforts in providing gainful employment to the youth of state, but it may not be possible for the government to provide government jobs to all. Under these circumstances possibilities have to be explored for absorbing the youth by way of creating work opportunities in the private sector as well. In this direction the sectors like agriculture and animal husbandry, handicrafts, tourism, and Information Technology, etc. of economy have been identified for generation of gainful employment opportunities in the state on sustainable basis.

## Sectoral Initiatives

### Agriculture and Animal Husbandry

The state is predominantly an agricultural economy with about 70 per cent of the population deriving its livelihood from agriculture and allied activities. However, the lack of private investment, distance from major markets, several layers of intermediation and virtual absence of postharvest infrastructure have restricted the development of agriculture. In the recent past, policy focus on increasing productivity in agriculture has led to the launch of a number of central government schemes like *Rashtriya Krishi Vikas Yojana (RKVY), Macro Management of Agriculture (MMA), National Bamboo Mission, and Integrated Scheme* of Oilseeds, Pulses, Oilpalm, and Maize. The funds allocated to J&K under the schemes of the Department of Agriculture have been increased Rs. 76 crores to almost Rs. 200 crores during 2007–08 to 2010–11 period—an increase of 250 per cent (Agriculture Production Dept, 2011–12). The state currently engages agricultural graduates on a contractual basis to carry out agricultural extension effort. The Rehbar-e-Zirat employees are responsible for disseminating improved agricultural technologies and practices and further for monitoring the implementation of the various rural development programmes.

## Animal Husbandry

The livestock sector, with a contribution of 11 per cent to the GSDP is making deep inroads in the rural economy of J&K by providing gainful employment to about 12 lakh small and marginal farmers. There is a large untapped potential in this sector since the high demand for meat, poultry items and milk in the state far outstrips the supply.

The highly labour intensive livestock sector with its capacity to cater to the poor and absorb large number of skilled and unskilled workers. For instance, increased public investment in the poultry sector will increase the growth potential and attract private investments. The government has taken a number of initiatives in this sector, some of which are working well. The *first* initiative in the poultry sector the centrally sponsored *Rural Backyard Poultry Scheme,* under which the state government provides low input technology birds (easy to rear and disease resistant) to BPL farmers for rearing in the backyards. The *second* intervention, which will also lead to direct employment generation, is the *Private Paravet Scheme.* According to the report of Planning Commission, 2011, the state established 3000 centres and introduced a paravet scheme in which educated unemployed youth from rural areas are to be trained in artificial insemination and veterinary first aid to animals.

Thus, agriculture and animal husbandry with their large employment potential need investments for production. The sector supports vulnerable sections of the population and can be an important employment creator for unskilled workers.

## Horticulture

Horticulture contributes 7–8 per cent of the GSDP and provides employment to around 30 lakh people in J&K. It has been growing in importance contributing to land productivity, employment and exports. Moreover, the forward and backward linkages in the sector which include inputs, packing, processing and transportation have significant untapped employment potential in the state.

A Centrally Sponsored Scheme MIDH has been launched for the holistic development of horticulture in the State from 2014 which integrates the ongoing schemes of National Horticulture Mission, Horticulture Mission for North East & Himalayan States. Mission for Integrated Development of Horticulture (MIDH) is a Centrally Sponsored Scheme for the holistic growth of the horticulture sector covering fruits, vegetables, mushrooms, spices, flowers, aromatic plants, etc. (Report: Horticulture Department, Govt. of J&K, 2018). High Density Apple Plantation scheme is 100 per cent state funded scheme launched in 2017 to achieve the objectives of enhanced production and productivity and raising the income of the farmers (Report: Horticulture Department, 2012).

## Tourism Sector

The tourism sector with its potential for employing people across the skill spectrum and positive externalities for other sectors like handicrafts, handlooms, and transport occupies an important place in the development and employment strategy of J&K. The tourism sector with a revenue generation of more than Rs. 3000 crores provides employment to about 5 lakh people (JK Economic survey, 2014). This sector will require significant private investment which is currently constrained by negative perception regarding the security situation and the lack of clarity on the land policy. Researcher recommended development and expansion of tourism infrastructure, transportation, communication, and other facilities to make tourism a successful sector in the state. Moreover, more and more tourist spots should be explored. The other strategy that can give quick returns to religious tourist spots requires development of recreational activities like investment in water sports, creation of shopping malls, cultural festivals, and exhibitions as potential tourist magnets and fast connectivity of bus services.

The most important on the tourism front is to inspire the confidence of potential tourists as a safe and secure destination. The most urgent task is to prepare a tourism vision document. Besides, there is a need to have a Master Plan with clear timelines to operationalize the vision. The state government on its part has set up 20 development authorities for regulated development of select tourism destinations (Tourism Department, Govt. of J&K, 2012). Ministry of Tourism, GOI have launched the SWADESH Darshan scheme in 2014 with the vision to develop theme-based tourist circuits on the principles of high tourist value, competitiveness, and sustainability in an integrated manner by synergizing efforts to focus on needs and concerns of all stakeholders to enrich tourist experience and enhance employment opportunities (Survey, 2016, DES).

## Handicrafts

The handicraft sector in J&K occupies an important place with a fine tradition of craftsmanship, employing 4–5 lakh artisans, 179 major craft clusters and revenue generation of Rs. 1000 crore plus annually (JK Digest, 2016–17). The central and state governments have taken number of initiatives to address these growth bottlenecks like established *Carpet Mega Cluster* in Srinagar area. (The scheme envisages training 10,000 artisans.) The state government consider, an embroidery crafts cluster in the state, based on the experience of *Narsapur Lace Mega Cluster'* in Andhra Pradesh. The advantage of this would be a large participation by women who are engaged in this craft.

The Ministry of Textiles has recently launched an *Integrated Skill Development Scheme* that proposes to train 26.75 lakh persons over a period of 5 years. The objective of the scheme is to address the trained manpower needs of the textile sector including handicrafts, handlooms, and sericulture by developing a cohesive and integrated framework of training based on industry needs. This will increase the employability of the target population. The scheme also seeks to create a trainers pool by conducting advanced training programmes at a cluster level and also training in design development programmes to help produce diversified products to meet contemporary market trends (DHDD, J&K, 2016–17).

Although unemployment in the state is a major challenge and government is taking every step to overcome this problem by focusing on employment potential sectors. Even former Chief Minister (Mehbooba) said 'private sector should be encouraged to invest in the state and the sectors like tourism, handicrafts and horticulture which has high employability rate must stress, she said' (Article by PTI, 13 August 2017).

## Medium Scale and Micro Enterprises

The role of Micro, Small, and Medium Enterprises (MSME) in the economic and social development of the country is well established. The MSME sector has not done well in the state and has been rendered uncompetitive due to a number of reasons like violence, inadequate local demand, poor credit flows and distance from markets. According to the estimates by the state government (MSME-DI Annual Report, 2015–16) there are a total of 39.44 thousand industries consisting of 39.36 small and 0.77 medium and large-scale units which provide employment to almost 1.24 lakh persons in J&K. However, according to the *Task Force Report* (2010) on MSME, the employment numbers are much higher at 4.3 lakhs.

The PMEGP (Prime Minister Employment Generation Programme), a centrally sponsored credit linked subsidy scheme launched recently envisages the generation of employment opportunities through establishment of micro enterprises in rural as well as urban areas. The scheme has a total outlay of more than Rs. 4000 crores, and has been working very well in J&K since 2009. This scheme also has a component for skill development to build capacities of the rural artisans (Economic Survey, 2016). The National Skill Certification & Monetary Reward (STAR scheme) scheme launched in 2015 for encouraging skill development among the youth by providing monetary rewards for successful completion of approved training programmes.

## SECTORAL INITIATIVES

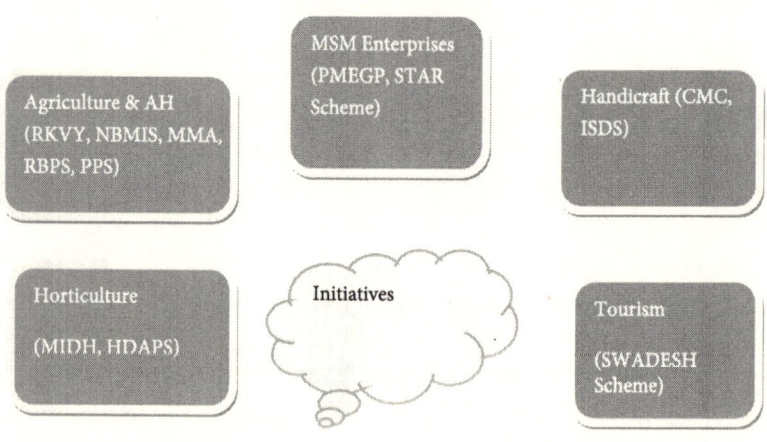

### Potential and Scope for Employment Generation

While preparing any plan for sustainable employment generation, it has to be kept in view that the prospects of any large-scale expansion in the public sector jobs are not very bright. Even if steps are taken to fill all the gaps in manpower required to deliver public services in crucial areas, the contribution of government jobs at the margin would not be more than 17 per cent as per the calculations worked out by the Task Force constituted by the Ministry of Home Affairs (GoI) in the year 2003 for creating one lakh employment and self-employment opportunities in the state of J&K. Taken together with the jobs in other formal establishments, the share of regular salaried jobs in the employment generation programme is not expected to be substantial. Therefore, other avenues would have to be explored for providing sustainable employment to the people of the State particularly through the following two routes:

- *Accelerating the rate of economic growth of the state.*
- *More effective implementation of employment-oriented schemes and programmes.*

Extending support to entrepreneurs to set up small and medium enterprises for self-employment would appear to be the most effective and durable way of doing this. A large number of workers in J&K have traditionally been self-employed in activities such as Handlooms and Handicrafts, Horticulture etc. The disturbed conditions prevailing in the State have affected them adversely to varying degree. Also, in many of the identical areas, especially horticulture and food processing, a large potential for growth lies untapped waiting to be exploited.

The comprehensive employment policy launched by J&K State in December, 2009 envisages a holistic programme to tackle unemployment problem laying emphasis on employment in private sector, self-employment, and skill development for enhancing employability. The District Employment & Counseling Centers had been conceived to have a dynamic and proactive approach in dealing with the changing scenario of unemployment at each level. In 2016–17, 4.13 lakh youths are unemployed youth of the state have registered themselves with these DECCs (J&K in India Economy 2017, DES).

Different sectors and sub-sectors of the State's economy would require different kinds of interventions for revival depending upon the nature of the activity that are in place to encourage or promote growth. Specific interventions through Government schemes and the special employment programmes like PMRY, REGP, SGSY, NREGS, and JK Self Employment Scheme would be important for giving better employment orientation to growth of the state economy.

In order to provide gainful employment opportunities on sustainable basis and tackle the disturbed condition of State, Central government and State government made many schemes in order to engage J&K youth. Depending upon the different situations and unrest circumstances, many employment generating programs were launched from time to time. The researcher is culpable of some important successful schemes. The first and foremost scheme during the early turbulent phase was the *J&K State Self Employment Scheme* implemented in 1995 by Employment Department provides loan assistance to the educated unemployed youth of the State for establishing their own employment generating units.

Secondly, the State Govt. launched a *State Help Group Scheme* in 2003 for allotting work contracts to Self-Help Groups (SHG) of unemployed Degree/Diploma engineers. The size of each Self-Help Group should not be less than 5 and not more than 10. The SHGs should be registered with the Registrar of Firms as firms. Under the scheme so far 302 groups have been registered with Registrar of Firms involving 1548 engineers besides, 802 number of works were allotted so far costing Rs. 4314.70 lakhs (JK Economic Survey, 2013–14).

Established in 1997, the J&K *Entrepreneurship Development Institute* started its regular activities in February 2004 and has already set up three regional centres of the State. The main objective of the Institute is to create awareness and facilitate entrepreneurship in J&K by imparting entrepreneurship education, skill up-gradation trainings, disseminating knowledge, and bringing about behavioural changes towards the concept of entrepreneurship at the social level. Besides, the Institute conducts and facilitates entrepreneurship research to help aspiring, budding or established entrepreneurs in their successful enterprise creation. The aim is to make entrepreneurship one of the most important components of the state's economic development and progress.

Besides, JKEDI implements a host of government sponsored employment schemes, which inter-alia include Seed Capital Fund Scheme (SCFS) of the Sher-e-Kashmir Employment and Welfare Programme for Youth and the Youth Start-up Loan Scheme. It also implements Education and Term Loan schemes of the National Minorities Development and Finance Corporation (NMDFC), Ministry of Minority Affairs.

The *Overseas Employment Corporation* was launched *in 2009* with an authorized share capital of 100.0 *lakhs* with the purpose to facilitate the educated and skilled labour force of the J&K State to seek employment within and outside the country.

The proposed Corporation shall also create a knowledge bank for aspirers of overseas employment, particularly on matters of legal requirements for migration, work environment in foreign lands, mandatory formalities, and formats prescribed by employer countries and organizations etc. The Corporation shall also handle matters of employment opportunities with other countries as well. A target of creating 1.25 *lakhs* people annually under wage employment schemes in the state has been set by the Govt. For this purpose, *State Employment Guarantee Council* in 2010 has taken up the matter with the Ministry of Rural Development, GoI, for extending the scope of schemes by incorporating relevant activities in the list of already available *Permissible Works.*

The Expert Group in consultation with the Ministry of Rural Development, GoI has developed a special placement linked, market-driven skill training programme for the J&K youth. The scheme will provide placement-linked, market-driven skill training to 50,000 to 100000 youth in 3–5 years. The objective of the special scheme is to provide options and opportunity to all youth in J&K regardless of their educational qualification to select training programmes for salaried or self-employment as per their interest.

Udaan, the *Special Industry Initiative* (Udaan) for J&K is founded by Ministry of Home Affairs and implemented by National Skill Development Corporation. Udaan programme is a special initiative to address educated unemployed in J&K and focus on graduates, postgraduates and three-year diploma engineers. The aim is to provide skill and job opportunities to 40000 youth over a period of 5 years and to provide exposure to move outside state. It also aims to corporate India with rich talent pool available in the J&K State. J&K State has a large talent pool of youth who are well educated but are unable to find employment due to lack of soft skills or hands-on training.

The *Mahatma Gandhi National Rural Employment Guarantee Scheme* helps create food security, prevent distress migration and generate

**Table 6.4**  Achievements of MGNREGS

| Year | Finance (Rs. In crores) | | Physical (lakhs) | |
|---|---|---|---|---|
| | Total Availability | Expenditure | Targets (Person day generation) | Achievement (lakhs PDs) |
| 2015–16 | 796.25 | 786.69 | 311.90 | 316.31 |
| 2016–17 | 859.71 | 853.89 | 263.65 | 312.68 |
| 2017–18 | 667.83 | 651.94 | 119.01 | 106.17 |

*Source*: Directorate of Economics and Statistics, J&K Govt. 2017–2018.

durable economic assets in the rural communities and provide 100 days wage employment in a year to the rural households who register themselves for unskilled manual labour. The activities like providing of wage employment to the Job Card holders who volunteer to do manual work on the notified wages and Creation of assets like foot bridges, flood protection structures, road connectivity, play fields, land protection, etc. is being carried out under the scheme.

The main aim of the scheme is to provide 100 days wage employment in a year to the rural households who register themselves for unskilled manual labour.

Besides, the results of EUS *(Employment and Unemployment Survey)* 2015–16 reveal that about 20.4 per cent of the households have been benefitted from MGNREGA. This programme arrests stress migration and provides job opportunities at the doorstep of people.

The most importantly and priority, the Government of J&K, conscious of the unemployment situation, especially unemployment among educated youth in the state, announced the launch of Sher-e-Kashmir Employment & Welfare Programme for the Youth (SKEWPY). SKEWPY is the state policy on Employment aiming at addressing all the issues relating to unemployment. The policy was launched on the 5th of December 2009, which marks the 105th birth anniversary of Sher-e-Kashmir, Jenab Sheikh Mohammad Abdullah, and hence named as 'Sher-e-Kashmir Employment & Welfare Programme for the Youth'.

Under it, the Government of J&K has planned to create some 5 lakh job opportunities in the state in the next coming 5 years. For creating 5 lakhs job opportunities, sound institutional arrangements and effective operational strategies are to be put in place by the Government. The focus of the new policy is not only to creation of self-employment in the private sector but on creation of job opportunities in other sectors including Govt. sector and creation of other employment avenues as well. The policy no doubt lays focus on self-employment but welfare aspect has not been forgotten at all.

The plan/arrangements made by the government are presented in the form of flow-chart shown below:

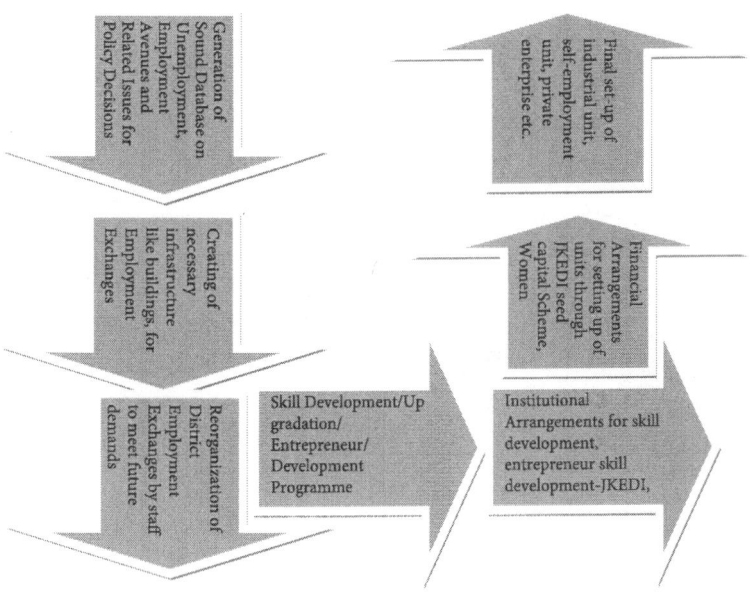

Union Government provides an important support to the economy of the State and focus on to engage and training to unemployed youths of the State in various employment programmes. To achieve targets, Government is implementing following Centrally Sponsored Schemes in the state:

Evaluation of Most Important Employment Schemes and Achievements

| Scheme/ Programme | Begin Year | Objectives | Target* (Annually) | Achievement (Mean) | Percentage |
|---|---|---|---|---|---|
| J&K SES | 1995 | Loan assistance to the educated unemployed youth | Up to 5 lakhs | 386240 | 77.2 |
| EST&P | 1998 | Employment through Skill training & Placement | Up to 2,500 | 1015 | 40.60 |
| State Help Group Scheme | 2003 | SHG of unemployed Degree/Diploma engineers. | Up to I lakh | 37453 | 36.9 |
| J&KEDI | 2004 | Create awareness and facilitate entrepreneurship | Up to 1 lakh | 6363 | 63.63 |
| PMEGP | 2008 | Employment opportunities through micro enterprises. | Up to 1 lakh | 41226 | 41.22 |
| SKEWPY | 2009 | Addressing all the issues relating to unemployment | Up to 1.25 lakh | 84277 | 67.2 |
| J&K Overseas Employment Corporation | 2009 | Facilitate educated and skilled labour force to seek employment within and outside the country. | Up to 1.25 lakh | 76448 | 61.12 |
| MGNREGA replaced NREGA | 2009 | Provide at least 100 days wage employment in a year | Up to 15 lakh | 965426 | 64.36 |
| VSA | 2010 | Financial support to the unemployed educated youth | Up to 1 lakh | 42458 | 42.45 |
| SEES, J&K | 2011 | Skill training to Youth | Up to 15,000 | 11552 | 77.01 |
| SIIJ&K/ Himayat | 2012 | provide skill and job opportunities & exposure to move outside state | Up to 41,000 | 12566 | 30.64 |

| Scheme/ Programme | Begin Year | Objectives | Target* (Annually) | Achievement (Mean) | Percentage |
|---|---|---|---|---|---|
| NRLM (Umeed) replaced SGSY | 2012 | Gainful self-employment and skilled wage employment opportunities through SHGS. | Up to 6,000 SHGS | 4619 | 76.93 |
| NULM replaced SJSRY | 2014 | Employment through Skill Training & Placement | Up to 10,000 | 7443 | 74.43 |

*Sources*: www.indiastat.com; www.nrega.nic.in; Ministry of Rural Development, GOI, Annual Report 2012–2013; Directorate of Economics and Statistics, (Govt. of J&K) (Various Reports); MSME-DI Jammu Annual Reports; Report of Expert Group to Formulate a Jobs Plan For State of J&K 2011.

SKEWPY = Sher-E-Kashmir Employment & Welfare Programme For Youth

J&KSES = J&K State Self-Employment Scheme

SEES, J&K = Skill, Empowerment and Employment Scheme for J&K

EST & P = Employment Through Skill Training & Placement

SII J&K = Special Industry Initiative for J&K or Himayat

NRLM = National Rural Livelihood Mission

NULM = National Urban Livelihood Mission

VSA = Voluntary Services Allowance

PMEGP = Prime Minister Employment Guarantee Programme

SGSY= Swarnajayanti Gram Swarojgar Yojana,

SJSRY= Swarnajayanti Shahari Rozgar Yojana

*Monitorable targets set by J&K Govt.*

In spite of various initiatives from time to time government fails to fulfil the targets or provide gainful employment opportunities on sustainable basis. What is important at this moment to decipher is to look into the reasons for the ever-increasing unemployment in the state. Every year the literacy rate is increasing. This number is increasing and will continue to inflate year after year. Since neither the requirements in different government offices nor the resources of the state would do and would permit to create as many jobs, therefore, the unemployment of educated young men will continue to attain dangerous proportions. The high proportion of unemployment of the educated youth leads different destructive activities. The problem calls for immediate attention.

Fostering Peace in Kashmir is very momentous. The effort to build a free-trade area in South Asia over the period of a decade offers a unique opportunity for laying the groundwork to resolve the problem. The aim was to develop an integrated market in the region, which could develop into a common market. Such a market could later encompass other parts of South Asia. Trade liberalization is expected to improve exports which generate employment. However, it depends on whether the benefits percolate to unskilled workers or skilled workers.

Based on the study work, the following broad two recommendations are given:

1. **Appropriate Macro Policies:** Appropriate macro policies are important for generating employment. In other words, one has to examine whether macro policies in the State are pro-employment and pro-poor in the post reform period. Investments are important for higher growth which can improve employment if invested in labour intensive sectors. One of the reasons for the low growth in employment in the post reform period could be low growth in public investment. Fiscal reforms are supposed to reduce fiscal deficit, improve social sector expenditures, and capital expenditures. These are expected to improve employment prospects.

Improvement in Education has not been able to take advantage of 'demographic dividend' because of low skills. It is important to realize however that we can only reap this demographic dividend if we invest on human resource development and skill formation in a massive way and create productive employment for our relatively young working (Approach to 11th FYP). Modern industry needs skill education and that is why educated find it hard to get jobs.

Although J&K Government has established an institutional mechanism for planning and management of state's labour force and also for implementation of various legislations through various institutions like the State Labour Department, Provident Fund Organization, State Insurance Corporation (ESIC), and J&K Building and Other Construction Welfare Board, however, the situation on ground is very grim. An appalling situation has aroused wherein locals are starving for work and outsiders are getting absorbed with ever increasing pace. There is an immediate need to adopt globally used policies of labour economics in order to recognize the dynamics and functions of the labour markets.

Education system is a mindset. We are unable to break the shackles of British education system. It is regrettable to get current students teaching through age old technology when the world is striding towards technological development every day, every hour.

2. **Active Labour Market Policies Skill** improvement is one of the important things needed in active labour market policies. Expanding capacity through private sector initiatives in higher learning needs to be explored while maintaining quality. Conditions of work and promotion of livelihoods are important for raising the incomes of youth workers. Since majorities are in the informal sector, protective measures are also required. Minimum Level of Social Security like life insurance, health insurance has to be given to unorganized workers.

Self-help groups and micro finance institutes should be encouraged for livelihood promotion. Cluster development should be undertaken for improvement in productivity of self-employed. Existing self-employment programmes (e.g. Prime Ministers Rozgar Yojana and wage employment programmes (National Rural employment Guarantee Scheme) should be strengthened.

Employability of youth has to be increased through skill development and vocational training. The Government has realized the importance of skills. The mid-term appraisal of 11th Plan says *improved training and skill development has to be a critical part of the employment strategy.* A Coordinated Action Plan for skill development has been approved by the Cabinet to have a target of 500 million skilled persons by 2022 (Chandrasekhar et al., 2006).

Unemployment has become such a complicated issue, that it requires urgent steps to eliminate its scourge. Half-hearted measures or temporary solution will not yield any fruitful results. The foremost requirement is the overhauling of the existing educational system. We have to change the system from producing white-collar job seekers, to practical job oriented technocrats, capable to start their own ventures. There should be perfect co-ordination and integration between education and industry.

We have to plan and exploit our industrial potential to the fullest extent, to provide jobs to our fellow youths. If there are more industries, there will be more avenues for employment. If more and more industries are established and more commodities are produced, there will be vacancies not merely for technically trained men but also for labourers—skilled and unskilled. Thus, rapid industrialization alone opens up new avenues for the educated people.

Thus government has announced a package of incentives under its New Industrial Policy of 1998. Through this initiative, the government aims to attract industries in the state and create new employment opportunities for the local youth. The state government should take steps immediately to remove all the obstacles in order to get rapid industrialization and overall economic development. For this purpose, there is a need of permanent agreement between two countries so that peace full environment will be created once for all and encouraged all sectors including industrial sector rapidly.

Keeping the above recommendations in view, researcher discusses premier measures that can help us in eradicating or minimizing unemployment evil.

I. **Expanding Volume of Work.** Foremost solution to the problem of unemployment lies in enlarging the opportunities for work. This needs to be done to clear the backlog of unemployment and to provide jobs to the large additions being made to labour force. The work to be expanded has to be both in the sphere of wage-employment and self-employment.

The ultimate avenue of more employment has to be found in the industrial sector, as also in the service sector. Even the high industrial growth in the J&K has not been of much help in this regard. Hence for a fairly long time to come, the key-role for employment needs to be assigned to the growth of agriculture. Significant contribution in this sphere can also be made by small-scale and cottage industries. Growth rate of economy has to be raised to a higher rate. However, in promoting an employment-oriented production-structure, it is important to ensure that it is consistent with the comparative advantage of the state and has a built-in bias for modernization and technological upgradation.

II. **Raising Capital Formation.** It is also necessary that the accumulation of capital is stepped up. It helps employment expansion in two principal ways: *One,* it becomes possible to maintain the existing activities, as also to expand the current activities and to set up new ones. An increase in agricultural production depends much upon new irrigation facilities, more implements, etc. In the same way, setting up of industrial and service activities requires capital assets as buildings, machinery, etc. *Secondly,* capital formation directly generates employment in capital goods sector. The production of 'mother machines' that is, the machines which produce machines, give rise to employment. This also provides capital goods for the production for consumer goods and services.

III. **Appropriate Mix of Production Techniques.** It is also necessary to choose such a combination of capital-intensive and labour-intensive technologies of production as may generate maximum employment. On the face of it, labour-intensive activities such as cottage/household activities and also many agricultural operations, promise much by way of employment. But such an argument should not be carried too far. In the choice of technologies, another important thing to be kept in view is the total impact, direct and indirect, that a technology produces on employment. From this angle, capital-intensive technologies, are by and large, more employment-creating. This is so for several reasons: *One,* the secondary and tertiary employment-linkages are larger than in labour-intensive technologies. *Two,* labour when employed in capital intensive industries, give rise not only to capital goods, but also generate employment in industries which provide inputs to them. Labour-intensive industries do not produce such like employment-effects. *Three,* capital intensive technologies being more productive, give rise to large surpluses for additional investment. As such, these technologies become a continuous source of additional employment. *Four,* since capital intensive industries ensure higher wages, these lead to higher demand for wage-goods. This, in turn, leads to the generation of employment in consumer goods industries. One has to choose the right mix of technologies which may provide maximum employment at higher wage rates and provide surplus for further investment.

IV. **Special Employment Programmes.** Till the economy matures to a level where every one finds job as described above, it is necessary, as an interim measure, to undertake special employment programmes for those who do not have benefit from this type of growth in the short run. The number of persons to be helped in this way will be large. The need for supplement programmes is all the more important for poor people, residing mostly in rural areas and small towns. There are large many seasonally unemployed, mostly those associated with agriculture, which need supplementary seasonal employment. Quite many, though employed such as artisans, do not earn enough to meet their needs even for necessities. They also need supplement employment.

Different types of people for whom special employment programmes are needed, are landless agricultural labourers, marginal farmers, village artisans, tribal people living in the remote areas of state as also the people living in the hilly areas. Specific employment programmes have to be such as suit specific group of people and specific areas. These programmes may be in the form of direct employment as rural capital works, or in the form of providing assets like animals, sewing machines, hand/power-driven looms, etc., or these may be in the form of the supply of infrastructural facilities like marketing, credit, etc. to help them.

V. **Manpower Planning.** For achieving the aim of employment for all, it is necessary to manage human resources in a scientific manner. *One,* it is essential to adopt effective remedies to cut down the growth rate of population. This will no doubt reduce the growth rate of labour supply, notwithstanding only after some time, but it will make for the adoption for an appropriate employment policy and the solution of unemployment problem. *Two,* the supply of skilled labour needs to be tailored to the requirements of the rate and pattern of employment-oriented development. This should also take care for the imbalances. *Three,* while high-level skill-formation through education and training will be confined to a small proportion of labour force, it is essential to improve upon the capabilities for the development of vast masses of people. *Four,* in providing employment under special programmes, it is necessary to ensure that these accord with the characteristics of the target group/area as also with the overall development plans for various sectors.

Therefore measures have been suggested which allow program administrators and policy makers to continually monitor progress across multiple programs. Furthermore, additional flying measures has been suggested by the researcher are:

VI. Resolution of conflict via peaceful dialogue should be preferred. There is need of peace full environment. CM (Omar Abdullal) said, *The youth must explore other options other than Govt. jobs. But for that, peace has to return to the state* (Greater Kashmir, 22 May 2012).

VII. Demilitarization is the need of the hour. As productive and cultivated areas are deployed on military forces.

VIII. Need of political stability. Instability turns productive resources into unproductive.

IX. Implement the New Pension Policy (No Pension for Fresh Recruits). Youth explore jobs equally in the private sector.

X. Rapid industrialization in accordance with natural resource endowment position.

XI. Invite FDI for large scale employment generation in Kashmir.

XII. Efforts uninterrupted power supply. All business runs by electricity.

XIII. Develop unexplored tourism destinations. J&K tourist police Force to be enhanced at all the tourist destinations.

XIV. To develop linkage between industry and university.

XV. Modernization and mechanization of agriculture should be done.

XVI. Necessary measures to get registered with employment exchanges so that exact magnitude of educated youths can be known.

These measures can go a long way in solving most of the problems. The basic task is to provide additional employment opportunities through skills. General improvement in the working conditions, enforcement of legislative measures, provision of social security, etc. are all the secondary measures.

To maintain the pace of gainful employment growth, achieve broad based, sustainable, and fast economic growth. To achieve such growth rates, government will need to work with business leaders to implement reforms. The digital economy could unlock work opportunities and flexibility for lakhs of workers. Cross-sector collaboration can be pursued between government and industry to remove barriers to digital adoption. This collaboration would aim to expand the ability of workers and harness digital technologies in order to become more productive. It is high time for policy makers to think and eradicate unemployment in J&K and overhaul the system for urgent action.

Furthermore need to address demand-supply mismatches and lack of detailed information about geography-specific employment opportunities. It will also need to tackle challenges such as low awareness and aspiration, high dropout rates during training, inadequate employer linkages, and a passive approach to seeking employment. Demand-driven models for skills training can establish a higher return on investment for skills training programmes and could result in more sustainable benefits to both workers and employers.

In the foregoing chapter, it can be concluded that the way of success or failure in creating employment depends on the governance system that are crucial for overall development and destiney maker of respective state. The policy makers and politicians should make an attempt to ensure that each young person is able to shape positive and desirable identity. Therefore, attempt should be made to draw attention by outlining some of the essential way out.

# 7

# Summary and Conclusion

This book provides a comprehensive analysis of the state economy in connection with employment generation and the way conflict situation changed its nature in the militancy and post-militancy period. The volume of work also shows the hidden factors responsible to the changing nature of employment.

It can be concluded that the workforce growth is accompanied and assisted by structural transformation unevenly in the sectors due to unpretentious development. The decline of workforce share in primary sector is compensated by the increase in the share of tertiary sector gives fillip to the process of urbanization by way of migration from rural to urban areas. This dynamic nature accelerated more State Gross Domestic Product and employment generation. Work participation rates among districts show high disparity over time. To be very brief, two major challenges that state is confronting are ferocity and lackadaisical or imprudent policies, pursued by the subsequent governments that eroded our strengths and potential. There is a dire need of permanent agreement for the resolution of conflict between India and Pakistan so that peace full environment will be created once for all and all economic sectors will be encouraged rapidly. The state must make a radical shift in its policies especially in the education sector in order to remove its impediments so that we can give birth to capable workforce. Actually the remedy lies in revamping the education sector by crafting appropriate policies for appropriate skills in line with the socio-economic requirements of the society.

Underdevelopment and unemployment in J&K are the manifestation of mismatch between physical and human resources technically known as structural unemployment. This exists when a large segment of working age population does not possess the appropriate skills and knowledge.

*Jammu & Kashmir.* Bilal Ahmad Khan, Oxford University Press. © Oxford University Press 2022.
DOI: 10.1093/oso/9780192849656.003.0007

The book began with an attempt to understand the 'J&K Economy in Historical Perspective' through an interpretation of demographic features in terms of its growth, trends, patterns as well as spatial distribution. It attempted to analyse the historical development of state. Chapter 2, 'Current State of Economic Growth and Development' gives brief account of state's performance in terms of growth and development.

The initial chapters understand a modest effort by analysing the pace of population with workforce and other parameters. J&K is passing through the phase of population explosion and economic development has failed to maintain pace with population growth. The study tried to elucidate one of the challenges the state however continuous to wrestle with is 'violence' which has reduced the efficacy and efficiency of natural resources bestowed upon region.

Chapter 4, 'Occupational Pattern and Levels of Workforce' reveals the broad pattern of workforce and deep introspection regarding structural breaks, secular acceleration, or deceleration that could have been present in the series and number of alternative methodologies applied fit and useful for the analysis.

The 1970 period was a period of near-stagnation for J&K Economy. From time immemorial, land was treated as the property of ruler and was cultivated by tenants down to the pre-reform period. It was overwhelmingly primary producing economy where large proportions of people were engaged in cultivation. About seventy-five people are directly and indirectly dependent on agriculture which reflects backwardness of J&K economy. However, there seems appearance of developmental path after every decade due to dynamic nature of workforce that generates more GDP and employment. This gives fillip to process of urbanization by way of migration. Synchronously migration took place from rural to urban areas as urban areas are the hub of various economic activities.

The area-wise change in workforce from rural to urban areas and sectoral shift of workforce from primary sector to non-primary sector is related with Simon Kuznets Hypothesis implies that as a region undergoes industrialization, the centre of region's economy will shift to cities for better jobs and higher wages in urban areas.

Chapter 5, 'Issues of Unemployment and Underemployment' made an attempt to explore the problems confronting state. The Kashmir being a conflict-ridden zone has far less opportunities for employment than rest of the other states of the country. Violence is the basic problem from which other problems emanate. It became the stumbling block for economic development. There are virtually no engines of job creation and resources are used inefficiently for maintaining law and order. Apart from ferocities the State faces lackadaisical policies, pursued by the subsequent governments which converted state economy into fragile economy.

Chapter 6, 'Prospects of Employment Generation in J&K' explores job avenues and schemes launched for gainful employment opportunities on sustainable basis and tackle the disturbed condition of State. In spite achievements of various schemes, major challenges remain. Although a lot of damage has been done so far, yet there seems to be some ray of hope and situation can be reversed when prudent policies are put in gear through enlightened institutions. In such a situation the state must make a radical shift in its policies especially in the education sector to remove its impediments so that we can give birth to capable workforce on modern lines, that is, equipped with entrepreneurial abilities necessary to vibrate all the potential sectors of economy. There is also dire need of permanent agreement for the resolution of conflict between the two countries so that peace full environment will be created once for all and all economic sectors will be encouraged rapidly.

The foremost requirement is the overhauling of the existing educational system. We have to change the system from producing white-collar job seekers, to practical job oriented technocrats, capable to start their own ventures. The measures can go a long way in solving most of the problems. The basic task is to provide additional employment opportunities through skills. General improvement in the working conditions, enforcement of legislative measures, provision of social security, etc. are all the secondary measures.

The last chapter has the concluding observations of book. This chapter has summarized the main points of book.

## Salient Findings

A conclusion of the study work is summarized into following finding points.

1    An increase of 14.4 per cent of workforce against 23 per cent of population between the period of 2001 and 2011 delineates low pace of workforce.

2    The female working population decelerated (33.35 per cent to 28.38 per cent) due to increase of girls' enrolment in the schools during 1981 to 2011.

3    The work participation rates fluctuated between 37 per cent to 45 per cent during the reference periods of 1981 and 2011.

4    Working population at the time of 1981 (63.88 per cent) was over-whelmingly rural and agricultural in character.

5    Migration took place from rural to urban area for high job opportunity and high wage.

6    Unbalanced occupational structure is examined with 71 per cent of labour force absorbed during 1981 and less than 50 per cent during 2011 in primary sector.

7    According to census 1981, the J&K State constitutes 44.26 per cent of workforce, 30.37 per cent as main workers, and 13.89 per cent marginal workers.

8    According to census 2001, the State constitutes 37.0 per cent of workforce, 26.30 per cent are main workers, and 10.70 per cent marginal workers.

9    According to census 2011, the State constitutes 34.44 per cent of total workers, 21.07 per cent constitutes main workers, and 13.36 per cent marginal workers.

10   The size of the workforce has been increased since 1981. In 1981 census, 26.50 lakh, 37.53 lakh in 2001, and 43.22 lakh in 2011.

11   Matric and above (up to graduation) accounts highest proportion of job seekers. That is, 38.10 per cent in 1991 and 58.11 per cent in 2016.

12   Labour force towards tertiary sector generates more GDP and employment.

13  The decline of employment share in primary sector has been mostly compensated by the increase in the share of tertiary sector.

14  Synchronously output and employment share move in the same direction from primary to the non-primary sector.

15  Since 1981, the main workers poked large proportion than marginal workers (more than 60 per cent).

16  Age group 1559 absorbs maximum per cent of workforce, i.e. more than 80 per cent during all the reference periods.

17  The unemployment trend increased from 66.74 thousand to 111.07 thousand between 1984 and 2016.

18  With the passage of time, Labour force moved towards tertiary sector.

19  The tourism sector recorded fluctuated trend in absorption of employment. The year 1990, 1995 and 2010 reflected negative growth rate of -97.87, -20.35, and -0.68 due to unavoidable circumstance prevailed in the state.

20  Less productive investment taking place i.e. no manufacturing sector or foreign direct investment (DFI) exists.

21  No internal resource mobilization. Huge resources spent on internal security.

22  J&K State has highest Unemployment rate of 4.9 per cent than its neighbouring States viz. Punjab (2.8 per cent), Himachal Pradesh (2.0 per cent), Delhi (4.7 per cent), Haryana (3.2 per cent) as per 68th Round based on UPS.

23  There is no long run employment generation policy due to lack of investment in both private and public sectors.

24  Out-migrants account more against in-migrants due to lack of job avenues. Disparity Index calculated 0.17 during the reference period of 2001.

25  Lack of linkage between industry and the university.

26  Manifestation of mismatch between physical and human resources.

27  Imprudent or lackadaisical policies, pursued by the subsequent governments converted state economy into fragile economy.

28   The Expert Group, 2011, set up in the context of enhancing the employment opportunities suggested two pronged strategy. The first to identify sectors with large employment generation potential and the second, human resource development initiative focused on improving skill sets.

29   Resolution of conflict via peaceful dialogue should be preferred.


This chapter in nutshell makes a thoughtful effort to understand some important issues. This gains significance as it attempts to reflect the change in trend and pattern of workforce in quick glance. The cursory problems and important suggestions for employment generation by author for improving the system have been highlighted and summarized in this chapter. This chapter makes the assessment of the book in short form.

# Bibliography

## Books

1. Lewis, A. (2010), *Economic and Unlimited Supplies of Labour*, 40th Edition. Mayur Vihar, Delhi: Vrinda Publications Private Limited.
2. Anand, A. S. (2006), *The Constitution of Jammu and Kashmir: Development and Comments*. New Delhi: Universal Law Publishing Co. Pvt. Ltd., p. 223.
3. Baba, A. M. (2012), *General Knowledge of J&K*. Srinagar: Kashmir Book Depot.
4. Baba, A. M. (2012–13), *General Studies Manual of J&K*. Srinagar: Kashmir Book Depot, pp. 28–42.
5. Puri, B. (1981), *Jammu and Kashmir: Triumph and Tragedy of Indian Federalization*. New Delhi: Sterling Publisher, 1981.
6. Bamzai, P. N. K. (2008), *History of Kashmir*. Srinagar: Gulshan Publishers.
7. Chandra, B. (2007), *India since Independence*. New Delhi: Penguin Books Pvt. Ltd.
8. Bhargava, R. C. (1969), *Economic Background*. Srinagar: Universal Publications, p. 119.
9. Bhattacharya, A. (1994), *Kashmir: The Wounded Valley*. New Delhi: UBSPD, p. 129.
10. Bookman, M. Z. (1991), *The Political Economy of Discontinuous Development: Regional Disparities and Inter-Regional Conflict*. New York Press.
11. Darpun, P. (2016–17), Indian Economy. *Annual Magazine*.
12. Ganguly, and Bajpal (1994), India and the Crisis in Kashmir. *Asian Survey*, 34 (5), 401–416.
13. Harris-Todaro (2008), *Model of Migration and Unemployment*, 40th Edition (Ed. M. L. Jhingan). Mayur Vihar, Delhi: Vrinda Publications Private Limited.
14. Copland, I. (1991), *The Abdullah Factor: Kashmiri Muslims and the Crisis of 1947*. The Political Inheritance of Pakistan. London: Macmillan, p. 233.
15. Jamwal, S. (1994), Economy of Early Kashmir. *Published by Indian History Congress*, 57 (1996), 154–158, Available at www.jstor.org
16. Jasbir, S. (1998), *The Economy of Jammu & Kashmir*. Srinagar: Wattan Publications.
17. Jasbir, S. (2004), *The Economy of Jammu and Kashmir*. New Delhi: Radha Krishan Anand and Co.
18. Joseph, K. (1992), *Danger in Kashmir*. Jammu: Vinod Publishers and Distributors, pp. 7–22.
19. Kaldor (2010), *Model of Distribution*, 40th Edition. New Delhi: Vrinda Publications Private Ltd.
20. Kalhana (1148 AD), Rajtarangani: A History of Kashmir. *QUORA*. Available at www.quora.com

21. Khan, B. A. (1981), *Economic Consequences of Land and Kashmir State*. Unpublished Ph.D. thesis. Department of Economics, University of Kashmir.

22. Malik, I. (2005), *Kashmir: Ethnic Conflict, International Dispute*. Karachi: Oxford University Press, p. 26.

23. Mishra, S. K., and Puri, V. K (2008), *Labour Force Growth and Occupational Pattern*. Indian Economy, 28th Edition. Darya Ganj, New Delhi: Himalayan Publishing House.

24. Mishra, S. K., and Puri, V. K. (2010), *Employment and Unemployment in India*. Indian Economy. Darya Ganj, New Delhi: Himalayan Publishing House, pp. 157–175.

25. Misri, M. L., and Bhat, M. S (1994), *Poverty, Planning and Economic Change in J&K*. New Delhi: Vikas Publishing House Pvt. Ltd., p. 28.

26. Naqshbandi, M. (2011), *Child Labor in Kashmir*. LAP Lambert Academic Publishing.

27. Ali, N. (1987), *Growth and Development of small scale Industries*. New Delhi: Deep and Deep Publications, p. 52.

28. Norris, D. (1994), *Kashmir—the Switzerland of India*. Srinagar: Gulshan Publishers.

29. Papola, T. S. (2008), *Labour Regulation in Indian Industry*. Vol. 1–10, New Delhi: Bookwell Publishers.

30. Pati, R. (1991), *Rehabilitation of Child Labourers in India*. New Delhi: Ashish Publishing House.

31. Ramachandra, G. (2008), *India after Gandhi*. New Delhi: Picador India, p. 255.

32. Rekhi, T. (1993), *Socio-Economic Justice in J&K*. New Delhi: Ideal Publications.

33. Roy, S. (2008), *Structural Change in Employment in India Since 1980s*. New Delhi: ISID Vasant Kunj.

34. Sehgal, R. (2011), *Kashmir Conflict and Self-Determination*. New Delhi: LAP Lambert Academic Publishing, pp. 30–32.

35. Gupta, S. (1967), *Kashmir: A Study in India-Pakistan Relationships*. Bombay: Asia Publishing House, p. 29.

36. Srivastava, O. S. (1966), *Theory of Structural Changes in Economy and the Process of Economic Growth*. New Delhi: Vikas Publishing House.

37. Dyson, T. (1988), *The Cause of Demographic Change*. Experiment Research in South India. Madison: University of Wisconsin Press.

38. Dyson, T. (1988), *India's Demographic Transition and Its Consequences for Development*. [Edited by Kapila in Indian Economy, 2013–14]. New Delhi: Acad. Foundation.

39. Kapila, U. (2013–14), *Employment Problem in India and the Phenomenon of Missing Middle*, 24th Edition. Indian Economy Since Independence, pp. 903–906.

40. Vaidyanthan (2005), *Indian Economy since Independence 1947-70*. New Delhi: Orient Longman Pvt. Ltd. 2005, p. 348.

41. Schofield, V. (2001), *Kashmir in Crossfire*. London: B. Taurus Publishers.

42. Vyas, V. S. (2012), *Challenging of Transforming Indian Agriculture*. New Delhi: Academic Foundation.

43. Thomson, W. S., and Notestein, F. W. (2008), *Theory of Demographic Transition*, 40th Edition. Mayur Vihar, Delhi: Vrinda Publications Private Limited.

## Research Articles and Journals

44. Azeng, T. F., and Yogo, T. U. (2013), *Youth Unemployment and Political Instability in Selected DCs*. Working Paper Series No 171, DRDADB, Tunis, Tunisia.
45. Akanda, M. A. (2005), Structural Changes in Land Use and Rural Livelihoods of Bangladesh. *Medwell Journals (Pakistan Journal of Social Sciences)*, 3 (1), 175–181.
46. Hazari, B., and Krishanmurthy, J. (1970), Employment Implications of India's Industrialisation: Analysis on Input- Output frame Work. *Review of Economics and Statistics*.
47. Barry, E. (1989), *Unemployment & Underemployment in Historical Perspective*. Berkeley: IRLE, Working Paper No. 18-89, University of California.
48. Bhalla, G. (2008), Globalization and Employment Trends in India. *IJLE*, 51, 9–10.
49. Bhattacharya, B. B (1997, March 15), Changing Composition of Employment in Tertiary Sector. *Economic and Political Weekly*.
50. Bose, S. (1999), Kashmir: Sources of Conflict, Dimensions of Peace. *EPW*, 34 (13).
51. Bossaert, D., Demmke, C., and Moilanen, T. (2012), *The Impact of Demographic Change and Its Challenges for the Workforce in the European Public Sectors*, cited by European Institute of Public Administration. Working paper 2012/W/01 EIPA.
52. Burki, S. (2007), *Kashmir: A Problem in Search of a Solution*. Washington, DC: United States Institute of Peace, p. 15.
53. Butt, K., and Pandow (2012, January), Investment, Industrial Growth and Conflict in Kashmir: An Analysis. *SSRN Electronic Journal*. DOI: 10.2139/ssrn.2944651
54. Chandrasekhar, C. P., Jayati, G., and Roychowdhury, A. (2006), The Demographic Dividend and Young India's Economic Future. *Economic and Political Weekly*, 41 (49).
55. Development Strategies for J&K (1960), New Delhi: Observer Research Foundation, pp. 21–25.
56. Economic Features of J&K (2013), Published by *International Journal of Engineering Development Research*. Available at www.ijedr.org/Papers/IJEDR1704091
57. Fallen, P. R. (1983), *Education and the Duration of Job Search: An Empirical Analysis Based on Delhi Job Seekers. Journal of Development Economics*, 12 (3), 327–336.
58. Rather, F. (2013), Armed Conflicts in J&K and Its Impact on Society. *IJSRP*. 3 (2).
59. Bhatt, G. M., and Anwar, S. (2013), Higher Education and Educated Unemployment in Jammu & Kashmir. *UPJSSR*, 4 (1), 1–14.
60. Habibullah, W. (2004), *The Political Economy of the Kashmir Conflict: Opportunities for Economic Peace building and for U.S. Policy*. Retrieved on 22 April 2010.
61. Habibullah, W. (2009), *Political Economy of the Kashmir Conflict: Opportunities for Economic Peacebuilding and for US Policy*. DIANE Publishing.
62. Kanjwal, H. (2017), *Building a New Kashmir: Politics of State-Formation in a Disputed Territory*. Ph.D. Thesis, University of Michigan. ORCID ID: 0000-0002-5879-9906.
63. Khalid, H. (2009), *History Revisited: Narratives on Political and Constitutional Changes in Kashmir (1947–1990)*. Working Paper 233, ISEC, Bangalore India.

64. Hoover, C. (1944, 27 August), *Older Men Declare War. But It is Youth that Must Fight and Die.* Speech in Chicago, 23rd Republican national convention.
65. Inequalities in J&K. *EPW*, 18 February 2018.
66. Islam, A. (2014), Impact of Armed Conflict on Economy & Tourism. *IOSR-JEF*, 4 (6).
67. Ahmad, J. (2016, August), Unemployed Youth in Kashmir: Social Policy Issues Revisited. *International Journal of Research in Humanities, Arts and Literature (IMPACT: IJRHAL) ISSN(P): 2347–4564*, 4 (8), 117–132.
68. Jones, Z., Corey, S., and Farha, T. (2010), *Economic Development as a Tool to Reduce Secessionism in J&K.* Publications Office: La Follette School of Public Affairs Madison.
69. Kalis, N., and Shaheen, D. (2013), *Geo-Political Significance of Kashmir: An Overview of Indo-Pak Relations. IOSR-JHSS*, 9 (2), 115–123. Available at www.Iosrjournals.Org
70. Kashmir Study Group. (1997), *The Kashmir Dispute at Fifty.* Larchmont: KSG.
71. Khan, B. (2013), Violence & Turmoil Adversely Effected J&K Economy. *IJERT*, 4 (1).
72. Khan, B. (2015), Occupational Structure of Kashmir: Case Study of block Kupwara. *European Academic Journal*, II (6). ISSN 2286-4822.
73. Bilal, K. (2016, December), Trends in Growth of Workforce in Kashmir since 1980. *Journal-NAIRJSS&H*, 2 (12). ISSN 2454-9827.
74. Kraska, J. (2003), Sustainable Development is Security: The Role of Trans-boundary River Agreement as a Confidence Measure in South Asia. *Yale Journal of International Law.*
75. Lewis, S., et al. (1996), *Sub-National Movements in South Asia.* Oxford: Westview Press.
76. Lovass, Mastrone, Skafte, and Wiederkehr (2014), *Conflict in Kashmir.* Department of Culture and Global Studies, Aalborg University.
77. Dev, M., and Motkuri, V. (2011, April), *Youth Employment and Unemployment in India.* Indira Gandhi Institute of Development Research, Mumbai. Working Paper.
78. Moinak, M. (2014), Understanding the Employment Challenges in India. Published by *International Research Journal of Social Sciences.*
79. Martin, G., and Alicia, M. (2006), Why Have Urban Poverty and Income Inequality Increased So Much? Argentina, 1991–2001. *JEDCC*, 55, 109–138.
80. Miguel, E., et al. (2003), *Economic Shocks and Civil Conflict: An Instrumental Variables Approach,* Duke University. Retrieved 22 April 2010.
81. Showket, N. (2011), Land Reform Measures in Kashmir During Dogra Rule. *JSTOR*, 72 (PART-I), 587–603.
82. Naqshbandi, M. M. (2011), *Child Labor in Kashmir.* LAP Lambert Academic Publishing.
83. Nengoo, A. (2015), Employment and Unemployment Scenario of J&K. *IJSRST*, 1 (3).
84. Papala, A., and Sharma (2006, 27 May), Flexibility, Employment and Labour Market Reforms in India. *EPW.* Retrieved 2012.

85. Papola, T. S. (2008), *Employment Challenge and Strategies in India*. International Labour Organization Publications.

86. Patnaik, P. (2004), *On Changing Course: In India: An Agenda for 2004*. New Delhi: Social Scientist—Sahmat.

87. Rahman, M. (1996), *Divided Kashmir: Old Problems, New Opportunities for India, Pakistan, and the Kashmiri People*. Boulder: Lynne Rienner.

88. Ramotra, K. C. (1989), Female Work Participation: A Geographical Perspective with Special Reference to Marathwada. *Indian Geographical Journal*, 64 (1), 80–87.

89. Bhagat, R. B., and Dass, R. C. (2008), Levels, Trends & Structure of Workforce in India, Census Based Study 1981–2001. *International Institute for Population Sciences*.

90. Rao, R. (2009, 13 July), *New Target for Banihal Rail Line: 2017*. Retrieved 21 April 2010.

91. Sehgal, R. (2011, June), Kashmir Conflict: Solutions and Demand for Self-Determination. *International Journal of Humanities and Social Science*, 1 (6).

92. Reynaldo, F., and Fabiana, F. (2005, July), The Entry of Wild into Labor Force in Response to the Husbands Unemployment. *JEDCC*, 53, 887–911.

93. Wilson, R., and Briscoe, G. (2004), *The Impact of Human Capital on Economic Growth*. Luxembourg: Office for Official Publications of the European Communities.

94. Qadril, B., and Kasab (2017), Educational Unemployment in J&K: Causes, Consequences and Remedial Measures. *Asian Journal of Managerial Science*, 6 (2), 58–66.

95. Anuva, S. (2000, January–March), Employment Pattern of Rural Women: A Case Study in Jorhat District of Assam. *Journal of Agricultural Economics*, 59 (1).

96. Sandaram, K. (2001, March 17–23), Special article, Employment-Unemployment Situation in the Nineties. *Journal of EPW*, 36 (11).

97. Schofield, V. (2002, January 16), Kashmir: The Origins of Dispute. *BBC News UK Edition*.

98. Schaffer, T. C. (2005), *Kashmir: The Economics of Peace Building*. Washington, DC: The CSIS Press.

99. Shekhawat, D. A. (2008), Peace Process and Prospects for Economic Reconstruction in Kashmir. *Peace and Conflict Review*, 3 (1).

100. Prakash, S. (2000), Political Economy of Kashmir since 1947. *EPW*, 2054.

101. Singh, R. N (1981), Occupational Structure of Urban Centers of Eastern Uttar Pradesh. Published by *IOSR*, 23 (1).

102. Mahendra Dev, S., and Venkatanarayana, M. (2011), *Youth Employment and Unemployment in India*. Published by Indira Gandhi Institute of Development Research (IGIDR).

103. Gill, S. S. (1966, December), Unemployment and Under-Employment of Permanent Farm Workers. *Arthavijnana*, 2 (4), 255–260.

104. Kapila, S. (2002, January), United States Obsession with the Kashmir Issue: An Analysis. *SAAG*.

105. Rafael, T., and Macculoch Robert, J. (2002), The Determination of Unemployment Benefits. Published in *Journal of Labor Economics*, 20 (2).

106. Thurik, A., Roy, C., Martin, A., Stel, A., and David, B. (2008), Does Self-Unemployment Reduce Unemployment. *Journal of Business Venturing*, 23 (6), 673–686.

107. Habibullah, W. (2004), *The Political Economy of the Kashmir Conflict: Opportunities for Economic Peace Building*. United States Institute of Peace. Retrieved 8 April 2013.

108. Korpi, W. (2001, September 9), *Distributive Conflict and The Great Trough in Unemployment*. Published by Swedish Institute for Social Research, Stockholm University.

109. Wani, S. (2015, May), Nature of the Dogra State and the condition of the Muslims of Kashmir (1846–1930). *IJSR*, 5 (5). ISSN 2250-3153.

110. Wazir, T. C. (1996–1997). *Life Story*, 232–234.

111. Yasmeen, E. (2007), *Employment Scenario in Jammu & Kashmir: An Analysis of Causes and Strategies*. PG. Dept. of Economics, University of Kashmir, Srinagar.

112. Yasmin, E. (2013, July), An Evaluation of Handicraft Sector of J&K. *European Academic Research*, I (4). ISSN 2286-4822.

## Government Reports and Documents

113. Census of India 1921, J&K, Part I, Vol. XXII, Lahore, 1923, pp. 1612.

114. Reorganization Report of 1942.

115. Census of India 1941, J&K, Parts I and II, Vol. XXII, Jammu, 1943, p. 7.

116. Land Committee Report, J&K Govt., 1951–1952.

117. Census of India 1971, Vol. I, India Part II A, Union Primary Census Abstract.

118. Census of India 1981 Series 8, Jammu & Kashmir, Registrar General of India.

119. Census of India 2001, Series 2, J&K Provisional Population Totals, Paper 1.

120. Census of India 2001, Series 2, Jammu & Kashmir Provisional Population Totals, Paper 2 of 2001, Rural Urban Distribution of Population.

121. Census of India 2001, Directorate of Census Operations (J&K), 2001, Series II, Part XII-B.

122. Census of India 2011, J&K, Series 02, Part XII-B, Primary Census Abstract.

123. Census of India 2011 (Jammu & Kashmir), Office of the Registrar General and Census Commissioner, India, Ministry of Home Affairs, GoI.

124. 2th Economic Census (1980), Ministry of Planning & Programme Implementation (Department of Statistics), Central Statistical Organization, New Delhi.

125. 3th Economic Census (1990), MOPPI (Department of Statistics), CSO, New Delhi.

126. 4th Economic Census (1998), Ministry of Statistics & Programme Implementation (Department of Statistics), Central Statistical Organization, New Delhi.

127. 5th Economic Census (2005), MOSPI (Department of Statistics), CSO, New Delhi.

128. 6th Economic Census (2013), MOSPI (Department of Statistics), CSO, New Delhi.

129. NSS 32nd Round (1972), National Sample Survey. However, in 1972, NSS replaced to NSSO under Ministry of Planning & Programme Implementation (Department of Statistics), Central Statistical Organization, New Delhi.

130. NSS 38th Round (January 1983–December 1983), National Sample Survey. In 1972, NSS replaced to NSSO under Ministry of Planning & Programme Implementation (Department of Statistics), Central Statistical Organization, New Delhi.

131. NSSO 50th Round (July 1993–June 1994), Employment & Unemployment Survey, MOSPI, Department of Statistics, Central Statistical Organization, New Delhi.

132. NSSO 55th Round (January 1999–June 2000), Employment & Unemployment Survey, MOSPI (Department of Statistics), CSO, New Delhi.

133. Statistical Abstract of India (1999), MOSPI, CSO, New Delhi, New Delhi.

134. NSSO 59th Round (January 2003–December 2003), Employment & Unemployment Survey, MOSPI (Department of Statistics), CSO, New Delhi.

135. NSSO 60th Round (January 2004–June 2004), Employment & Unemployment Survey, MOSPI (Department of Statistics), CSO, New Delhi.

136. NSSO 61th Round (2004–2005), Employment and Unemployment Situation in India, Report No. 515, Government of India.

137. NSSO 63rd Round (July 2006–June 2007), Unorganized Services Enterprises, MOSPI (Department of Statistics), CSO, New Delhi.

138. NSSO 64th Round (July 2007–June 2008), Employment & Unemployment Survey and Migration, MOSPI (Department of Statistics), CSO, New Delhi.

139. NSSO 65th Round (July 2008–June 2009), Domestic Tourism, MOSPI (Department of Statistics), CSO, New Delhi.

140. NSSO 66th Round (July 2009–June 2010), Domestic Tourism, MOSPI (Department of Statistics), CSO, New Delhi.

141. NSSO 67th Round (July 2010–June 2011), MOSPI (Department of Statistics), CSO, New Delhi.

142. NSSO 68th Round (July 2011–June 2012), Domestic Tourism, MOSPI (Department of Statistics), CSO, New Delhi.

143. NSSO 71st Round (January–June 2014), Social Consumption: Education, MOSPI (Department of Statistics), CSO, New Delhi.

144. NSSO 72nd Round (July 2014–June 2015), Domestic Tourism, MOSPI (Department of Statistics), CSO, New Delhi.

145. JK Economic Survey, Directorate of Economics and Statistics, Govt. of J&K, 1980–1981.

146. Economic Review of J&K, Directorate of Economics and Statistics, Govt. of J&K, 1984–1985.

147. JK Economic Survey, Directorate of Economics and Statistics, Govt. of J&K, 1995–1996.

148. JK Economic Survey, Directorate of Economics and Statistics, Govt. of J&K, 1999–2000.

149. JK Economic Survey, Directorate of Economic and Statistics, Govt. of J&K, 2001–2002.

150. JK Economic Survey, Directorate of Economics and Statistics, Govt. of J&K, 2006–2007.

151. JK Economic Review: Directorate of Economics and Statistics, Govt. of J&K, 2007–2008.
152. JK Economic Survey, Directorate of Economic and Statistics, Govt. of J&K, 2009–2010.
153. JK Economic Survey, Directorate of Statistics and Economics, Govt. of J&K 2011–2012.
154. JK Economic Survey, Directorate of Statistics and Economics, Govt. of J&K 2013–2014.
155. JK Economic Survey, Directorate of Statistics and Economics, Govt. of J&K, 2016–2017.
156. Digest of Statistics (1971–1972), Directorate of Economics and Statistics, Planning and Development Department (Govt. of J&K).
157. Digest of Statistics (1977–1978), Directorate of Economics and Statistics, Planning and Development Department (Govt. of J&K).
158. Digest of Statistics (1980–1981), Directorate of Economics and Statistics, Planning and Development Department (Govt. of J&K).
159. Digest of Statistics (1990–1991), Directorate of Economics and Statistics, Planning and Development Department (Govt. of J&K).
160. Digest of Statistics (1995–1996), Directorate of Economics and Statistics, Planning and Development Department (Govt. of J&K).
161. Digest of Statistics (2000–2001), Directorate of Economics and Statistics, Planning and Development Department (Govt. of J&K).
162. Digest of Statistics (2011–2012), Directorate of Economics and Statistics (Govt. of J&K).
163. Digest of Statistics (2016–2017), Directorate of Economics and Statistics (Govt. of J&K).
164. Annual Report 1997–1998, Ministry of Health and Family Welfare, GoI.
165. Annual Report 1999–2000, Ministry of Health and Family Welfare, GoI.
166. Annual Report 2008–2009, Ministry of Health and Family Welfare, GoI.
167. Annual Report 2013–2014, Ministry of Health and Family Welfare, GoI.
168. State Finance Commission Report, First Five Year Plan (1951–1956), Govt. of J&K.
169. State Finance Commission Report, Second Five Year Plan (1956–1961), Govt. of J&K.
170. State Finance Commission Report, Tenth Five Year Plan (2002–2007), Govt. of J&K.
171. State Finance Commission Report, Eleventh Five Year Plan (2007–2012), Govt. of J&K.
172. State Finance Commission Report, Twentieth Five Year Plan (2012–2017), Govt. of J&K.
173. A Review of Progress, 1961, Department of Information, Govt. of J&K.
174. A Review of Progress, 1969, Department of Information, Govt. of J&K, pp. 12.
175. A Review of Progress, 1998, Department of Information, Govt. of J&K, 1998.
176. Agriculture Census (J&K), 1970–1971, Department of Agriculture & Cooperation, Ministry of Agriculture, Govt. of India, Krishi Bhawan, New Delhi.
177. Agriculture Census (J&K), 2001, Department of Agriculture & Cooperation, Ministry of Agriculture, Govt. of India, Krishi Bhawan, New Delhi.

178. Agriculture Census (J&K), 2005–2006, Department of Agriculture & Cooperation, Ministry of Agriculture, Govt. of India, Krishi Bhawan, New Delhi.
179. Agriculture Census (J&K), 2015–2016, Department of Agriculture, Cooperation & Farmers Welfare, Ministry of Agriculture, Govt. of India.
180. Report from Department of Agriculture Kashmir, Govt. of J&K, 2001.
181. Report from Department of Agriculture Kashmir, Govt. of J&K, 2007.
182. Report from Department of Agriculture Kashmir, Govt. of J&K, 2010.
183. Report of the Land Compensation Committee, Govt. of J&K, 1951–1952.
184. Land Commission Report, 1968, Govt. of Jammu & Kashmir.
185. Techno-Economic Survey of Jammu and Kashmir. Published by NCAER, New Delhi, 1969.
186. Pocket Book of Population Statistics (MOSPI), India, 1983.
187. Report on Economic Reforms, Government of Jammu and Kashmir, 1998.
188. Report of the Committee on Economic Reforms for J&K, Govt. of J&K, 1998, p. 12.
189. Annual Report, 1999–2000, Animal Husbandry Department, Jammu Division, Govt. of J&K.
190. District Census Handbook 2001, DC Complex, Kupwara (J&K).
191. Investment Opportunities for Tourism: Vision 2020, June 2002, Tourism Department of J&K.
192. Report: Religion Data, Registrar General and Census Commissioner, India (2004).
193. Report of the Task Force on Development of Jammu and Kashmir, Growth Generating Initiatives, Government of India (2006). Retrieved 22 April 2010.
194. Report of Tourism Department, Govt. of J&K, 15 November 2007. Retrieved April 2010.
195. District Level House Hold Survey and Facility Survey (DLHS), 200708, India.
196. Socio-Economic Profile of J&K, 2008, Directorate of Economics & Statistics (Govt. of J&K).
197. Handloom Census of India, 2009–2010 Development Commissioner, Ministry of Textile, GoI.
198. World Trade Report (Annual Publication), World Trade Organization, 2010.
199. Report of Agriculture Department, SWOT Analysis, 10 April 2010 (Govt. of J&K).
200. Report of Expert Group to Formulate a Jobs Plan for the State of J&K (2011), Constituted by the Prime Minister on 18 August 2010.
201. Report: Jammu & Kashmir PHD Chamber of Commerce and Industry (Govt. of J&K), 2011.
202. Report: District Employment and Counseling Centers (2011) (Govt. of J&K).
203. District Census Handbook, 2011. Department of Planning, DC Complex.
204. Report of Comptroller and Auditor General (CAG) of India (J&K), 2011.
205. Report of Planning Commission, GoI. Development of Jammu & Kashmir, 2011.
206. Report from the office of Commissioner Commercial Taxes, Srinagar. Department of Commercial Taxes (Govt. of J&K), 2011.
207. Report from J&K Higher Education Plan (Govt. of J&K) 201112.
208. Indicators of Regional Development, 2011–2012 (Part-I), Directorate of Eco. & Statistics (J&K Govt.).

209. Report from Agriculture Production Department, Govt. of J&K, 2012.
210. Report from National Commission for Protection of Child Rights (2012), GoI, India.
211. Report from Department of Horticulture, Planning, and Marketing (J&K Govt.), 2012.
212. Report from Tourism Department (Govt. of J&K), 2012.
213. Annual Employment and Unemployment Survey Report (2014) released by Labour Bureau under Union Ministry of Labour and Employment.
214. Report Fifth Annual Employment Unemployment Survey 2015–2016, Ministry of Labour & Employment, Labour Bureau, GoI.
215. Indicators of Economic Development, 2015–2016, Directorate of Economics & Statistics (J&K).
216. Annual Report MSME-DI (2015–2016), Micro Small and Medium Enterprises Development Institute, Jammu.
217. Report from Directorate of Handicraft Development Department, J&K, 2016–2017.
218. National Family Health Survey, 2016–2017. Mumbai: International Institute for Population Sciences.
219. National Commission for Enterprise in the Unorganized Sector, The Challenges of Employment in India, Volume II, NCEUS, 2007–2012/2012–2017.
220. Employment Exchange Statistics, Directorate General of Employment & Training, Ministry of Labour & Employment, 2017.
221. J&K in Indian Economy, 2017, Directorate of Economics and Statistics (Govt. of J&K).
222. Economic Survey of India 2017 (Inter-State Migration in India), Organization for Economic Co-operation and Development.
223. Fifteenth (15th) Finance Commission, Department of Finance (Govt. of J&K), 2017–2018.
224. Handloom Industry: Vision 2020 (J&K Development Report of Planning Commission).

## Newspaper Clippings

225. Seth, S. (2018, 16 December), Employment Scenario in Jammu and Kashmir. *Daily Excelsior*.
226. Dar, B. (2016, 21 March), Challenges Kashmiri Youth Face. *Greater Kashmir*.
227. Ali, N. (2007, 24 September), How Chronic is Chronic Unemployment in Jammu and Kashmir. Local Newspaper: *Greater Kashmir*.
228. Youth Must Explore Other Options Other than Govt. Jobs. *Greater Kashmir*, 22 May 2012.
229. Ayoub, A. (2013, 29 January), Economic Structure of Jammu & Kashmir. *Greater Kashmir*.
230. Creation of Jobs for Political Interests and High Corruption in J&K. *GK*, 26 September 2013.
231. Imtiyaz ul Haq (2015, 28 April), Is Knowledge Society a Remedy to the Growing Structural Unemployment in J&K? *Greater Kashmir*, April 2015.

232. Sasi, A. (2016, 17 October), Jammu & Kashmir: An Economy in Turmoil. *Greater Kashmir*.

233. Mukeet, A. (2017, 22 January), In JK Unemployment Rate is Higher Than All India Level. *GK*.

234. Raymond Pur, N. (2017, 27 March), Managing Kashmir's Youth Bulge. *Live Mint*.

235. Less Opportunities for Employment in Kashmir. *Greater Kashmir*, May 2017.

236. Singh, S. (2017, 14 May), Is Unemployment Biggest Hurdle for Youth in Kashmir? *Times of India*.

237. State Government Must Address the Unemployment. *Rising Kashmir*, 3 July 2017.

238. Increase of In-Migrant Workers Leads Unemployment to Local Workers. *GK*, 4 July 2017.

239. Entrepreneurship Development in J&K. *Daily Excelsior*, 11 August 2017.

240. *Economic Significance of Horticulture, Handicrafts and Tourism*. Article by PTI, 13 August 2017.

241. Nazir, S. (2017, 21 September), Unemployment as Grave Social Problem. *Kashmir Reader*.

242. Less Productive Investment in J&K. *Business Today*, 5 November 2017.

243. Bhat, B. (2017, 9 December), Unemployment Ruining the Future of Youths in J&K. *Daily Hunt*.

244. Lal, B., and Sharma (2017, 13 December), Unemployment—Causes and Solutions in J&K. *State Times*.

245. Hussain, A. (2017, 22 December), Unemployment Scenario in Jammu Kashmir. *Rising Kashmir*.

246. Hussain, A. (2018, 29 January), Unemployment: An Ample Problem in Kashmir. *Brighter Kashmir*.

247. Malik, S. (2018, 4 February), J&K's Draft Trade Policy Envisions eTrade, Branding Handicrafts. *GK*.

248. Rustam (2018, 19 March), Unemployment Problem in Kashmir. *Early Times*.

249. Shortage of Capital and Entrepreneurial Abilities. *Greater Kashmir*, March 2018.

250. Lack of Awareness of Different Jobs Available at Centre Level. *Raising Kashmir*, 2 August 2018.

251. Low Job Opportunities Due to Lack of Multinational Companies. *Daily Excelsior*, 27 October 2018.